"Through the leadership and witne
see how the promise of 'mutuality
gress 1963) has taken root, transforming the life of the Anglican Church
of Canada, locally and globally. Ellie embodied that transformation and
launched our Church on a journey that continues today. These essays are an
encouragement and prophetic call born from her witness."

—LINDA NICHOLLS,
archbishop and primate, Anglican Church of Canada

"Kenneth Gray and Maylanne Maybe present this set of informative articles
featuring the life and work of Ellie Johnson. She was a moving force in the
evolving understanding of mission in the Anglican Church of Canada. From
her perch as Director of Partnerships at the church's national office, she led
in developing close ties—partnerships—with Indigenous communities and
overseas partner churches. This is a good book."

—JIM BOYLES,
retired general secretary, Anglican Church of Canada

"This volume of essays is a marvelous multi-hued window into a church in
transformation. At the heart of this living history is the life, work, and witness of an exceptional lay woman with her colleagues, family, and mission
partners. This book is a gift for reflection and challenge for any who seek to
more fully participate in God's mission in the world today."

—CATHY CAMPBELL,
retired Anglican priest

"Ellie Johnson persistently challenged us to move beyond our preoccupa-
tions with the mission of the institutional Church and focus instead on
God's mission of (in her words) 'healing, hope, and transformation' in the
world around us. This important collection of essays extends Ellie's missiological vision, locating the mission of God within the contexts of changing
ecclesiologies, the full personhood of indigenous peoples, and ecojustice
movements. It is a fitting tribute to Ellie's life, ministry, and dedication to
God's mission."

—IAN T. DOUGLAS,
former professor of mission and world Christianity, Episcopal Divinity
School

"The woman who inspired this book said, 'Our calling is to serve the world, as part of God's transforming action.' These essays testify to the ways in which the idea of 'mission 'has itself been transformed, in no small part by "Ellie Johnson's passionate persistence. The realities of global ecological collapse, homelessness, food insecurity, the scandalous history of residential schools are all faced firmly by the authors who yet inspire the reader to engage this world with hope."

—ALYSON BARNETT-COWAN,
retired Anglican priest

Partnership as Mission

Partnership as Mission

Essays in Memory of Ellie Johnson

Edited by KENNETH GRAY
and MAYLANNE MAYBEE

foreword by JAMES BOYLES

WIPF *&* STOCK · Eugene, Oregon

PARTNERSHIP AS MISSION
Essays in Memory of Ellie Johnson

Copyright © 2023 Wipf and Stock Publishers. All rights reserved. Except for brief quotations in critical publications or reviews, no part of this book may be reproduced in any manner without prior written permission from the publisher. Write: Permissions, Wipf and Stock Publishers, 199 W. 8th Ave., Suite 3, Eugene, OR 97401.

Wipf & Stock
An Imprint of Wipf and Stock Publishers
199 W. 8th Ave., Suite 3
Eugene, OR 97401

www.wipfandstock.com

PAPERBACK ISBN: 978-1-6667-7932-5
HARDCOVER ISBN: 978-1-6667-7933-2
EBOOK ISBN: 978-1-6667-7934-9

VERSION NUMBER 11/08/23

Scripture quotations are from New Revised Standard Version Bible, copyright © 1989 National Council of the Churches of Christ in the United States of America. Used by permission. All rights reserved worldwide.

The chapter "The Climate Crisis and the Church: A Landscape for Theological Education" by Sylvia Keesmaat was first published in *The Toronto Journal of Theology* (*TJT*) 38.2 (2022) 206–13. It is reprinted here under copyright with permission from University of Toronto Press https://utpjournals.press and the author.

The poem "Reconciliation" by Rebeka Tabobondung, which opens the book *Nation to Nation: Aboriginal Sovereignty and the Future of Canada* (Toronto, ON: Anansi, 1998) is used with the permission of the author.

To Dr. Christopher Lind (1953–2014), Colleague, Mentor, and Friend

Contents

Foreword

THE VENERABLE JAMES BOYLES

ELLIE JOHNSON WAS THE right person, in the right place, at the right time. The concept of Christian mission was evolving from mission tied to empire to mission focused on partnership and interdependence. She studied anthropology and had on-the-ground experience in Kenya, Nigeria, Trinidad, and Honduras. She worked as a Christian educator in an Anglican parish in New Brunswick, then later, joined the national Anglican staff in Toronto working in mission education, then became director of Partnerships in 1994, succeeding the director of National and World Mission. The change in title tells the full story (although the title *director* may need some additional reform).

In these pages, you will find frequent reference to two events in the 1960s that set us on this course:

The Anglican Congress in Toronto in 1963, a gathering of Anglicans from across the world, met in Toronto with a theme of "Mutual Responsibility and Interdependence in the Body of Christ." Its statement about mission was this: "The Church is not a club or an association of like-minded and congenial people. Nor is our Communion, named for its historic roots, a federation commissioned to propagate an English-speaking culture across the world. . . . The Church exists to witness, obey, and serve."[1]

Six years later, a study commissioned by the church and undertaken by Dr. Charles Hendry, *Beyond Traplines*, called for a dramatic change in direction for the church in its relations to Indigenous peoples.[2] It was the same year that the federal government canceled the contracts with the churches and took over full control of the Indian residential schools.

---

1. "Mutual Responsibility," §3.
2. Hendry, *Beyond Traplines*.

As these chapters will show, taking both these reports into its life, the Anglican Church of Canada began the slow, at times painful movement of casting aside a deeply flawed colonial model of mission towards a refreshing and creative partnership model.

It is a journey that has taken decades, and still has a long way to go, as much of the world still holds to a colonial and racist understanding of development and power.

Into this mix came Ellie Johnson. She understood from the ground up the importance of this journey. In the Canadian context, it meant deep listening to Indigenous voices, not just in the church but also those who had been painfully alienated from the churches, those who were just skeptical or distant, and those who had returned to former Indigenous spiritualities. In the overseas context, it meant slowly withdrawing from the old missionary pattern of sending devoted Anglicans out to distant points to proclaim the gospel, too often according more to the gospel of England than the gospel of Christ.

Ellie understood the mission to listen and build community at a human level both at home and abroad. She lived this understanding, whether working at Church House with the management team, or with the people she was "directing." She brought this understanding to the worldwide Anglican Communion at their gatherings, and in personal and church-to-church relations across the world. She had an innate skill of bringing people together, listening with deep respect, and dialoguing with them in a loving way.

As general secretary, I collaborated closely with Ellie as we worked toward a settlement agreement with the federal government on residential schools, 1995–2005. I was dealing primarily with the lawyers and the government while she was doing the important work of meeting with survivors, listening to their stories, exploring ways in which they could safely tell their stories in order to receive compensation, but also to record the Indigenous side of the residential school trauma. We held on, and proclaimed endlessly, that the mission of the church was to encourage and assist healing. Ellie understood profoundly that we, the church that had caused so much harm, were not in a position to fly in and fix things. Rather, we needed to sit with the survivors, listen, grieve, apologize, assist them in their own, personal healing journey.

I was delighted to hear that Ellie would succeed me as the church's interim general secretary in 2005 after I retired, and that she would be the one to work toward reaching the final settlement agreement with its financial terms involving both the common experience payment and a process to hear and compensate former students who had been abused. The agreement also called for the establishment of the Truth and Reconciliation Commission, which over the years has done so much to support the Canadian Indigenous community in telling their stories and enable their healing.

Nancy Hurn, the General Synod archivist, worked with Ellie and others in providing documentation of the commission, as required by the settlement agreement. The purpose was to collect the historic record of the schools and make it available to the public, but more importantly, to the survivors. At the seven national events sponsored by the commission across the country, one of the most popular spots was the archives tent, where Nancy and the other church archivists displayed pictures of the schools, the students, staff, and other records.

The mission of the Anglican Church of Canada also embraced ecumenical and Anglican initiatives of service, witness, and justice. The late 1990s were years of upheaval and structural transition for the twelve ecumenical coalitions. Financial support was declining, and the administrative and staff costs were taking up an increasingly large proportion of their budgets. They came together to form KAIROS in 2001, a more streamlined organization that would continue advocacy for social and economic justice, Indigenous issues, ecological justice, and human rights under one roof. Ellie's unique style of consultation helped to make this happen. She quietly but persistently raised the hard questions, and with others brought about change. Today, KAIROS continues with many of the mandates and programs of the former social justice coalitions, striving to bring a Christian voice to society in a clear and forceful way, on behalf of the churches.

Ken Gray and Maylanne Maybee have done an extraordinary job in bringing together a group of people to reflect on Ellie's work and on her contribution to the understanding of Christian mission that was in so much need of redirection. Ken retired recently as dean of St. Paul's Anglican Cathedral in Kamloops, and had worked with Ellie on the Ecojustice Committee of the General Synod. Maylanne was part of Ellie's staff at Church House in Toronto for several years with a focus on social justice issues. She went on to be principal of the Centre for Christian Studies in Winnipeg. They both knew Ellie well, and have brought together a number of writers to produce this work in her memory. The collection includes stories and memories of Ellie from her friends, coworkers, and family; essays about her presence, influence, and accomplishments in her years at Church House; contributions from people who didn't know her, but whose work and ideas today carry forward the principles and vision of partnership that she stood for; and a handful of presentations in Ellie's own words.

These memories, stories, and essays will provide insights into the evolution of Canadian Anglican thought and practice through two decades of turbulent life of the national church, and by extension, touching on all Anglican parishes, as well as various ecumenical bodies and partner churches. Ellie's work is the focus, but as she would demand, the relevance is seen in on-the-ground practices and action.

BIBLIOGRAPHY

Hendry, Charles Eric. *Beyond Traplines: Does the Church Really Care? Towards an Assessment of the Work of the Anglican Church of Canada with Canada's Native Peoples.* Toronto: Ryerson, 1969.

"Mutual Responsibility and Interdependence in the Body of Christ." Project Canterbury, 2009. Orig. pub. 1963. http://anglicanhistory.org/canada/toronto_mutual1963. html.

Contributor List and Biographies

Verna Andrews was born and educated in England, and trained as a registered nurse and midwife, with specialist qualifications in orthopedics, cardiology (in UK), and teaching and palliative care (Canada). Verna was a longtime and close friend of Ellie Johnson. An active mother, grandmother, and caregiver for many, including Ellie in her later years, they traveled the world together and shared many common life events together. She has been a member of the Rotary Club of Oakville Trafalgar since 1997. She has received many awards including the Golden Jubilee Medal of Queen Elizabeth II—in recognition of support for Global Landmine Eradication and Survivor Assistance, and a 2005 Ontario Government Volunteer Service Award.

The Reverend Canon Dr. Alyson Barnett-Cowan is a former colleague of Ellie's and fellow member of the management team of the General Synod of the Anglican Church of Canada. Alyson served there as director for Faith, Worship, and Ministry before becoming director for Unity, Faith, and Order at the Anglican Communion Office in London, England. Ordained priest in 1978, she is now retired and serves two parishes in Toronto as honorary assistant.

The Venerable James (Jim) Boyles served as general secretary of General Synod (1993–2005) where he led the church's response to the residential schools' litigation and ensuing negotiations with the federal government, which led to the settlement agreement. Since retiring he has worked as ombudsman for home health care in Toronto, and has volunteered for many years in the national church archives, initially in support of document collection for the Truth and Reconciliation Commission.

The Right Reverend Terry M. Brown taught theology at Bishop Patteson Theological College in Solomon Islands (1975–1981) and was Regional

Mission coordinator: Asia/Pacific of the Anglican Church of Canada (1985–1996). In 1996, he was elected and consecrated bishop of Malaita in the Anglican Church of Melanesia, serving twelve years in that position. From 2013 to 2020, he was bishop-rector of Church of the Ascension, Hamilton, Ontario. He is currently an honorary assistant at Christ's Church Cathedral, Hamilton, Ontario.

The Very Reverend Dr. Peter Elliott worked with Ellie Johnson at Church House from 1990 to 1994. He relocated to Vancouver after his time at the national office and served as dean of Christ Church Cathedral until 2019. In retirement he works as a consultant and coach, and teaches at the Vancouver School of Theology.

The Very Reverend Kenneth Gray recently retired as dean of St. Paul's Cathedral in Kamloops, British Columbia. A trained musician and keen amateur photographer, he was the first secretary of the Anglican Communion Environmental Network (ACEN). He blogs regularly on retirement, music, dogs, photography, and the arts. This is his first academic publication.

The Reverend Dr. Jeff Golliher, SSF, is the assisting minister provincial for Sacred Ecology, Third Order, Province of the Americas, Society of Saint Francis (Anglican). For about twenty-five years, he was environmental staff person at the Anglican Communion Office at the United Nations (AUNO). He also served as canon for the environment at the Cathedral of St. John the Divine in Manhattan, and is currently missioner in the Diocese of New York, working at St. John's Episcopal Church in Ellenville, New York. He is the author and editor of several books and numerous articles on ecology and spirituality.

Nancy Hurn has been an award-winning and well-recognized archivist in Canada for over forty years, serving as the archivist for the Canadian National Exhibition (1978–1989), senior archivist for the Municipality of Metropolitan Toronto and the amalgamated City of Toronto (1990–2003), and General Synod archivist of the Anglican Church of Canada (2004–2018). Retiring in 2018, Nancy spends her time at the Anglican National Archives working extensively to provide documents, register information, and photographs to assist survivors of the Anglican residential schools.

Dr. Sylvia C. Keesmaat is volunteer cochair of the Bishop's Committee of Creation Care for the Anglican Diocese of Toronto, teaches part-time at Trinity College, Toronto School of Theology, and is the founder of Bible

Remixed (www.bibleremixed.ca), where she teaches online. She is the co-author of *Romans Disarmed: Resisting Empire, Demanding Justice,* and *Colossians Remixed: Subverting the Empire.* Sylvia is working on a book *Ecological Grief and Biblical Hope* (working title). She lives on an off-grid permaculture farm in the Kawartha Lakes.

Dr. Andrea Mann is the director of the Anglican Church of Canada's Global Relations ministry. She began her work in the mid-1990s with the Anglican Church of Canada as a volunteer in mission with the Church of Ceylon, Sri Lanka. Andrea served in the Partnerships department with Dr. Ellie Johnson from 1997 until Ellie's retirement in 2008. Andrea lives with her family as guests on the unceded territories of the Musqeum, Salish, and Tsleil Waut.

The Right Reverend Logan McMenamie is the retired Bishop of Vancouver Island and the Gulf Islands, and the community of Kingcome, Wakeman, Hopetown, and Gilford Island, all of which make up the Diocese of British Columbia, now known as the Diocese of Islands and Inlets. He is married to Marcia, with whom he enjoys their seven children and seventeen grand-children. Logan has led pilgrimages to pre-Christian and Christian sites in Scotland and England. He continues to invite seekers to examine what it means to reenter the land and dismantle and disassemble colonial practices.

The Reverend Maylanne Maybee, deacon, recently retired from ministry as a community developer, social justice advocate, theological educator, and ecumenist. For fourteen years she served at the office of General Synod of the Anglican Church of Canada (1996–2011), first as coordinator of Mission and Justice Education, then as coordinator for Ecojustice Networks, and for a further ten years as principal of the Centre for Christian Studies, Winni-peg (2011–2017), and interim principal of the United Theological College, Montreal (2018–2021). She edited and contributed to *All Who Minister: New Ways of Serving God's People*, a collection of essays from across Canada on innovative approaches to ministry and congregational life.

The Reverend Canon Jeffrey Metcalfe is an avid birder, rock climber, and gardener, residing at the confluence of the St. Lawrence and St. Charles Rivers, in the territory of the Huron-Wendat. He serves as the canon theo-logian of the Anglican Diocese of Quebec and as a priest in an emerging bioregional ministry. As a PhD candidate at the University of Toronto, his research focuses on the theological intersections of land, identity, and race.

Alex Nelson is a proud member of the Musgamagw Dzawadaʼenuxw First Nations in Kingcome Inlet. At age seven, he was taken away from family and community and became a seven-year product and survivor of St. Michaels Residential School in Alert Bay. Today, he maintains a strong family foundation with his wife, Nella, his daughter, Natasha, his grandsons, Gigalis and Braden, and his great-grandson, Marcus.

Nella Nelson is originally from the N'amgis Nation of Alert Bay and married into the Musgamagw Dzawadaʼenuwx Nation. She is a mother, grandmother, and great-grandmother. Nella and her husband, Alex, have also cared for thirty-four First Nations young people from their home communities. She was a high school history teacher and counsellor for ten years and was the district administrator for the Aboriginal Nations Education Division, a position she held for twenty-nine years prior to her retirement.

The Reverend Michael Shapcott is ordained as a distinctive deacon in the Anglican Church of Canada, and serves as executive director of the Sorrento Retreat and Conference Centre. He is a passionate advocate for housing justice—serving internationally, nationally, and in a number of local communities across the country for several decades.

Esther Wesley, is a former Anglican Aboriginal Healing Fund coordinator, who fondly recalls her personal experience working with Ellie Johnson to mend and improve the lives of residential school survivors.

Susan Winn has enjoyed a career in education as a teacher and a school principal with the Lester B. Pearson School Board in Montreal, Quebec. She has been an active member of the Anglican Church of Canada, locally and nationally, serving on the Ecojustice Committee and on the Council of General Synod for two triennia. An active lay reader, Sue served on the executive of the Lay Readers' Association in the Diocese of Montreal. In 2019 she received an Anglican Award of Merit. Sue counts her friendship with Ellie Johnson as a pivotal relationship in her role as a church leader.

The Reverend Dr. Jesse Zink is principal of Montreal Diocesan Theological College and canon theologian in the Diocese of Montreal. His books include *Backpacking through the Anglican Communion: A Search for Unity, a Faith for the Future* and *Christianity and Catastrophe in South Sudan*.

Timeline

In the life of Ellie Johnson		In the life of the church and the world
	1893	Creation of General Synod
	1901	St. George's IRS opens in Lytton, British Columbia
Eleanor Jean Spence is born	1942	
	1948	United Nations Universal Declaration on Human Rights
Ellie discovers the writings of Albert Schweitzer	1956	
	1963	Anglican Congress, Toronto
Masters in anthropology, McGill	1964	
	1967	Pricewaterhouse report
	1969	Publication of *Beyond Traplines*
	1971	Ted Scott elected primate
Doctorate in social anthropology, Michigan State	1973	
	1973	National Housing Act debated in House of Commons
	1980	Derwyn Owen addresses the General Synod in Peterborough
	1981–1984	MISAG 1
Return to Canada from global study and travel	1982	

In the life of Ellie Johnson		In the life of the church and the world
	1985	Publication of *Justice as Mission: An Agenda for the Church*, Brown and Lind
	1986	Michael Peers elected primate
Mission education coordinator at Anglican Church of Canada	1987	
	1987–1992	MISAG 2
	1992	General Synod Healing and Reconciliation Fund established
	1992	Rio Earth Summit
	1993	Primate Michael Peers offers "The Apology"
	1993	MISSIO commences its work
Appointed director of Partnerships	1994	
	1994	The Covenant drafting commences
	1994	Pivotal Partners in Mission Consultation, Winnipeg
	1995	Anglican Church of Canada General Synod accepts invitation of The Covenant
	1995	Strategic Plan *Preparing the Way*
	1996	Maylanne Maybee commences work at Church House
	1996	Report of the Royal Commission on Aboriginal Peoples
	1996	Terry Brown consecrated bishop of Malaita
	1996	Ecojustice Committee 1
	1998	Church/government residential school conversations begin
Commences ADR process development	1998	
	1998	Jubilee Initiative launches
	1998	Canadian mayors declare homelessness a national disaster

In the life of Ellie Johnson		In the life of the church and the world
	2000	PWRDF becomes a separate legal entity
	2001	General Synod adopts "A New Agape"
	2001	Ecojustice Committee 2
Seminally involved in the creation of KAIROS	2001	
	2001	UN World Conference Against Racism, Durban, South Africa
	2002	Global Congress on the Stewardship of Creation, South Africa
	2002	Agreement between Anglican Church of Canada and the government of Canada
	2003	Residential Schools Settlement Agreement signed
	2003	Diocese of Keewatin first to ratify IRS agreement
Awarded the Order of Niagara	2004	
	2004	"Serving God's World, Strengthening the Church: A Framework for a Common Journey in Christ 2005–2010"
	2004	Ecojustice Committee 3
	2005	First Justice Camp: Food
Appointed acting general secretary	2005	
	2005	Survivor's group work begins
Honorary doctorate, Montreal Dio	2006	
	2007	UN Special Rapporteur on the Right to Adequate Housing visits Canada
	2007	Residential School Settlement Agreement comes into force
Retirement	2008	
	2021	ACC Auckland makes significant changes to the Five Marks

In the life of Ellie Johnson		In the life of the church and the world
	2013	Logan McMenamie elected bishop of the Diocese of British Columbia
	2015	Sacred Journey in Diocese of Islands and Inlets (B.C.)
	2015	Demolition of St. Michael's Residential School
	2019	"Apology for Spiritual Harm" offered by Primate Fred Hiltz
	2019	National Housing Strategy Act proclaimed
	2021	Discovery of graves at Kamloops IRS
	2021	Destruction of the Village of Lytton, British Columbia.
Death, January 7	2022	
	2022	Lambeth Conference Calls
	2023	Plan "Changing Church" presented to General Synod in Calgary

Abbreviations

ACC	Anglican Consultative Council
ACEN	Anglican Communion Environmental Network
ACIP	Anglican Council of Indigenous Peoples
ADR	Alternative dispute resolution
AFN	Assembly of First Nations
ARC	Aboriginal Rights Coalition
ATR	Anglican Theological Review
AUNO	Anglican United Nations Office
BPTC	Bishop Patteson Theological Centre
CCBP	Confederation of Church and Business People
CEARN	The Canadian Ecumenical Anti-Racism Network
CEP	Common Experience Payment
CMS	Church Missionary Society
COGS	Council of General Synod
COM	Church of Melanesia
CPJ	Citizens for Public Justice
IAP	Independent Assessment Process

IAS-COME	International Anglican Standing Commission on Mission and Evangelism
IRS	Indian residential schools
IRSSA	Indian Residential Schools Settlement Agreement
KAIROS	Canadian Ecumenical Justice Initiative
LFN	Lytton First Nation
MISAG	Mission Issues and Strategy Advisory Group
MISSIO	Mission Commission of the Anglican Communion
MDG	Millenium Development Goals
MRI	Mutual Responsibility and Interdependence
MSCC	Missionary Society of the Canadian Church
NRSV	New Revised Standard Version (biblical translation)
NGO	Non-governmental organization
PIM	Partners in Mission
PWRDF	Primate's World Relief and Development Fund
RCAP	Royal Commission on Aboriginal Peoples
SPCK	Society for the Propagation of Christian Knowledge
SSF	Society of St. Francis
TRC	Truth and Reconciliation Commission
TEAC	Theological Education for the Anglican Communion
WA	Woman's Auxiliary
WCC	World Council of Churches

Appreciations

THERE ARE MANY PEOPLE to thank who have provided assistance and guidance as this project evolved. First and foremost, we thank our chapter authors who accepted both timelines, advice, and in a few cases, significant revisions from one or both editors. We are so very grateful for your many contributions to this collection. Thanks to Ellie's daughters who provided both text and photographs of life with their mother, and to the three eulogists at her funeral.

Special thanks go to Terry Brown who first shared the image of Ellie which fronts this collection, an image made during his episcopal consecration in the Solomon Islands. This image sparked Ken's idea for a blog and a subsequent book project. Terry has been a constant source of inspiration and information at all stages of development.

General Synod archivist Laurel Parson, ably assisted by Nancy Hurn and Jim Boyles, have provided critical archival assistance. Our Anglican archives have been, and continue to be, well organized and accessible; this is a tribute to archives staff, both present and previous.

A number of people joined in early conversations, each providing comment and assistance. These include Jeanne Moffatt, Joe Mihevc, Terry Reilly, Sue Winn, Marjorie Ross, Cynthia Patterson, Chris Trott, and Joy Kennedy. Editor Kate Merriman met with us early on and provided invaluable strategic advice on how to approach and manage our work. Cathy Campbell assisted Ken with both research and insight as did the Rev. Angus Muir, who shared about life in the town of Lytton following the catastrophic fire of 2021.

Both Archbishop Linda Nicholls, primate, and Archdeacon Alan Perry, general secretary, have enthusiastically endorsed our project and have helped us obtain funding. Also helpful were the Rev. Malcolm French, the rector of Ellie's home parish of St. Simon's, Oakville, and the congregation itself.

We are grateful for the assistance in so many ways of Archdeacon Jim Boyles, general secretary of the Anglican Church of Canada from 1993 to 2005, who has contributed a foreword, drawing on his long working relationship with Ellie and other members of the General Synod management team, and for sharing his comprehensive knowledge of our church and its workings over many years.

We have enjoyed our working relationship with our publisher, Wipf and Stock, especially with coordinating editor, Matt Wimer, and copy editor Christopher Klimkowski.

Finally, we, Ken and Maylanne, are each grateful for the gifts, abilities, and creative passion the other has brought to this project. It is no surprise that editing this little volume ended up requiring a good deal more time, energy, and commitment than either of us anticipated. In so many ways it has been "infinitely more than we can ask or imagine."

We acknowledge with gratitude a grant from the Anglican Foundation of Canada, which allowed this project to proceed with confidence.

Ellie speaking with Bishop Willie Pwaisiho, second bishop of Malaita, at the consecration of Bishop Terry Brown in the Solomon Islands, 1996

Introduction and Overview

IF A PICTURE IS worth a thousand words, then the image of Ellie Johnson standing in a Solomon Islands village clearing is worth so many more. It was this picture shared on social media by Bishop Terry Brown which inspired this volume of essays. There she stands, feet firmly planted, on the occasion of the consecration of Terry Brown as bishop of Malaita in 1996. Malaita is an Anglican diocese within the global Anglican Communion, and though we write from an Anglican perspective, it is a perspective we share with many historic Eurocentric churches—Lutheran, Presbyterian, Christian Reform, and Roman Catholic, to name a few. We see a Western-clothed woman totally comfortable, not only in herself, but also in this place few of us will ever visit.

In previous times we would have described Ellie or Bishop Terry as being "out in the mission field," bringing Western European culture, technology, insight, and religion to those supposedly eager to receive such wisdom, and in some cases, financial assistance. Such an understanding was the strategy and practice of a colonial church, eager to share and impose its wisdom and religious practices, yet unaware of, or inattentive to, the experience of those already there. If we sing Sylvia Dunstan's hymn, "Go to the world, go in to all the earth," we can only do so with the greatest of caution.[1] Today's liturgical song can and must consider what people of faith in all cultures throughout the ages have already been singing—and for the record, Ellie did sing, a lot.

The contributors in this volume include some who worked closely with Ellie, and some who never knew her but share her approach to partnership and mission. Others worked with her for decades and counted her as a colleague, mentor, or friend. Some assisted her in making decisions and setting mission priorities for the Anglican Church of Canada. Others glimpsed her

---

1. Sylvia Dunstan, "Go to the World," in *Common Praise: Anglican Church of Canada* (Toronto, ON: Anglican Book Centre, 1998), 598.

activity from afar, knowing her best through her writings found in reports, addresses, *Anglican Journal* articles, and through partnerships conferences and experiences.

Our collection is both historical and analytical. While some biographies tell the stories of clergy leaders, such as Archbishop Ted Scott and Archbishop Michael Peers, there is a dearth of biographies that tell the story of lay leaders. In this volume, all of the chapters tell stories not only of Ellie, but of God's mission revealed in the wider church and its various ministries. With one exception all writers work in and through the Anglican Church of Canada—so this is a uniquely Canadian collection.

Since the Anglican Congress of 1963, through the years of the justice coalitions of the 1970s and 1980s, through the drastic restructuring of the national church in the first decade of the 2000s, which directly affected the work of domestic and international mission, change has been continuous and relentless. Indeed, one of the most critical changes that confronted the church then and now is climate change, a key mandate of the aptly renamed Ecojustice Committee, also under Ellie's watch. One of Ellie's mission principles was that "we must all embrace change and learn to live with it."

In assisting both residential school survivors and the wider church through the period of the residential school agreements, Ellie joined many in acknowledging the sin (Ellie's term) of systemic racism embodied in the forced assimilation process. There is so much to appreciate in her life and work, yet naming the sin of racism and calling the institutional church to repentance might be considered one of her greatest contributions. We hope that as you read the chapters that follow, you will find inspiration, comfort, and strength for today's demanding justice journey.

We asked our authors for contributions "more or less scholarly in subject, but full of beautiful aphorisms and leaps of imagination, a scholarship of evocation rather than definition."[2] Our authors have responded to this request in a wonderful variety of forms and styles, including formal academic essays, reminiscences, eulogies, and comments from her daughters.

The collection is organized into five sections.

In the first section, "Biography, Memories, Perspectives," Kenneth Gray remembers Ellie-the-educator as he recalls how his own vocational journey was transformed through his work on the Ecojustice Committee. We are grateful to Canon Alyson Barnett-Cowan, Verna Andrews, and Bishop Terry Brown who shared their eulogies from Ellie's funeral, appreciations both unique and profound. Finally two of Ellie's daughters, Sekoia

---

2. Rebecca Solnit, *Wanderlust: A History of Walking* (Westminster, MD: Penguin, 2001), 214.

and Kate, shared what their mum was like when she came home from work. Their intimate insights amplify and inform other more public reflections.

In section II, "Church House: Embracing Partnership," Ellie's longtime colleague Maylanne Maybee reflects on her years of working in the Partnerships department at Church House, especially on the combined impact of Ellie's leadership and *Preparing the Way*, General Synod's strategic plan from 1996 to 2006, on the justice work of the Anglican church. Former General Synod staffer Peter Elliott writes about the changes in the structure of the Anglican Church as it evolved from assuming a colonial approach to mission into a practice of mutual partnership and beyond. Bishop Terry Brown explains his role as a Canadian priest, academic, teacher, and then bishop of the Diocese of Malaita in the Solomon Islands, a ministry he describes as one of the most enjoyable of his life. We also hear from Dr. Andrea Mann, the sole contributor to this volume who is still employed by General Synod, who pays tribute to Ellie's role in shaping a "people-first" approach to mission partnerships.

In the next section, "Indigenous Voices and Stories of Solidarity," we turn to Ellie's role in the Residential Schools Settlement Agreement process, and most importantly in the development of Alternative Dispute Resolution agreements, which took healing and reconciliation so much further than initially imagined. Retired General Synod archivist Nancy Hurn and former Healing Fund coordinator Esther Wesley tell about their involvement and Ellie's in the complex and painful story of the church's relationship with residential school survivors. Rounding out this section, Bishop Logan McMenamie tells the story of "Reentering the Land" in the Diocese of Islands and Inlets (British Columbia), paired with an interview with his chief elder, Alex Nelson, who is joined by his wife, Nella.

In "Mission and Ecojustice: Reflections and Analysis," we jump forward to the present moment, looking for connections with those things that were important to Ellie—mission, partnership, moving beyond colonialism, confronting racism, and striving for justice and healing—which remain instructive for us and our church today. Jesse Zink considers a local Anglican response to global realities, making connections between the changing environment and population mobility. Sylvia Keesmaat proposes a dynamic curriculum for theological colleges so that students will be prepared to give leadership in a time of climate crisis. Jeffrey Metcalfe uses his daily walk to work in Quebec City as a way of comparing the threat of extinction of the woodland caribou to the demise of the Anglican church in Quebec. Michael Shapcott writes of the origins and significance of the universal right to housing in Canada and elsewhere. Kenneth Gray thinks about the language we use for mission today, arguing for use of the term *ecojustice*. Drawing on his work as an Anglican Franciscan, Jeff Golliher writes on mission and hope in the face of climate crisis. Such a focus allows us to consider how many religious orders have become visible and influential in their demand for justice for all of creation.

Finally we have included some of Ellie's own words and presentations: first, an address to the Convocation of Montreal Diocesan Theological College on the occasion of her receipt of the degree of doctor of divinity (*honoris causa*) in 2006; and secondly, in notes she prepared for a detailed presentation on mission, a template likely used for many presentations—to the councils of the church, to clusters of parishioners, and in communion-wide publications.

The fourteen years that Ellie directed Partnerships were pivotal in the life of the Anglican Church of Canada, and in the life of Canada as a country as it began the ongoing work of forging a new identity with the Indigenous peoples of the land. Currently, in the life of the planet itself, as it evolves toward a precarious future, our purpose in collecting these essays is not only to honor the mark that Ellie made in her lifetime, but also to invite you, our readers, to make your own mark, moving forward with purpose and hope while checking in the rearview mirror to see how far we've come.

Our title *Partnership as Mission* pays homage to an earlier publication, *Justice as Mission: An Agenda for the Church* (1985) edited by the late Christopher Lind (to whom this book is posthumously dedicated) and Terry Brown who also contributes to this collection. We hope and pray that our gathering of wisdom will be a worthy successor to this earlier collection as we seek to live out our baptismal calling in and through the church, honoring the Creator, following the path of Jesus, empowered and inspired by the Holy Spirit.

KENNETH GRAY

MAYLANNE MAYBEE

I. BIOGRAPHY, MEMORIES, PERSPECTIVES

I

Ellie, Ecojustice, and Me

The Education of a Climate Activist

KENNETH GRAY

"YOU SHOULD PUT YOUR name forward for nomination to a standing committee at this General Synod." In such words my journey towards ecojustice was born. I was one of a half-dozen synod delegates representing the Diocese of Kootenay at the thirty-sixth General Synod of the Anglican Church of Canada in 2001. Ever the astute politician, Archbishop David Crawley explained how to make ourselves visible on the floor of General Synod hoping to attract the attention of the nominations committee. At that time, I had no interest in the Pension Committee, and I knew that competition for the Faith, Worship, and Ministry Committee was fierce; I was, however, intrigued by the remit of the Ecojustice Committee, then in its third iteration since its inception in 1996.

General Synod in those days was large and long. Meetings spanned ten or so days with four hundred or more people in the room. It was a great privilege to participate in such an exciting meeting, peopled with talented Anglicans from all parts of our Canadian church. For a newcomer, the prospect of addressing such a crowd was daunting. With the archbishop's words ringing in my ears, I stood at one of three microphones, immediately behind the redoubtable Phyllis Creighton, an ethicist and seasoned advocate for peace and justice who had just spoken to an environmental resolution. I was shaking with aspirational intent. In the end, given some vacancies on the committee and being a male cleric from western Canada, I was nominated to the Ecojustice Committee on which I served for two terms from 2001 to 2007. It was a moment that transformed my ministry and my life—and at the center of it all was Ellie Johnson.

In her own quiet way, Ellie was the pillar around which our committee of approximately fifteen members gathered. Together, we learned, worshiped, prayed, schemed, expressed our frustrations, and celebrated the occasional victory together. As the General Synod's director of Partnerships, and gifted with a lifelong passion for mission and justice, the Ecojustice Committee fell within her remit. Ably joined by Deacon Maylanne Maybee, coordinator for Mission and Justice Education, the two were a calm though dynamic duo leading a cluster of lay and clergy leaders, academics, teachers, and activists, all gathered under an Anglican umbrella. We were Indigenous and settler folks, some were younger and some older, and we were from all across our Canadian church. It was a rich and talented team—many of us remain friends to this day.

GETTING DOWN TO BUSINESS

The committee's mandate from 2001 identifies a huge scope of work:

> To pursue vigorously the church's commitment to the integrity of God's creation, recognizing this generation's accountability to future generations;

> To challenge attitudes and structures that cause injustice, primarily in Canada, but also in a global context, recognizing the interconnectedness of conditions that affect us all whether at home or in other parts of the world.[1]

The minutes of our first meeting at Toronto's Scarborough Foreign Mission Centre describe an intensive six-day organizational and educational odyssey as we aligned our work with the evolving structure of KAIROS, a newly formed ecumenical justice network which sought to continue the work of the former ecumenical justice coalitions. Our work was organized under five headings: Canadian social development, environment/ecology, global economic justice, Indigenous justice, and peace/nonviolence.

At this stage, the committee identified relevant justice issues and considered advocacy possibilities across all five of these areas. Given Ellie's many roles and connections—with General Synod staff, with KAIROS, with

---

1. "Ecojustice Committee: Terms of Reference."

the Anglican Consultative Council, and given her connections with Anglican Dioceses across our church, her input and direction was vital to our discernment process. During our first triennium, we deliberated carefully what work was possible given the skill sets, passions, and callings of committee members. We also responded to requests from the General Synod and other church leaders, from the Anglican Communion and ecumenical partners. We adjusted our agenda accordingly. In time, economic justice was coupled with environment, a fruitful combination as it turns out, while Canadian social development became a catch-all category for issues that didn't fit elsewhere. We spent more time working on a response to a General Synod resolution on gambling, which was referred to us by a General Synod resolution, than we did to the current and pressing issues of housing and homelessness, which was not. Indigenous justice and anti-racism work grew in importance partly in response to the Residential School Settlement agreements and parallel Healing and Reconciliation initiatives.

RESOURCES AND RESPONSES

Two significant resources were published during those years. A small working group drafted a resource on peace building, "Just War? Just Peace!" in response to a General Synod resolution.[2] However, it was obsolete before it was printed, as its release was overshadowed by the September 11 attacks of 2001, forever changing the ethical discourse about war, terrorism, and peace. In contrast, "A New Agape: A Plan of Anglican Work in Support of a New Partnership between Indigenous and Non-Indigenous Anglicans," developed by the Anglican Council of Indigenous Peoples, enjoyed broad distribution and deep engagement.[3] "A New Agape" was an idea and a process laid out in an open-ended binder full of examples, prayers, liturgies, and tools. It was designed to build a new relationship with Indigenous people based on an Indigenous-led partnership focused on the cultural, spiritual, social, and economic interdependence of Indigenous communities.

The list of draft resolutions forwarded by the Ecojustice Committee to the floor of General Synod 2004 is a good indicator of how we interpreted our work within the five categories previously listed:

> Globalization and Trade—to urge a review of the North American Free Trade Agreement (NAFTA) prior to any signing of the Free Trade Agreement of the Americas (FTAA);

2. Eco-Justice Committee Just War Working Group, "Just War? Just Peace!"
3. Indigenous Ministries, "New Agape."

Peace-making—to monitor and assess the next stage of weaponization, national missile defense;

Anti-racism—to extend and broaden the mandate potentially working with the General Secretary's office;

Indigenous rights—to further promote the "UN Declaration of the Rights of Indigenous Peoples" (UNDRIP) jointly with the Anglican Council of Indigenous Peoples;

Ecology and the environment—to further encourage and support the environmental audits of church buildings, drawing on resources from dioceses and the Global Network on the Stewardship of Creation; and to bring forward a resolution from the World Council of Churches (WCC) regarding climate change and economic justice.[4]

Given her many connections and roles, Ellie was well positioned to bring analysis and experience from various councils—including ecumenical and communion partners—to our twice-yearly meetings. It is interesting to ask what projects and issues the Ecojustice Committee did *not* take up. Despite the fact that justice issues are paramount in conversations around human sexuality, such matters never appeared on our agenda. During the work of the International Standing Committee on Mission and Evangelism (IASCOME), the task group made a conscious decision to avoid this work so as not to distract from other matters. In Canada, the difficult conversation around human sexuality was delegated to the Faith, Worship, and Ministry Committee, to diocesan listening circles, and to the Primate's Theological Commission.

During the early 2000s it was Ellie's and Maylanne's job to shepherd the work of the Ecojustice Committee through a time of tremendous upheaval and reorganization at Church House, a transition triggered by a seemingly endless series of budget cuts and staff downsizing. The ecumenical justice coalitions had folded into KAIROS—the only one remaining at the time was the Aboriginal Rights Coalition. Precarious times required structural innovation and experimentation with different ways of meeting and developing projects.

---

4. Author notes. See also detailed summary in "Ecojustice Committee: Report."

KINGFISHER LAKE: AN IMMERSION EXPERIENCE

Our committee met twice annually in different locations across the Canadian church for multiday meetings. Our gatherings were intentionally immersive so we could meet with local partners to hear their stories and witness their many challenges and opportunities. One particular highlight was a visit to Kingfisher Lake First Nation, an Indigenous northern community located 451 miles north of Sioux Lookout in northern Ontario. Now part of the Spiritual Ministry of Mishamikoweesh, the community is deeply rooted in Anglican tradition and practice while proud of its Indigenous heritage.

Over eight days we experienced the rhythms of this isolated Indigenous community. We joined in the broadcasting of Morning and Evening Prayer on the community radio station; we experienced the hotel, a tourism venture in the early stages of development; we joined a community member in a sponsored walk; we watched Bishop David Ashdown, then a committee member and bishop of the Diocese of Keewatin, join community members in extinguishing a house fire; we participated in a large confirmation service; we met the parish priest, now Bishop Lydia Mamakwa; we drafted a letter to the Ontario government in consultation with the chief and council concerning the preservation of Aboriginal lands and traditional hunting rights in light of a planned provincial park; and finally, we enjoyed a dinner together in which I joined local musicians in leading a gospel jamboree.

While expensive and logistically challenging, the advantages of immersion into local church ministry settings, especially in Indigenous communities, cannot be overemphasized. As I write, the Eleventh Sacred Circle of the Indigenous Anglican Church in Canada affirmed "The Covenant and Our Way of Life" and other foundational documents of the self-determining Indigenous Church.[5] The Kingfisher Lake immersion provided me with firsthand experiences through which, as a descendant of settlers, I could glimpse a different future for our churches in the years which followed.

Ellie frequently reported back to the committee the daily realities facing Church House staff, including relocation to a new building. Many fiscal and human resources disappeared over time. Through this maelstrom, Ellie remained emotionally and resolutely strong, omnivorously well-informed, globally experienced, and personally authoritative. As a person of strong faith and conviction, she still had confidence in the church and in its leaders! She was no charismatic, spot-lit, performative leader; rather, she was the person holding the rope as you attempted to climb a steep cliff—something

---

5. "Eleventh Indigenous Anglican Sacred Circle."

she and Maylanne did with me, a complete neophyte in ecological issues, in the early months of 2002.

A SURPRISING INVITATION

In March of 2002, a few months into my first term on the committee, my phone rang midday in the British Columbia Interior—Ellie and Maylanne were both on the line. After sharing pleasantries they asked if I would be willing to attend a meeting, the first ever Anglican Global Congress on the Stewardship of Creation in South Africa. With my heart racing, I reminded them that another person was better equipped to go—but the suitable candidate had declined—so after some travel preparation, I was off to the Good Shepherd Retreat Centre near Pretoria. Once arrived (after a very long delay) I met with global Anglican environmental justice leaders. The congress was the brainchild of the Rev. Dr. Jeff Golliher from the Anglican Communion Office at the UN in New York. We were hosted by the so-called "Green Bishop," Geoff Davies, whose long-standing and very public concern for ecological justice dating back to the early 1980s caused Archbishop Desmond Tutu to later say, "We should have listened to you sooner."[6] Also present was the Rev. Eric Beresford, then consultant for Ethics and Interfaith Relations at the Anglican Church of Canada.

The congress included around fifty scholars, activists, clergy and lay leaders from around the Anglican Communion. Considering my limited knowledge of environmental issues it was a glorious, if intimidating baptism by fire (irony noted). Following this meeting, some of us moved over to Johannesburg to attend the United Nations World Summit on Sustainable Development (WSSD). It was the experience of a lifetime.

The congress proceedings are published in *Healing God's Creation: The Global Anglican Congress on the Stewardship of Creation*.[7] The congress developed a motion for presentation to the next meeting of the Anglican Consultative Council in 2004 urging the creation of the Anglican Communion Environmental Network (ACEN).

Personally, the conference presentations, the creative worship experiences, and the sharing of stories of environmental degradation, coupled with an analysis of how wealthy countries and corporate entities obstruct in whole or in part a just transition towards a healthier planet, provided me with a curriculum for ecojustice ministry. As I returned from South Africa,

---

6. As described to the author by Bishop Geoff Davies, who worked alongside the archbishop at the South African Council of Churches.

7. Golliher and Tuatagaloa-Matalavea, *Healing God's Creation*.

my priestly ministry had plateaued somewhat, so the opportunity to engage in ecojustice ministry arrived at just the right time for me. The congress had opened a door, wide. Quakers say that "when one door closes, another opens." In my case, this was and remains true. And Ellie—the educator, the networker, the animator—helped make it all happen. She was a good recruiter and a brilliant assembler of teams. She easily discerned potential in many of us. She did not work alone, but had a talent for connecting people "of all sorts and conditions" together, often in surprising ways.

My new role in the semiannual meetings of the Ecojustice Committee was to report on the environmental work of the Anglican Communion, reporting which increased following my appointment as the first secretary for the ACEN in 2005. The Communion work, however, was not the only Ecojustice Committee activity.

JUSTICE CAMPS

Arguably the most significant project during my time on the Ecojustice Committee was the creation of the Justice Camps Initiative. Based on models from the US, Justice Camps were each structured around a theme: food, advocacy, and environment were the first three, the latter facilitated by myself and a team at the Church of the Advent in Colwood, British Columbia, in 2006. The brainchild of the Rev. Dr. Cathy Campbell, aided by the Rev. Dr. Peter John Hobbs and myself, the Justice Camp project launched a grassroots movement within the Anglican Church of Canada. It brought together people of all ages (half under thirty years old, the other half over thirty) from across the country to encounter a variety of social and ecological justice issues up close and first hand. By design there was a careful balance maintained between the giving of information and the sharing of experience. Through a program of directed immersion experiences, biblical reflection, worship, and relationship building, participants formed friendships, discerned calls to various ministry orders, and developed skills to become effective justice leaders within their own local communities. Now paused, nine camps were developed between 2005–2019.

THE COMMUNION CONNECTION

The Ecojustice Committee functioned alongside the Partners in Mission Committee, staffed by Ellie Johnson, Jill Cruse, and Andrea Mann, all employees in the Partnerships department. Though our areas of work did not directly overlap, we learned much from Ellie about the participation of the

Anglican Church of Canada in global Anglican circles such as the Anglican Consultative Council and the International Anglican Standing Commission on Mission and Evangelism (IASCOME).

At our March 2005 meeting, Ellie reminded us of the Ten Principles of Partnership—local initiative, mutuality, responsible stewardship, interdependence, cross fertilization, integrity, transparency, solidarity, meeting together, and acting ecumenically—which helped to underscore our missional justice work. At one point she recalled for us the words of Bishop Simon Chiwanga, onetime chair of the Anglican Consultative Council, who, in 1999, addressed the Council in Dundee, Scotland:

> The world is dying to hear, to know, and to experience the Good News that we have found in Jesus Christ. . . . The divisions that we wrestle with in the Church are minuscule in relation to the evils and pains of the world. Capitalism and international debt, militarism, religious persecution, civil wars, the drugs trade, the environmental crises and the devastation of this fragile earth, and nuclear arms proliferation, the continuing marginalization of women and youth in some of our cultures, all seek to undermine the commonality of creation we have with and in God.[8]

Ellie often reminded members of the Ecojustice and Partners in Mission committees of the Five Marks of Mission, which had been around for a while, but were finally gaining recognition not only in the Anglican Communion, but also in the Anglican Church of Canada under the primacy of Archbishop Fred Hiltz, who championed them at every opportunity:

> The mission of the Church is the mission of Christ
>
> 1. To proclaim the Good News of the Kingdom
>
> 2. To teach, baptize and nurture new believers
>
> 3. To respond to human need by loving service
>
> 4. To transform unjust structures of society, to challenge violence of every kind and pursue peace and reconciliation
>
> 5. To strive to safeguard the integrity of creation, and sustain and renew the life of the earth[9]

Having endured a stream of diocesan and parish attempts to craft mission statements over the years, a process which often produced imprecise and

---

8. Douglas et al., "Chairman's Address," para. 5.
9. "Anglican Communion's Five Marks."

confusing directives, I appreciate the elegant simplicity of these marks. I continue to believe that, with the addition of local contextual flesh, they remain relevant, robust, and practical. Since their first appearance in 1984, the marks have been revised or updated in two ways that intersected with our ecojustice work. In 1990, the Anglican Consultative Council added the fifth mark about the integrity of creation, stating, "We now feel that our understanding of the ecological crisis, and indeed of the threats to the unity of all creation, mean that we have to add a fifth affirmation."[10] Additionally, in 2012, the original text of the fourth mark, "to transform the unjust structures of society," was expanded with additional language, "to challenge violence of every kind and pursue peace and reconciliation," influenced by a joint resolution of the Ecojustice and Partners in Mission Committee to General Synod.

These opportunities to connect with Ellie's work and deliberations with the Anglican Communion were invaluable. For Ellie, mission education was the goal not only for Partnerships but for the whole church. Those of us who were privileged to participate in such partnerships were blessed with the education of a lifetime.

SAFEGUARDING THE INTEGRITY OF CREATION AND RENEWING THE LIFE OF THE EARTH

Having reflected on Ellie's role in the pursuit of justice and in the practice of partnership-as-mission through to her retirement in 2008, I now want to apply her understanding of mission and partnerships to today's missional landscape. In an undated mission workshop overview Ellie describes mission "as first and foremost what God is doing in the world. God is at work in the world, bringing healing, hope, [and] transformation in many different places and many different ways." She next challenges workshop participants to "first and foremost . . . name mission as God's transformative action in the world. And in addition . . . acknowledge that God is calling all of us to active participation in that transformative action."[11] So the question Ellie poses is similar to that posed by the prophet Micah: "What does God require of us" (Mic 6:6) as church leaders and activists at all levels who faithfully seek justice for all—justice for creation itself and humanity within it?

10. Anglican Consultative Council, *Mission in a Broken World*, 101.

11. Ellie's notes for an undated presentation on mission; personal papers of Maylanne Maybee.

Canadians Anglicans respond in various ways to the global climate crisis, in some cases working hard to mitigate climate risks and adapting to new environmental realities. Alternatively, many continue to minimize or deny the connection between climate change and economic and industrial activity. Nationally and within our church, such diverse views are not easily reconciled, especially considering Canada's historic dependance on resource industry wealth (forestry, mining, fishing) and more specifically on our dependence on fossil fuel extraction, transmission, export, and combustion locally and abroad for economic growth. An often polarizing debate ensues, with unfortunate results. Productivity, however, can be managed sustainably. The work of the Pembina Institute[12] and Iron and Earth[13] are two examples of an integrated and mutually respectful approach. These organizations have found a way to balance the legitimate needs of workers with sustainable development goals. While our church has been unreservedly outspoken in its condemnation of racism, sexism, and xenophobia, and our work with refugees and safe-church initiatives command international respect, by comparison, our track record on climate crisis response garners considerably less praise.

I often return to Jesus's parable of the rich man, Lazarus, and Abraham (Luke 16:19–31). The rich man has consistently mistreated Lazarus and others like him who begged at his door during his lifetime. Both are now dead—Lazarus with Abraham in heaven, and the rich man in a place of torment. Concerned about the welfare of his family, the rich man from his place of torment asks Abraham to send Lazarus to his brothers to warn them of the consequences of their callous and unjust behavior. Abraham replies, "They have Moses and the prophets; they should listen to them." The rich man persists: "No, Father Abraham; but if someone goes to them from the dead, they will repent." Abraham replies, "If they do not listen to Moses and the prophets, neither will they be convinced even if someone rises from the dead."

In the context of the climate crisis, I wonder who will describe to all humanity the error of our ways before it is too late? Within our church, how should our demand for climate justice be shaped? Must we wait until further calamities occur—increasingly severe floods, explosive and unrelenting wildfires, rising oceans and deteriorating fresh water supply, food security threats? How should we organize our advocacy in a resilient public witness?

---

12. See https://www.pembina.org/.

13. See https://www.ironandearth.org/.

During the early 2000s I cochaired the Creation Matters Working Group, a representative collection of diocesan environmental leaders from about half of our thirty Canadian dioceses. We met monthly by conference call to share information on activity and events in our dioceses, and to consider recommendations to General Synod and other councils of our church. It was a modest though well intentioned group. We lacked the ability to gather in person, let alone to initiate and sponsor gatherings or training sessions. It felt like we could endorse whatever activity we found around us but lacked the resources to take any project to the next level. We found more resources and greater efficiency in programs of the United Church of Canada. We deferred to numerous excellent KAIROS resources around the stewardship of water. We turned to the ecumenical group Greening Sacred Spaces having faltered with our own Greening Anglican Spaces work—the acronym "GAS" was possibly unhelpful. In many instances it felt like we had contracted out our work. Other Anglican provinces, such as the Episcopal Church and the Church of England, each produce webinars, informational sessions, worship experiences, event broadcasts, and frequently highlight the insights of prominent Anglicans such as Archbishops Michael Curry and Rowan Williams, Rachel Mash (my successor as ACEN secretary), and Ruth Valerio, author of the Archbishop of Canterbury's 2020 Lenten book *Saying Yes to Life*.[14]

Many argue, myself included, that environmental justice is the most urgent matter and concern for our time: there is no area of life it does not touch. It concerns not only the individual human but extends to compassionate care and healing for all species and to creation itself. What I see elsewhere, I seek for ourselves. As with most ethical reflection and commentary, when we "follow the money" we see the relationship between the environment and economics for what it is—a persistent and chronic abuse of power. As with the rich man and Lazarus, there is a profoundly inequitable balance of power between those who have little and those who continue to seek their own welfare. So then, where might we turn for leadership, comfort, and direction?

A PERSISTENT SPIRIT!

In her Magnificat, Mary knows that the lowly will be lifted up and the mighty brought low (Luke 1:52). So when and how, we cry, might that happen in the struggle for environmental justice? What people, processes, or procedures will lead to such a reversal of fortunes? In worship at EJC meetings we often

14. Valerio, *Saying Yes to Life*.

sang a song by Colleen Fulmer, SSF, based on the parable of the persistent widow (Luke 18:1–8).

> Choose life, that we might live
> Choose peace that we might see a tomorrow
> Let justice roll, roll like a river
> Roll like a river down.[15]

How then might we take this hopeful, persistent spirit into our climate crisis justice advocacy as a church? Through what kind of partnership do we work today? I fear we have been too quiescent. One reason for our dormancy may be that as a church we *continue to deny responsibility for our part in the destruction of the planet.* We have come to such a reckoning regarding racism and the residential schools' legacy. We can do something similar with justice for and within creation.

As a church and a nation we can alter the way we do business and live together, globally and locally for the sake of creation, God's gift for God's world. Historically, Canadians have altered economic and environmental practices—tobacco in southern Ontario, asbestos in Quebec, the fishery in Newfoundland and Labrador. One recent (2016) and noteworthy piece of work at the General Synod level has been the production of *Investing with a Mission*, an attempt to align Church investment practices at all levels with the evolving financial industry standards of environmental, social and governance functions (ESG).[16] We have moved through difficult economic transitions. Change is possible, if painful, along the way.

To whom then should we look for inspiration and climate crisis leadership today? Well if General Synod 2019 is any indicator, I would say youth are leading the way. In the last minutes of that Synod, three youth-generated motions arrived on the floor: Resolution C003 dealing with the climate emergency, and Resolution C004, climate change, which resolved in part "that this General Synod . . . encourage dioceses and parishes to support and participate in the global climate justice rallies occurring for young Canadians."[17]

Jumping ahead to 2023, at the time of writing, three environmental motions have been sent to General Synod by the Council of General Synod: one seeks to move the Anglican Church of Canada toward net-zero carbon

---

15. Fulmer, *Cry of Ramah.*

16. Responsible Investment Task Group, *Investing with a Mission.*

17. Due to time constraints, Resolution C004 was not presented at the General Synod but considered by the Council of General Synod at a later date when some of the content was no longer relevant. For the text, see "C004—Climate Change." For a list of resolutions, see "Resolutions."

emissions; another addresses climate change; and a third promotes clean and safe drinking water for all. The second motion calls on General Synod to declare, "in solidarity with the most vulnerable of our society" that there is a global climate emergency; to encourage Anglican parishes to work on reducing greenhouse gas emissions to help Canada reach a target of keeping global temperature increases at or below 1.5 degrees Celsius; and to endorse a "broad-based approach to investing which considers people, society, and the environment as important as financial performance."[18]

To the present generation of young adults, the fifth mark of mission directs us towards a timely and essential response to the climate crisis. As they see things, their very lives are on the line. Again, here is an activist voice, not unlike that of Phyllis Creighton mentioned above. Youth are demanding that Anglican Christians acknowledge Canada's "disproportionate role in the climate crisis" and *take responsibility for the protection of the most vulnerable*. These are mighty words of action, spoken by the present generation of younger Anglicans now taking their place in the leadership structures and public witness of our church. Theirs is the voice of mission today.

In a foreword to *Welcoming the Stranger: Mission as Transformation*, Ellie Johnson wrote: "Our calling to be sojourners on this earth means that we are challenged to keep moving and to travel lightly. God is at work transforming the world, and we are all called to be willing helpers in that mission. We need to have our bags almost packed so that we can respond quickly when God nudges us, telling us it's time to move on to a new challenge."[19]

The common ground of this collection of essays is that the gifts Ellie brought to the church in her day continue to affect and inspire us today. She believed that accurate information, information that was culturally aware, formed the basis for good education. Such learning leads to the personal transformation of both leaders and followers. Faith matters, and informs and supports our actions. Each of these, collectively, can and will reform the church. The church, rightly postured and resourced, can then transform the world. Rest well Ellie, and thank you. Your work is done; it is now handed on to us.

BIBLIOGRAPHY

"The Anglican Communion's Five Marks of Mission: An Introduction." Anglican Communion News Service, Feb 4, 2020. https://www.anglicannews.org/

18. Puddister, "This Is Still God's World," para. 6.
19. Johnson, *Welcoming the Stranger*, 7.

features/2020/02/the-anglican-communions-five-marks-of-mission-an-introduction.aspx.

Anglican Consultative Council. *Mission in a Broken World: Report of ACC-8 Wales 1990*. London: Church House Publishing, 1990.

Douglas, Ian, et al. "The Chairman's Address to the Anglican Consultative Council." Anglican Communion News Service, Sep 16, 1999. https://www.anglicannews.org/news/1999/09/the-chairmans-address-to-the-anglican-consultative-council.aspx.

Eco-Justice Committee Just War Working Group. "Just War? Just Peace! An Educational Resource on Peace and Nonviolence." Toronto: Anglican Church of Canada, 2001.

"Eleventh Indigenous Anglican Sacred Circle." The Anglican Church of Canada. https://www.anglican.ca/im/sacredcircles/sc11/.

Fulmer, Colleen. *Cry of Ramah*. Albany, CA: Loretto Spirituality Network, 1985.

"C004—Climate Change." General Synod 2019. https://gs2019.anglican.ca/wp-content/uploads/C004-Climate-Change.pdf.

Golliher, Jeffrey Mark, and Taimalelagi Tuatagaloa-Matalavea, eds. *Healing God's Creation: The Global Anglican Congress on the Stewardship of Creation*. Harrisburg, PA: Moorehouse, 2004.

Indigenous Ministries. "A New Agape: Plan of Anglican Work in Support of a New Partnership between Indigenous and Non-Indigenous Anglicans." The Anglican Church of Canada. https://www.anglican.ca/im/foundational-documents/anewagape/.

Johnson, Eleanor, ed. *Mission as Transformation: Welcoming the Stranger*. Toronto: Anglican Book Centre, 2007.

"Minutes of the Ecojustice Committee: Report to General Synod 2004–2007." Anglican Church of Canada, 2004, Anglican Church of Canada Archives.

"Minutes of the Ecojustice Committee: Terms of Reference." Anglican Church of Canada, Sep 2001, Anglican Church of Canada Archives.

MISAG 2 (Mission Issues and Strategy Advisory Group 2). *Towards Dynamic Mission: Renewing the Church for Mission*. London: Anglican Consultative Council, 1993.

Puddister, Matthew. "'This Is Still God's World': Canadians Respond to the Lambeth Call on Environment and Sustainable Development." *Anglican Journal*, Jun 1, 2023. https://anglicanjournal.com/this-is-still-gods-world-canadians-respond-to-the-lambeth-call-on-environment-and-sustainable-development/.

"Resolutions." General Synod 2019. https://gs2019.anglican.ca/cc/resolutions.

Responsible Investment Task Group. *Investing with a Mission: A Guide to Responsible Investment and Church Funds*. Toronto: Anglican Church of Canada, 2018. https://dq5pwpg1q8ruo.cloudfront.net/2021/03/15/09/57/05/44903f35-1f24-484a-9070-941e591c3b2f/Investing-with-a-Mission.pdf.

Rosenthal, James M., and Susan T. Erdey, eds. *Communion in Mission: Final Report of the Inter-Anglican Standing Commission on Mission and Evangelism*. New York: Church Publishing, 2006.

Valerio, Ruth. *Saying Yes to Life: The Archbishop of Canterbury's 2020 Lenten Book*. London: SPCK, 2020.

Zink, Jesse. "Five Marks of Mission: History, Theology, Critique." In *Journal of Anglican Studies* 15 (2017) 144–66.

2

Celebrating Ellie
Funeral Eulogies

VERNA ANDREWS: THROUGH THE LENS OF FRIENDSHIP

I am grateful to Ellie's daughters for the invitation to offer this eulogy, through the lens of friendship. The word "eulogy" comes from the Greek, meaning "good words"! So I have crafted a tribute of good words for my friend Ellie, reflecting on the goodness of her life as I encountered it. It is a statement of gratitude on my part.

These are the good words that surface immediately in my mind and memory of Ellie, and are woven throughout the many years of our friendship: Ellie was *generous, loyal, supportive*, and such a *good listener*. She was *hopeful* and *joyful, compassionate,* and *passionate.*

Ellie has three beautiful and talented daughters, who gave her so much joy. We loved to share our children's talents, achievements, and escapades, which were many! She played an active part in any event, be it weddings, baby showers, or fundraising parties. Any social gathering was incomplete unless Ellie was present. She was so kind. The word "generosity" keeps popping into my mind. So how did this wonderful friendship come about?

Going back to the early 1980s, we were fellow parishioners at St. Jude's, and often found ourselves sitting close by in the congregation. Our friendship blossomed later, after the Rev. Alec Hewitt, who was rector at that time, connected us, because we were travelling similar journeys, and he thought we could help each other. He was very right. Thank you Alec, you initiated a beautiful friendship which lasted for more than thirty years.

In those early years we were somewhat reckless in our activities. I remember many a summer's night going on mini "pub crawls" around downtown Oakville, Ellie encouraging me to participate with her in the Karaoke at various venues! Ellie loved to sing and was always a member of a choir, most recently here at St. Simon's. We had so much in common, we used each other as "sounding boards." I relied on Ellie to keep me grounded and she guided me to always "do the right thing." Don't get me wrong though; our friendship was not one-sided and that's why it endured. We proofread each other's presentations, speeches, and job applications, although hers needed little improvement! We organized fundraising dinners, for the eradication of land mines, for instance, and had great fun at murder mystery events with friends. Ellie threw herself in with great enthusiasm. I couldn't have wished for a more supportive friend and mentor. There wasn't a thing she wouldn't do.

During the hard times we spoke on the phone every evening to chat and debrief each other on the happenings of the day—we got everything off our chests, feeling lighter for the sharing, feeling more hopeful and able to sleep. All that "getting stuff off our chests" was a form of exercise, we thought—of fitness, of working out, and indeed it kept us in very good shape! During this period, we took a holiday together in Cozumel. I believe it was 1994. Ellie's language skills made her very popular and got us preferential treatment with the waiters! She was a very proficient snorkeler, too, though I nearly drowned! That holiday was so therapeutic and so much fun! Much later, in 2016, I returned to Cozumel as I accompanied my daughter to the World Triathlon Championships. Coincidentally, we stayed at the very same resort hotel that Ellie and I had stayed in over two decades previously. For me many memories were rekindled there.

Ellie was an adventurous, fun-loving, and compassionate person. If she felt it was important to do something, her determination made it happen. Those qualities are her legacy to me and all who knew and loved her. The best tribute to her would be to strive to be that kind of friend. When Ellie became unwell, during the early stages of degenerative brain disease, I was glad to support her more than ever. We drank tea together and talked and talked. I drove her on various shopping trips . . . but only under her precise directions! Bruce, my husband, was also Ellie's friend and advised her on all things financial. When Ellie was told of her diagnosis, she asked him for help. Ellie had a strong desire to have everything in order as best she could . . . this gave her some peace of mind.

Ellie had incredible intellectual strength, wisdom and knowledge . . . this made her diagnosis all the more tragic and especially hard to bear. Ellie taught me that being humble means recognizing that we are not on earth to see how important we can become, but to see how much difference we can make in the lives of others.

Ellie, your wings were ready. But our hearts were not. Thank you!

ALYSON BARNETT-COWAN: INTEGRITY, JUSTICE, AND PARTNERSHIP

Ellie and I were colleagues at Church House from 1991 to 2008, first as second-tier executives and then as directors and members of the management team. We spent many long hours together with colleagues working out budgets—mostly reducing them—and staffing, as well as preparing for meetings of General Synod. Ellie had a real flair for management, and one of the things I learned from her is how to exercise leadership in a collegial yet firm way. She wrestled with hard decisions by always considering the work priorities, not personalities. Yet she always encouraged her staff, paying attention to their personal needs, helping them to play from their strengths.

That was part of her integrity. She was well grounded in herself and so could place principles first. Ellie was always thinking of how to do work better. That meant also thinking about how to grow herself, always seeking, always learning, and always enthusiastic about finding new insights.

Justice, forever justice. First it was in seeking justice with and for overseas partners, then helping to integrate the social justice coalitions into KAIROS so that they could be more efficient and effective, more readily interpreted together to the churches. Then it was Indigenous justice. Through the time of the residential schools apology, the development of the settlement agreements, and then in truth and reconciliation long before the commission, she sought justice for survivors, and developed ways, always in partnership, to use the resources raised by the church for projects that would in some ways try to restore right relationships and recover language and culture.

Then more broadly, racial justice. Ellie was passionate about bringing the church, and its leaders, to an awareness of deeply instilled racial bias and of the damage of empire. Taking on the difficult and often unpopular task of racial justice education, sometimes with great resistance, she helped us all see the need for a truly just community, within and outside the church, and the need for personal transformation.

Then ecojustice emerged as a theme in General Synod's priorities, and Ellie took leadership in this as well. Moving well beyond teaching the church to use renewable plates at coffee hours, she pushed for an understanding of ecological justice as right relationship with the earth, walking lightly, respecting and upholding the dignity of every creature, and doing so never at the expense of those most suffering from climate change.

And, always, partnership. Ellie was passionate about moving the church from mission as a sending of aid to poor folks, to true collaboration. From the Anglican Communion's program of Partnership and Mission she drew insights about how to move to mutual mission, to hearing the gospel from the margins and living it out in right relationships of mutual learning and respect. At General Synod, but also at the Anglican Communion, she helped develop and live out the Five Marks of Mission. Ellie served the World Council of Churches on the Commission on Mission and Evangelism and was a major contributor to their shift in the understanding of mission as well. You will not see her name in the WCC's reports, because they are always consensus documents, but I can read Ellie in them.

Whether it was in church or just in life, Ellie valued each person and community, always seeking to learn and understand from those who came from different experiences and contexts. She modelled and exemplified what it means to be a genuine global neighbor.

I was reminded of Ellie as I was saying my prayers this morning. Three petitions from one of the litanies in the *Book of Alternative Services* stand out as being prayers that she honored and prayed:

> Give to all nations an awareness of the unity of the human family.
>
> Cleanse our hearts of prejudice and selfishness, and inspire us to hunger and thirst for what is right.
>
> Teach us to use your creation for your greater praise, that all may share the good things you provide.[1]

Thank you, Ellie, from all of us who had the privilege of knowing you. I picture you now continuing to animate the realm of God, maybe pushing even the saints into deeper partnership with one another for the sake of truth and justice and love.

---

1. *Book of Alternative Services*, 112.

TERRY BROWN: HER ACHIEVEMENTS WILL ENDURE

"And what does the Lord require of you but to do justice, and to love kindness, and to walk humbly with your God?" (Mic 6:8b)

What better words to describe Ellie's life and work, and what better words for us as we seek to live authentic Christian lives in a very violent, corrupt, and often hopeless world. "Do justice." "Love kindness." "Walk humbly with your God." In her various roles of doing justice through participation in God's mission, Ellie always did so with great kindness, and with genuine vulnerability, aware of her own weaknesses, never really lording over others.

The passage we heard from a couple of earlier chapters in Micah describes the ingathering and restoration of all nations and peoples in the final Davidic reign, which later for the church became the Messianic reign brought in through Jesus's life and ministry, later continued in Christian mission. What are the main elements? Ingathering, restoration, instruction, judgment, peacemaking, and the removal of fear.

Each of these (or combinations of them) might be a description of Ellie's ministry at different times in her life. She was often gathering, bringing together different peoples with different experiences. She worked at restoration, for example, of Canada's Indigenous peoples after so much trauma and destruction by both church and government. She was a mission educator and moved from teaching to action. As funds lessened and priorities came into conflict with one another, she had to exercise great judgment; she did not flee from difficult decisions. Her remit included many situations of peacemaking, locally, nationally and globally. John Keble's hymn, "When God of Old Came Down from Heav'n" ends with the line, "Save, Lord, by love or fear."[2] The theology of that line is a bit suspect, as causing fear in another is not the best way to express God's love. "Perfect love casts out fear" (1 John 4:18). Ellie's style removed fear and replaced it with support and encouragement.

Again, all models for us all: ministries of ingathering of all peoples, regardless of race, creed, national origin, religion, gender, sexual identity, age, ideology, or lifestyle; ministries of restoration, where, in the words of the great Cranmerian prayer, "things which were cast down are being raised up, and things which had grown old are being made new, and that all things are being brought to their perfection"[3] in Christ; ministries of teaching that bring together both old and new insights; discernment in this age of false

2. *Book of Common Praise*, 180.

3. *Book of Common Prayer*, 39–40.

news, demonic gaslighting, and fake identities, but also new insights and awareness; and finally, ministries of encouragement and forgiveness rather than enshrinement of victimhood or oppression: in the words of the hymn, there is "a wideness in God's mercy" (though I sometimes sing "wildness") that often needs to be recovered in our era of quick and irreparable judgements, from whatever ideological perspective.[4] We are called to all of them: ingathering, restoration, instruction, judgment, peacemaking, and the removal of fear.

Today's Gospel (John 10:11–16) speaks of Christ as the Good Shepherd, harkening back to God's shepherding Israel in Ezekiel, and forward to our looking after one another in our various capacities of leadership, whether in family, church, or society. Ellie was certainly a good shepherd, sacrificing her time and self for the church, in and out of all sorts of situations. Like the shepherd with responsibility for "other sheep," those of us who were shepherded by her at Church House realized that there were others besides ourselves that she looked after with great care; for example, her family, and she was delighted and shared, as they successfully worked through sometimes difficult struggles.

Many years ago, I had a conversation with late Bishop K. H. Ting, sometime Anglican bishop of Nanjing, survivor of the Cultural Revolution and later chair of the China Christian Council. We were talking about metaphors of Christian leadership, including the Good Shepherd passage. He commented that for many Asians, the Good Shepherd metaphor was too intrusive and interventionist, particularly in the light of colonial mission history. He suggested another biblical metaphor, that of the Gardener and the garden. Just as God is the Gardener, caring for us, the vines, hoping that we will bear good fruit, so we, created in God's image, are gardeners to one another. The gardener prepares the ground, plants the seed and waters it, and then goes away, letting the sun and rain (indeed, God) do their work, sometimes checking, sometimes watering, if necessary, but often staying away, not overtending, not overwatering, not dumping tons of fertilizer but letting God give the growth, with the hope that there will fruit. Certainly, that is another description of Ellie's style of ministry, at least as I experienced it. She did not micromanage but let you do your work. She was not threatened by others but offered encouragement without being overbearing. Surely the divine Gardener is also a model for us: offering the support and encouragement that is needed, but not control or manipulation.

Two other points: As an anthropologist, Ellie, I am sure, would be interested in the emergence in secular anthropological circles of the

---

4. *Common Praise*, 606.

"anthropology of Christianity." One of the principal debates there, especially in Oceania, is whether religious change takes place through continuity or what is termed "rupture." Both are biblical: whether the continuity of the slow growth, maturity, and fruitfulness of the Gardener's vine, or the rupture of St. Paul's conversion on the road to Damascus, or of apocalyptic destruction. I have spoken of the continuity of Ellie's justice and mission ministry. But sometimes, often delightfully, Ellie could be a bit "off the wall" or unpredictable and there were moments of great changes, or ruptures, in her life, surprising and unexpected. Sometimes she disappeared. Sometimes she seemed to be in a slightly different world.

But as Jesus said to Nicodemus, "The wind blows wherever it pleases. You hear its sound, but you cannot tell where it comes from or where it is going. So it is, with everyone born of the Spirit" (John 3:8). Like Ellie, may we too have an element of unpredictability and, indeed, as appropriate, rupture, born of the Spirit. I think this sense of the unpredictability of it all gave Ellie her great sense of humor, especially as she worked with others who could also be quite unpredictable. (I think of the "Three Musketeers," the late Father John Rye, the now-bishop David Hamid, and myself, covering the whole globe, always scheming. She accepted us and knew what was happening.) We are born of the Spirit, not of boredom and sadness but of excitement and laughter.

Finally, the last rupture was her loss of memory, a tragedy—and the greatest of thanks go to you who looked after her so well in those last years. And although Ellie may have lost the memory of her achievements, we have not—they will endure. May we too be encouraged and strengthened despite the present or coming depredations of age and further loss.

Ellie, "may the Angels lead you into paradise; may the martyrs greet you at your arrival and lead you into the holy city, Jerusalem. May the choir of Angels greet you and like Lazarus, who once was a poor man, may you have eternal rest. Amen."[5]

BIBLIOGRAPHY

The Book of Alternative Services of the Anglican Church of Canada. Toronto, Canada: Anglican Book Centre, 1985.

The Book of Common Praise: Being The Hymn Book of the Anglican Church of Canada. Toronto, Canada: Anglican Book Centre, 1938.

The Book of Common Prayer. Toronto, Canada: Anglican Book Centre, 1962.

Common Praise: Anglican Church of Canada. Toronto: Anglican Book Centre, 1998.

"In paradisum." Wikipedia. https://en.wikipedia.org/wiki/In_paradisum.

5. "In paradisum."

3

Presenting Doctor Johnson

SUSAN WINN

CITATION FOR DR. ELEANOR JEAN JOHNSON FOR THE DEGREE OF DOCTOR OF DIVINITY HONORIS CAUSA CONFERRED BY THE MONTREAL DIOCESAN THEOLOGICAL COLLEGE, MAY 18, 2006

Madame President, honored guests, members of the board, graduands, ladies and gentlemen.

I am honored to be able to present Dr. Eleanor Jean Johnson for this well-deserved recognition of her leadership in the life of the Anglican Church in Canada, and in her role as our Canadian director of Partnerships.

"Ellie," as she is known to friends and colleagues, is a lady with many gifts that she shares generously and with patience. I know this because I needed to learn so much from her when I became a member of the national EcoJustice Committee some years ago. Ellie is a woman of deep faith, a teacher, and a caring mentor to so many people. Ellie's ability to listen to the heart of each individual enables her to give guidance towards resolution to even the most difficult matters.

Ellie has lived her life in many interesting places. She was born in Canada, arriving in Montreal during her elementary school years. Following the attainment of her bachelor of education degree in physical education and her master of arts degree in anthropology from McGill University, Ellie, as a Canada Council Scholar, conducted her research for her PhD dissertation in Benin City, in Nigeria. In 1973 she was awarded her degree of doctor of philosophy in social anthropology from Michigan State University. She then returned to the University of Benin in Benin City, Nigeria, as a research fellow in child health.

In 1975 Ellie returned to high school classroom teaching. I can only imagine how wonderful it must have been to sit in her classroom and to benefit from her sensitivity, her knowledge, and her ability to discover the gifts in each individual student. From 1975 until 1980, Ellie taught in a secondary school in San Pedro Sula, in Honduras. Her next stop was two years of teaching in Naivasha Harambee Secondary School in Naivasha, Kenya. She was always able to find her place among other cultures, and I believe she was an ambassador for peace and understanding from her earliest years.

Returning to Canada in the 1980s, Ellie and her family lived in Fredericton, New Brunswick where she became a lecturer at the University of New Brunswick, and the director of Christian education at Christ Church Parish Church.

It was in 1987 that Ellie became coordinator of mission education for the Anglican Church of Canada. Living and working in Toronto from that time, Ellie has led our Canadian Church in the area of Partners in World Mission and as director of Partnerships. These partnerships have been developed within Canada, throughout North America and in countries around the world.

Since 1994 our Anglican Church of Canada has benefited from Ellie's participation as a member of the senior management team. Key initiatives include the strategic plan adopted by General Synod in 1995, and the "Framework" adopted in 2004. She has used her expertise to develop and nurture an integrated approach to the various areas of work in the Partnerships department. Her participation on commissions of the Anglican Consultative Council and the World Council of Churches have enabled her to foster a clearer understanding of the place of partnerships in the wider work of General Synod. She helped us to develop new understandings of God's mission in the current world context, and has taught us much about the role of our church in that mission.

In recent years, the churches in Canada and around the world have come to realize the benefits of working in ecumenical coalitions, especially in the work of justice initiatives. Ellie gave her leadership and vision towards bringing together twelve coalitions into what we now know as KAIROS: Canadian Ecumenical Justice Initiative. She nurtured worldwide inter-Anglican mission networks. Such deep and strong ties will serve us well as we work through the disagreements and divisions that currently exist within the Anglican Communion on issues such as homosexuality.

A major focus of Ellie's work has been her efforts as a leader to find a just resolution to the legacy of the Indian residential schools system in Canada. She has supported the Anglican Council of Indigenous Peoples as they have developed their vision of self-determination, and she has served on the government's Working Caucus on Alternative Dispute Resolution. At the same time Ellie has been a key player on the churches' ecumenical working group on residential schools. These roles have enabled her to provide invaluable assistance to Anglican dioceses across the country. Her ability to interpret the history of our church's participation in the residential school system and to provide strategic support to all parties has played such an important role in the Indian Residential Schools Agreement process.

With the resignation of the general secretary, Archdeacon Jim Boyles, in 2005, Ellie assumed the role of acting general secretary for two years, functioning as the chief operations officer of the national office of the Anglican Church of Canada.

At this time (2006), Ellie continues to serve on the Inter-Anglican Standing Commission on Mission and Evangelism, the Governing Board of the Canadian Council of Churches, the Commission on Justice and Peace of the Canadian Council of Churches, and the Working Caucus on Alternative Dispute Resolution for Indian Residential Schools Resolution Canada.

I have heard Ellie referred to as one of our national church's unsung heroes. Ellie is a quiet, conscientious person whose primary focus is to involve individuals in the life of the church, to pass on her knowledge and understanding and to nurture lasting partnerships among Christian people. Today we are here to sing of her successes and to express our very real appreciation. She is surrounded today by family, two of her three daughters and her sister in particular, and many friends and colleagues who are proud to share in Ellie's recognition.

For her more than twenty years of service in participating in and fostering the church's global mission, and for her leadership at the national level in social justice initiatives, including resolution of the residential schools legacy, I present Eleanor Jean Johnson, bachelor of education, master of arts, doctor of philosophy for the degree of doctor of divinity *honoris causa*.

4

Our Mother, Ellie
Turning on a Dime

SHE WAS ALWAYS THERE, BY KATE JOHNSON

My mum's colleagues have told me how they admired her professional passion and commitment, but she always said her most important job was being a mother. She didn't approach this as her duty; it was her devotion. Her kids, and then grandkids, were the center of her world. Her term of endearment for us was "lovey," and she used this word generously and unconditionally for all three of her daughters. In that word she expressed love, but also support: "I'm so proud of you, good for you lovey!" And with that devotion she boosted me over my self-doubts to be the best person I can be. Now that she is gone, I realize how uplifting her belief in me was, and still is. It made me who I am, but it also continues to shape me. I still hear her voice in my head telling me I'm OK. Love, for my mum, was not just a feeling she had, it was an energy she transferred, and that energy is still here in me, radiating now to my own child. When our family was fractured by divorce, my mum's spirit faded temporarily, but through the pain, we strengthened our mother-daughter bonds.

My mum was not a "traditional" wife, or mother. She got engaged to my dad, whom her parents had never met, and they ran off to Africa. But still, traditions were important to her. Since we grew up far away from any of our extended family, we made our own traditions: a cottage week in the Honduran hills, Christmas Day on the beach. But she also warmly embraced her British husband's traditions. She loved to cook, and made a point of learning how to make his favorite English plum pudding and fruitcake with marzipan. She finally drew the line at pies, which were my paternal grandmother's trademark. Try as she might, Mum could not roll the pastry (blame it on the African heat) and apparently flung it across the kitchen in a rage. In the end, she changed plans for a more appropriate specialty: home-made ice cream, with fresh cream from our local dairy in Naivasha, Kenya.

Changing plans was a great skill of my mother. If something didn't work, she just found an alternative. In her speech upon accepting an honor-ary doctorate from the Montreal Diocesan Theological College, she talked about the value she'd learned in being able to "turn on a dime." For me, that says so much about her: if something got in her way, she just changed course. There were lots of twists and turns in her life and she had a great phi-losophy about simply forging ahead and not worrying too much about the past. In my early career as a news reporter this attitude was what saved me from paralysis in the face of tight deadlines and breaking stories. Sometimes you just have to churn it out and not let perfectionism drag you down. My mum called this "mailing it in," and it serves me well even now.

But Mum also recognized when something required her full commit-ment and effort. You could rely on her if you needed accuracy and thorough-ness. I was reminded of this when I recently found an old letter from her, written thirty-five years ago, on January 18, 1988, when I had just become engaged to my Catholic husband, Bob. I had many questions about the dif-ferences between Catholicism and Anglicanism, and Mum jumped into that challenge with great gusto! "How can I ever respond to all these questions without writing a whole book?" she wrote modestly, but then proceeded with three full pages of her small, neat handwriting. "I think there are two equally important 'ends' to religion," she began. "One is your personal re-lationship with God. The other is your relationship with other people. The vertical and horizontal arms which, when placed together, form the cross." She ended with perfect "Mum" advice: "I think it is important to come to your own conclusions and always to remain open to new interpretations. Once you close your mind, you stop growing."

Mum rarely closed her mind—but she was known for her pronounce-ment of "fiddlesticks" on all things she felt were trivial or unimportant. Barbies, bad boyfriends, teenage diets, makeup, and fashion generally all fell into this category. But when something was deemed worthy, she was enthusiastic. She urged and helped me learn how to type because "you'll always need that" (how right she was!) and showed me how to change a tire on the side of an African dirt road. She infused her love of cooking into me without ever "teaching" it, and I also absorbed her love of adventure and travel. She spent hours reading to the three of us, which took some patience since there is a six-year span in our ages. When things took an unexpected turn she could take it in her stride—like giving birth to me in a small African clinic with no pain control because she couldn't make it to the Nairobi hospital in time. She loved to take us on safaris and snorkeling on coral reefs. She had no problem with us running around barefoot in our tropical backyards, despite any number of snakes, spiders, and other potentially dangerous critters, and it was an almost daily ritual to share the local Nigerian pool with frogs, tadpoles, and a thick layer of grime on the bottom. We were not overprotected in our childhood: my youngest sister, Em, broke her arm, my middle sister, Sekoia, fractured her skull, and I got seven stitches and fourteen rabies shots after being bitten in the face by a potentially rabid dog.

My mum was my professional role model. As a young woman entering the broadcast media at a time when it was dominated by older men, I often turned to her for advice. Although our careers were different, she and I also shared a similar motivation in our work: the desire to make a difference. She once showed me the results of her Myers—Briggs Personality Type Indicator test—we were delighted to discover our similarities. At the root of our work, for both of us, was the drive to disseminate information and to illuminate "the truth."

I don't remember much about my mum retiring. Our daughter, Melanie, was twelve at the time and I was busy trying to be a full-time mother, wife, and journalist. Mum seemed initially very busy, between her local church, two choirs, aquafit, Zumba, and walking groups. But she started to retreat, becoming more distant and less communicative—the first signs of her mild cognitive impairment and eventual dementia. Instead of recognizing my cue to reverse our roles and check in more often, I told myself not to be selfish or feel hurt that she seemed less interested in my life. I'm sad about that now, but still convinced that this is what she would have wanted. She did not believe in burdening her kids—she loved seeing us getting on with our lives—and she didn't want to dwell on her eventual diagnosis of mild cognitive impairment. In fact, she seemed thankfully unperturbed. Perhaps it was denial, or perhaps it was the disease.

Mum died at seventy-nine years old after living in a nursing home for four years with severe dementia. There were many times that my sisters and I had prayed for her release from the grip of that disease. But in her last few days we were blessed with a few fleeting moments of her old self. She had not really spoken or even smiled much in the past year and disliked any form of touch, but in her last days she held our hands, stroked our faces, and whispered, "I love you." On one occasion, waking up as the pain meds wore off, her face lit up to see us all there. "This is fun!" she insisted, with a big smile, as we sat around her deathbed. It was a comfort knowing she had always looked forward to being with God and was not afraid of death.

I miss my mother and the instant boost that she could give me. In losing her I have lost the horizontal arm of the cross she described. But the vertical arm—my relationship with God—is still intact, and in that vertical connection I can still feel my mother's love, in the intersection where the two arms meet.

MUM'S GRACE AND KINDNESS ENRICHED OUR LIVES, BY SEKOIA JOHNSON

Mum had two separate and distinct lives. A devoted mother to her brood of three girls and wife to her husband, Tim, and a fiercely independent thinker, teacher, and leader in her career. She did not let one life interfere with or muddy the other. There was a flow of enrichment between the two, although we don't know the effects of her career on her marriage, which ended in her late forties.

She was a stay-at-home mum in the early years of her married life. We lived in a tiny student family apartment in Lansing Village, Michigan. She must have been itching to resume a life in the outside world during those years. When she did return to complete her master's and PhD degrees in anthropology, I was probably two or three years old. When I was four, we moved to Nigeria as Mum began her anthropological field work with the market women in the area. We accompanied her to the bustling marketplace many times. I remember the drama when a market woman threw cayenne pepper powder in the face of a pickpocket. The market women were astute and successful, valuing their independence, qualities Mum respected a great deal.

We girls went to the local school at first, but it was soon decided we needed to be driven into Benin City for better quality education. The drive was not easy—mud, potholes, wild drivers. Mum became an expert at changing flats and we seemed to get one almost daily.

Mum passed on a love of reading to her girls. She read to us daily— *Narnia*, *Lord of the Rings*, *Paddington*, *A Wrinkle in Time*—many books we read repeatedly. She always had a number of books on the go, for us and for herself. The house was lined with bookshelves, the library an essential destination. When we experienced a huge earthquake in the mid-seventies while in Honduras, the bookshelves all came crashing down in the middle of the night creating terrifying drama. Though we moved often over the years, the books always came with us.

Mum took her first degree in education at McGill where she trained as a phys ed teacher. She participated in gymnastics, track and field, basketball, and ballet through school and university. Mum was an all-round athlete.

She would have loved to have been a ballet dancer if it weren't for her flat feet and broad shoulders (both of which she was wont to mutter about under her breath occasionally). One of my fondest photos of Mum, which is sadly hiding out somewhere at the moment, is of her at a dance, her skirt twirling and her head held high toward her partner, a look of delight on her face.

Mum loved music. She trained on the piano as a girl. Her musical tastes crossed all genres. Being an avid choir participant in two choirs in her later years gave her the social and artistic outlet she so needed. When we took a road trip as a family around northern Nigeria in the seventies, we listened to music and sang most of the way. If one song brings back the sweetest memories of Mum it would probably be "Joy is Like the Rain" by the Medical Mission Sisters.

Mum suffered from strong anxiety, probably passed down from her genetic line. She felt deeply and empathized with the suffering of the world. One of the darkest periods of her life was when Dad made the decision to abruptly end their marriage. Though broken and wounded for a time, she soldiered on with her life. She taught me the importance of "showing up," even in times of great turmoil. For her, in sharing our pain we lighten our load, for ourselves and for others. It takes great courage to bare an injured heart. Thank you Mum.

I was a single mother for many years and Mum never failed to strongly support me every step of the way. I felt understood, accepted, and respected by her. She sent me a small monthly check that would always arrive just when it was needed the most. She spent many holidays visiting with us on Gabriola Island, British Columbia. Her words of encouragement were constant and she loved my boys, Adrien and Ray.

Thank you, Mum, our lives have been enriched immeasurably by your grace and kindness.

Emily, Kate, Ellie, and Sekoia, Great Whelnetham, Suffolk, England, 1979

Ellie in her thirties

Ellie with granddaughter Devon

II. CHURCH HOUSE

Embracing Partnership

5

Partnerships and Preparing the Way

MAYLANNE MAYBEE

"Partnership itself is a relationship that is characterized by strange multiplication tables. A new focus of relationship in which there is continuing commitment and common struggle in interaction with a wider community context displays characteristics of synergy, serendipity, and sharing. The relationships are not just quantitative, but are qualitative. They produce an overspill of energy greater than the sum of the parts and unexpected gifts that need to be shared."

—LETTY M. RUSSELL, *THE FUTURE OF PARTNERSHIP*[1]

THIS VISIONARY CONCEPT OF partnership was the organizing principle behind *Preparing the Way*, the 1995 strategic plan for the General Synod of the Anglican Church of Canada. Partnerships was also the name of the department at the national office (Church House) that brought together three areas of work—international mission, ecojustice, and Indigenous relationships—between 1994 and 2008. It was the creative and practical application of the concept of partnership that became the legacy of Dr. Eleanor Johnson (Ellie) who was on staff at Church House for twenty-one years, fourteen as Partnerships director. I knew her as my boss and mentor for eleven of those

---

1. Russell, *Future of Partnership*, 24.

years (1996–2008) and as a friend for many more. I believe her particular style of leadership, used within the framework of *Preparing the Way*, helped create a web of relationships, at home and abroad, that led to "an overspill of energy" in the Anglican Church of Canada, and left us with "unexpected gifts that need to be shared."

In this chapter, I reflect on Ellie's approach to mission, ecojustice, and Indigenous relationships through a partnership lens, and on the successes and learning arising from implementing the ten-year strategic plan known as *Preparing the Way*. I do this through the lens of General Synod's work relating to ecojustice, and how that work evolved through the combined influence of the strategic plan and Ellie's leadership from 1996 to her retirement in 2008.

THE CHURCHES AND SOCIAL JUSTICE IN THE SEVENTIES AND EIGHTIES

For decades, prior to the implementation of *Preparing the Way,* the office of General Synod had functioned as a source of financial services and staff support to parishes and dioceses of the Anglican Church of Canada for Christian education, leadership development, youth ministry, women's concerns, and congregational vitality, as well as international mission, ecumenical relations, social justice advocacy, and communication. During the 1950s and 1960s, a maze of boards and councils had grown up: the Missionary Society of the Church of England in Canada (MSCC), the General Board of Religious Education (GBRE), and the Council of Social Service (CSS), each with its own set of subcommittees and taskforces. Following the recommendations of a 1967 Pricewaterhouse report, these structures were consolidated into a system of standing committees responding to a single program department.

In the 1970s, when Ted Scott was primate, the program department thrived under the direction of Clarke Raymond. It was an era when the spirit of ecumenism and social activism among Canadian churches was at its peak, inspired by the Lund Principle, first articulated at the 1952 Faith and Order Conference of the World Council of Churches held at Lund, Sweden: that churches should act together in all matters except those in which deep differences of conviction compel them to act separately. The idea of the church as a national institution capable of influencing government and business prevailed. In the aftermath of the failure of union between the Anglican and United Churches in 1975, they redirected their energy into striving together with other denominations to address the social and economic injustices of the day. These efforts gave rise to a growing cluster of ecumenical justice coalitions,[2] formed to address injustices at home and abroad—human rights abuses in Latin America, Indigenous rights to land and resources in northern Canada, the anti-apartheid struggle in South Africa.

SOCIAL JUSTICE AND ANGLICAN THEOLOGY

Recognition was growing that the task of church leadership, social activism, and theology was to counteract the impact of colonialism and neocolonialism on Christian thought.[3] "Contextual theology" was a movement to become aware of inherited Eurocentric assumptions about God and the church and to do the hard work of paying attention to one's own context, to seek answers to one's own questions, and to formulate responses to one's own perspective.

One of the ecumenical coalitions, the Taskforce on Churches and Corporate Responsibility (TCCR), was applying pressure to churches and the public to boycott banks and corporations with investments in Pinochet's Chile and apartheid South Africa. Their stand led to growing tensions between church activists and more conservative members from affluent congregations who formed the Confederation of Church and Business People (CCBP). Against this backdrop, the Rev. Dr. Derwyn Owen, retired Provost of Trinity College, Toronto, was invited to address General Synod at its meeting in Peterborough in 1980. He articulated an Anglican understanding of social action that we would do well to revisit in our time.

Owen held that there was a characteristically Anglican method in theology, found in the works of Richard Hooker (1554–1600), F. D. Maurice (1805–1872), and William Temple (1881–1944), which attached a high value to reason, found expression in striving for mutual understanding, reconciliation, and mediation between opposing views, and emphasized the theological basis of the church's social action. If God is creating the world and loves the world and seeks to save it, then "Christians therefore must not turn their backs on the world and try to escape from it."[4] He spoke of

---

2. Aboriginal Rights Coalition, Inter-Church Coalition on Africa, Taskforce on the Churches and Corporate Responsibility, Canada-Asia Working Group, Ecumenical Coalitions for Economic Justice, Canada China Program, PLURA, Ten Days for World Development, Inter-Church Committee on Human Rights in Latin America, Project Ploughshares, Inter-Church Committee for Refugees, and Inter-church Fund for International Development.

3. Lind and Mihevc, *Coalitions*, 6.

4. Owen, *Social Thought*, 32.

the "plethora of ecumenical groups involved in social action," noting that what they held in common was a conviction that the church's place was to be involved in social, political, and economic concerns of the day, and that churches needed constantly to articulate the theological basis for taking social action. He referred to the Anglican conviction that being converted and faithful to "the Christian way" must involve challenging unjust policies and structures and raising moral and ethical issues in the public arena.[5] (These words were echoed years later in the definition of mission formulated by the 1984 Anglican Consultative Council, "to seek to transform the unjust structures of society,"[6] now familiar to us as the fourth mark of mission.)

PREPARING THE WAY FOR A NEW MILLENNIUM

Michael Peers became primate of the Anglican Church of Canada in 1986, at a time when the days of affluence, privilege, and largesse as a church were coming to an end. It was no longer possible for the "national office" to be all things to all people. It was in that period, at the Native Convocation of Indigenous Anglicans in 1993, that Archbishop Peers offered a formal apology on behalf of the whole church for the harm done by the residential schools system, in which the Anglican Church of Canada was complicit: "I accept and I confess before God and you, our failures in residential schools. We failed you. We failed ourselves. We failed God."[7]

In the face of shrinking membership, declining resources, and the emergent demand to repair the damages of colonialism, the 1995 strategic plan proposed to establish a clear division of labour: General Synod was to concentrate on "what it could do best"—nurturing and building overseas partnerships, advocacy for social justice issues, attention to Indigenous rights, communication and financial services for dioceses, ecumenical relationships, and Anglican identity. Local work was to be done locally, and domestic work such as congregational development, leadership development, and stewardship education was to be done by dioceses.

It was a plan built around the principle of subsidiarity, which provides that a central authority should perform only those tasks which cannot be performed at a more immediate or local level, provided there is capacity to perform these tasks adequately at such levels. At its best, subsidiarity is

---

5. Owen, *Social Thought*, 34.

6. "Anglican Communion's Five Marks."

7. "Anglican Church of Canada's Apology," para. 1.

about ensuring that decisions are made at the most appropriate level, so that all those most affected can contribute.

The *Anglican Journal* coverage of the strategic plan highlighted its focus on international partnerships and social justice as the central priorities of General Synod (though interestingly, less so on the church's obligations to Indigenous peoples). Compared to strategic plans before or since, *Preparing the Way* was exceptionally detailed and specific. Regarding international mission and development, the emphasis was less on sending resources and personnel overseas, and more on "increased collaboration at home and abroad by fostering and nurturing partnerships." Regarding social justice, the emphasis was on "engaging people in the pew in social justice issues and encouraging action at the local level." Regarding work with Indigenous peoples, the emphasis was on "healing, reconciliation and justice issues in aboriginal communities." General Synod was to act less as a legislative body working through standing committees and councils, and more of as a partner, working through networks, consultations, and ad hoc gatherings.[8]

As director of Partnerships, Ellie held together a complex organizational structure. She was part of the management team at Church House, responsible for strategic planning, coordination, and budgeting. She gave oversight to the Partners in Mission (PIM) Committee and its programs—Volunteers in Mission, Diocesan Companionships, and theological student internships. She supported the staff and volunteers of the Ecojustice Committee, who in turn connected with the justice work of parishes, dioceses, provinces, and our ecumenical partners. Her work with Indigenous Justice and the Anglican Council of Indigenous Peoples grew into a much larger portfolio, working toward a settlement agreement on residential schools and finding ways to listen to, receive, record, and compensate for the experience of Indigenous survivors.

ECOJUSTICE

By the late 1990s, the landscape of Anglican and ecumenical justice work had become very complicated. There were at least twelve ecumenical coalitions with their own offices, boards, and staff, and some uncertainty about who actually employed them. In addition, each of the mainstream national churches employed their own cluster of justice staff, and each in turn related to the Canadian Council of Churches and its affiliates (such as Project Ploughshares), to many other para-church groups and organizations, and to the World Council of Churches with its era of justice, peace, and the

8. *Preparing the Way*, 13.

integrity of creation, and the decade to overcome violence. There was the Primate's World Relief and Development Fund, which until the late sixties had been joined with international mission work under the umbrella of the World Mission department. The Anglican Church of Canada, as part of a worldwide communion, also related to the Lambeth Conference, the Anglican Consultative Council, and to global Anglican networks such as the Anglican Peace and Justice Network, the Inter-Anglican Women's Network, and the Anglican Communion Environmental Network.

In early 1996, the newly constituted standing committees and councils prescribed by *Preparing the Way* met at an airport hotel in Mississauga. The task at that first Ecojustice Committee meeting was daunting: to establish areas of work and identify priorities, taking into account this landscape of justice organizations and events in the world around us. Cynthia Patterson, a community organizer and activist from the Gaspé area of Quebec who had been part of the discontinued Public Social Responsibility Unit, recalls that the Ecojustice Committee "rose out of the noise and toxicity of a jet and automobile carbon-soaked atmosphere. The expansive character of our earlier justice work was out of necessity funneled into a very different context, not only financially but culturally, out of institutional and individual reflections and into a vortex of deepening challenges. No one knew what was happening or what would come out of the process, other than that we had no money."[9]

I was hired in August 1996 as coordinator for Mission and Justice Education, just as the strategic plan was coming into effect with its new emphasis on networking, education, and engaging people "in the pew" in social action and advocacy. My background in cross-cultural experience, education, and urban ministry seemed to suit me for the position. As the child of a career diplomat, I had grown up in Ottawa; Australia; Washington, DC; and Lebanon; I had traveled widely, and become fluent in French. As a young adult I taught religious education in Anglican schools and coordinated a Christian education program in a Toronto parish. I had worked as deacon-in-charge of the struggling congregation of St. Mark the Evangelist in the Parkdale neighborhood of Toronto, while also trying to animate a response among local churches to people affected by the 1982 recession. I was a "grad" of the Canadian Urban Training Program for Christian Leadership, and for ten years worked with the Urban Core Support Network, building strategic connections among church- and faith-based community services in urban centers across Canada. However, I had little involvement with the work of ecumenical coalitions, almost no awareness of Anglican mission,

9. Cynthia Patterson, email message to Ken Gray, June 22, 2022.

and limited exposure to Indigenous justice issues. There was a lot to learn on the job!

FROM PLAN TO REALITY—DIFFICULTIES OF TRANSITION

According to the strategic plan, the purpose of the Ecojustice Committee was "to advocate social justice and prophetic mission within Canada; to promote networks and develop discussion frameworks; to develop a new relationship with Indigenous peoples."[10] Applying the principle of subsidiarity meant working in ways that would empower local communities to take meaningful action on issues that concerned and affected them, while making the most of the resources and connections available to General Synod at the national level.

Minutes from that first Ecojustice Committee meeting in 1996 give an overview of General Synod resolutions requiring advocacy action relating to ecojustice: land mines, fish stocks, child prostitution in Asian tourism, land claims negotiations, nuclear weapons, Canadian foreign policy, international financial institutions, free trade in the Americas, prostitution, low-level flying mediation discussions in Labrador. There were requests to endorse and sign an ecumenical statement on an alternative budget (prepared by the Centre for Policy Alternatives in partnership with the Ecumenical Coalition for Economic Justice), to proclaim a day of fasting on April 1 in witness against the enactment of the Canadian Health and Social Transfer, and to endorse the climate change petition campaign of the World Council of Churches. While individual committee members had some connection with most of these issues and actions, it is not clear whether or how many "people in the pew" would have understood or supported them.

One of the great challenges of implementing the strategic plan was cutting back or letting go of pieces of work that had been important but were losing importance, or for which there were no longer resources. Some of the national work that had to be dropped were women's issues, urban ministries (close to my heart), and the close working relationships between the justice work of General Synod and that of the Primate's World Relief and Development Fund (PWRDF) and Ten Days for World Development, a justice coalition that connected people of faith across Canada with people engaged in development across the globe.

Another challenge was the overlap of work involving more than one committee or working group. For example, a 1997 General Synod resolution

10. *Preparing the Way*, 2.

requested the Ecojustice Committee; the Faith, Worship, and Ministry Committee; and the Anglican Council of Indigenous Peoples to develop an educational resource and policy framework on gambling, taking into consideration ethical concerns about addiction, centuries-old practices of gaming among Indigenous communities, and the place of raffles and auctions at the parish level. It was not always possible to keep pace with the changing context. By the time the work was near completion, events had overtaken us and interest had shifted to other issues. A similar thing happened when the Ecojustice Committee produced a study guide on "Just War," released within days of the 9/11 attacks in the USA, requiring a complete rethinking of the resource and a rewrite, which simply wasn't possible.

FROM PLAN TO REALITY—NEW WAYS OF WORKING

Over the next decade, the Ecojustice Committee and the Partnerships team would strive to narrow the gap between national priorities and those of dioceses and parishes. However, five years in, the strategic plan would be "preparing the way" for yet more reductions to budget and staff. In 2001, General Synod initiated budget cuts that would reshape the mission relationships of General Synod, ending the position of mission coordinator for Africa and the Middle East, and slashing $370,000 from funds available for mission partners. These changes marked the beginning of the ongoing task of streamlining the regional mission coordination desks into a single position of Global Mission coordinator—the work of Andrea Mann, then regional mission coordinator for Asia and the Pacific.

That same year my colleague Joy Kennedy, ecojustice coordinator, was let go after twelve years on the staff of Church House. Significantly, she had represented the Anglican Church of Canada at meetings of the Anglican Peace and Justice Network, sat at the table of many coalition boards, and worked with ecumenical partners on Building a Moral Economy, a three-year training program that paved the way for the Canadian Ecumenical Jubilee Initiative. Ecumenical staff would now carry out this level of justice work, and my role would change from coordinator for Mission and Justice Education to coordinator for ecojustice networks. The change in title represented an important change in both the style and scale of the justice work of General Synod.

Two other events stand out during the change of the millennium—the launch of KAIROS: Canadian Ecumenical Justice Initiative in 2001 as the successor to the ecumenical justice coalitions, and the formal signing of the Residential Schools Settlement Agreement in March 2003. That spring I returned from a four-month sabbatical to a Partnerships department in disarray, just as members of the Anglican Council of Indigenous Peoples had spoken out against the signing of the agreement. Ellie was not prepared for this reaction, and took many months to recover a sense of equilibrium.

The transition from the ecumenical justice coalitions into what was to become KAIROS: Canadian Ecumenical Justice Initiatives took years and months of planning and negotiations. Jeanne Moffat, who had staffed the Ten Days for World Development coalition and directed Greenpeace, was approached to manage the personnel and structural changes required to create a single organization. She initially declined, and when asked what would convince her to accept, she replied, among other things, that she would need the full support of the churches together and the assurance that the board was behind her. This was the kind of work that Ellie did so well. My cubicle was next to hers, and I have memories of overhearing her persuasive but diplomatic phone calls to colleagues in the other mainstream churches, listening to their concerns, making the case for a way forward. It was not the sort of action that received front-page coverage in church newspapers, but I know that Ellie was instrumental in building a common supportive stance among the churches for the direction KAIROS was taking and for winning their unequivocal support for this work.

I can only imagine the stress that Ellie must have been going through in those years. I marvel at her resilience, and at the achievements she facilitated over the following years, which were considerable. Four examples come to mind of projects that I think succeeded in narrowing the gap between the national office and the dioceses and parishes: the Canadian Ecumenical Jubilee Initiative, the Blanket Exercise and the Blanket Train campaign, the ongoing Justice Camps Initiative, and the Anti-Racism Working Group.

Canadian Ecumenical Jubilee Initiative

Canadian churches and ecumenical organizations launched the Jubilee Initiative in 1998 as a call to Christians and the general public to realize the vision of the biblical concept of Jubilee. Across Canada, church groups and partners joined with a global campaign seeking to cancel the debts of the world's fifty poorest nations in the form of a petition and bring an end to structural adjustment programs, the crippling austerity measures that were impoverishing billions of people worldwide. In Canada, denominational offices and coalitions collaborated to adapt the debt-cancelation campaign to the Canadian context, building on existing pieces of work and relating them to the Jubilee theme.

As Canadians learned about the issues, people began to write to, or meet with, their members of Parliament to push for change. Finance Minister Paul Martin reportedly received more mail on the debt issue than on anything else that year, and declared the campaign a "phenomenal success."[11] Christian communities were invited to take a "Jubilee pledge," personally committing themselves to specific actions at a personal, local, and global level. No longer was it a small collection of denominational staff acting in isolation from "people in the pew," but a concerted collaboration of churches and justice organizations that captured the attention and imagination of Christians at every level.

The Blanket Exercise and the Blanket Train

In November 1996, my first year on the job, I attended an event releasing the report of the Royal Commission on Aboriginal Peoples (RCAP),[12] an eye-opening moment for me and one that would increasingly define the priorities of General Synod and shape the work of Partnerships. In response to that report, the Aboriginal Rights Coalition (ARC) brought together elders and educators to develop the Blanket Exercise, an experiential learning tool whereby participants would revisit the history of relationships between Indigenous and non-Indigenous peoples in Canada. Blankets were laid out to represent Turtle Island—North America before the arrival of Europeans— and as people stood on it, a person representing European colonizers would recite the moments of war, disease, trickery, and legislation that eventually combined to separate Indigenous peoples from their land and isolate them from each other.

The third year of the Jubilee campaign was about restoring right relations with Aboriginal peoples, and with the earth. In order to highlight this theme, the idea emerged to reverse the Blanket Exercise in an action that would demonstrate the reclaiming of land and relationships. With the cooperation of Via Rail, staff from the Jubilee Initiative and ARC gathered blankets from communities across the country over a five-day train trip from the four directions, bringing them to Ottawa to lay out on the grounds

11. *Anglican Journal*, "Jubilee Continues."

12. "Indigenous peoples" is preferred to "Aboriginal people," as it recognizes more than just one group of individuals, and its Latin meaning, "sprung from the land: native," reinforces the connection of Indigenous peoples to their lands. See "Why We Say 'Indigenous,'" para. 10.

of the Supreme Court. I had the privilege of riding the train from Windsor, the southernmost point in Canada, stopping on the way at stations where people clustered to hand their blankets over and to cheer us on.

My single companion on that trip was a man from Walpole Island who shared his story of residential school abuse on the way. It was devastating. We arrived at Toronto Union Station before heading on to Ottawa in time to join a smudging and drumming ceremony, echoing through the halls of the station. It was an unforgettable experience of learning at a gut level, of cooperation, hope, and giving public witness to Indigenous land rights from coast-to-coast-to-coast.

Justice Camps Initiative

One of the first things I tried to do after starting at Church House was to collaborate with the Magnificat Network to organize and convene a national event with the goal of fostering and strengthening a network of justice activists and advocates. "Ancient Roots, New Routes" took place in Winnipeg in 1998. It was an inauspicious beginning: the conference ended in conflict, precipitated by a contingent of participants who walked out in protest over the historic and present treatment of Indigenous people.

Fortunately, the Ecojustice Committee came up with a more effective and lasting national/diocesan partnership: Justice Camps, the brainchild of the 2001–2004 Ecojustice Committee, led primarily by Cathy Campbell, Peter John Hobbs, and Ken Gray. Cathy Campbell pulled together the first Justice Camp in 2005 in Winnipeg on the theme of food security with less than half a year to plan, an incomplete budget, and not much more than a great idea. It was an intergenerational event, cosponsored by the Ecojustice Committee and the Diocese of Rupert's Land, that drew together youth and seasoned activists from across Canada for experiential learning through immersion, Bible study, informational input, and the sheer joy of community.

Journalist and activist Murray MacAdam wrote that Justice Camps "embody what our church should be about—and what it rises to, when we cast off our fear about trying courageous ways of 'making all things new' and look at Jesus' message with fresh eyes."[13] This was national/diocesan collaboration (subsidiarity) at its best, with General Synod providing leadership, resources, and a national perspective, while dioceses provided on-the-ground logistical support, hospitality, contextual insight, and the involvement of local youth, interest groups, and community organizations.

---

13. MacAdam, "Shalom Justice Camp," para. 6.

Racial Justice

In 2001, the UN convened a World Conference Against Racism, Racial Discrimination, Xenophobia and Related Intolerance in Durban, South Africa. Esther Wesley, the newly hired Indigenous Healing Fund coordinator, attended on behalf of the Anglican Church of Canada. Bishop James Cruickshank of Cariboo, taking his cue from that event, brought a resolution to the floor of General Synod to convene an Anti-Racism Working Group, to hold an anti-racism training session for the joint meeting of standing committees, councils, and boards, and to make recommendations for continuing the work of anti-racism.[14]

In her encounters with Indigenous communities in Canada, and with global partners in the worldwide communion, Ellie had undergone a conversion in her understanding of racism: she began to see it not just "over there" in apartheid South Africa, or "back then" in Europe during the Second World War, or "down there" in the southern USA, but as a sin, a symptom of brokenness within and among us, in our church and in Anglican parishes and communities across Canada. When she summoned Esther Wesley and me to her office to tell us, "You're on first for anti-racism," she was not just acting on a directive from General Synod. She was acting from a deep personal commitment.

I had no idea where to start, but as I moved forward, convening the working group, researching the anti-racism work of churches in the USA, hearing the stories of people who had endured racism and discrimination, and above all, working alongside Esther, who became a mentor and friend as well as a colleague, I began to undergo a similar kind of conversion. Learning about and teaching others about racism in our midst was hard, hard work. Not only did I come face to face with my own biases, privilege, discouragement, and vulnerability, but I also met up, more than once, with resistance and hostility from those on the receiving end of our efforts to provide training.

As our working group looked at what other churches and denominations were doing, we came up with the idea of writing a "Charter for Racial Justice," something to help develop a common lens for analyzing racism and strategizing for positive change. We soon discovered we were in for the long haul. When the first draft came to COGS in March 2004, it was clear that it was not going to fly. Ellie worked behind the scenes to change the motion from having the charter approved or adopted, to having it received

14. "Anti-Racism."

as a "working document," to be referred back to the Anti-Racism Working Group for "further refinement," and to be used for future educational work.

The results of our efforts were slow in coming, and we often felt as if we were taking one step forward and falling two steps back. Though our mandate was to work with committees, boards, and councils of General Synod, we began to receive invitations to lead anti-racism training events in dioceses across Canada. The work was demanding and exhausting. None of this had been in our original job description! Esther and I laughed when we revealed to each other that, unbeknownst to the other, we had each gone to Ellie to ask to be released from this work. It was just too difficult. And Ellie had just listened and encouraged us to keep going. It worked—and we did.

LOCAL VS. NATIONAL

In Derwyn Owen's 1980 address to the General Synod in Peterborough, he asked a question I often wonder about: whether the Anglican Church of Canada can truly call itself "national." Unlike The United Church of Canada, whose very structure and identity is rooted in its national origins and reach, the Anglican Church in Canada was not "made in Canada" and is not centralized; it is not a federation of provinces and dioceses; and its "head office" has only a very defined and limited jurisdiction in the dioceses. On one hand, Anglicans in Canada are a minority group among Christians, and an even greater minority within a pluralistic and highly secularized society. On the other hand, Anglicans have a compelling historic and geographic presence in Canada, a strong ecumenical tradition, and an incarnational theology that is oriented toward being a presence in the world.

According to Owen, Anglicans can surely claim to be "national" in their moral orientation, their ecumenical relationships, and their theological worldview.[15] Nevertheless, I am always careful to refer to Church House not as "the national church" but as "the office of General Synod" or "Church House." The challenge at the national level is to discern the appropriate distribution of resources and leadership to ensure that local churches will thrive, while also acting as the Anglican Church of Canada in relation to other churches and the global communion in ways that parishes and dioceses cannot.

In the later years of my time at Church House, I watched the erosion of the principle of subsidiarity underlying the strategic plan, a "mission creep" back to the unsustainable pattern of trying to be all things to all people. The March 2004 document "Serving God's World, Strengthening the Church: A

15. Owen, *Social Thought,* 33–34.

Framework for a Common Journey in Christ 2005–2010" recommended the continuation of the core mission identified in 1995, but with the addition of congregational development, stewardship education, youth ministry, and leadership development "as resources become available"—those very areas that had been dropped in 1995![16]

LESSONS AND LEGACY

When I consider the "transformational aspirations" of the 2023 plan for General Synod, "Changing Church," I can see the footprint of Ellie Johnson and Partnerships. The graphic and related videos for "Changing Church" identify four themes: (1) "works to dismantle racism and colonialism"—naming work that was painstakingly initiated by the Anti-Racism Working Group under Ellie; (2) "embraces mutual interdependence with the Indigenous church"—echoing the 1963 vision, so strongly championed by Ellie, of mutual responsibility and interdependence, especially in relation to Indigenous peoples; (3) "nurtures right relationships . . . at the local, national, and global communities and networks"—recalling the path set by *Preparing the Way* for partnerships and networking, though alas, lacking in clarity and detail; and (4) "stewards and renews God's creation"—continuing the wholistic trajectory of the Ecojustice Committee, yet erring in the direction of impossible generalities by aspiring to "pursue justice for all."[17]

"Changing Church" is neither a plan, nor is it strategic—and does not claim to be. Regardless of its intent or detail or merit, a plan, strategic or otherwise, is only half the picture. The other half is *what kind of person* actually does the planning and the implementing.

The years I spent working with Ellie as my "boss" were years of creativity, collaboration, and a sense of purpose, in spite of being a time of great anxiety and uncertainty. *Preparing the Way* was only part of what accounted for that spirit of creativity and collaboration; Ellie's leadership was the other. She was an educator with a passion for mission and a heart for justice, who discovered over time that she had a talent for organization and management.

I learned much from her way of moving people and projects forward, softening resistance or opposition and building up support and buy-ins. She structured the Partnerships department to work in self-directed teams, equipping us to make decisions within a budget, expecting accountability but not controlling our work.

16. "Anglican Church Adopts Plan."
17. See https://changingchurch.anglican.ca/.

Ellie made space for others—staff, colleagues, committee members, and volunteers—to see their work as ministry, to be creative, to contribute, and to act on their own ideas. She typified a style of "management by wandering around"—leaving her desk and walking around the workplace to speak with and understand her staff. She would gather information on issues, routines, workflows, and volunteers while sending a clear signal of being available with an open door and listening ear. She gave constructive feedback with great skill and sensitivity; she did not shy away from correcting mistakes, her own and others, and was quick to forgive. She had a knack for getting things done without alienating people, for making difficult things seem clear and doable, for finding common ground when there seemed no way forward.

For me, Ellie was a true partner in ministry—a boss, mentor, and friend, whose spirit continues to energize me and whose example I still aspire to follow. Pray that we may raise up more leaders like Ellie Johnson, who did indeed "produce an overspill of energy greater than the sum of the parts."

BIBLIOGRAPHY

"Anglican Church Adopts Plan with Focus on Local Development." The Anglican Church of Canada, Jun 4, 2004. https://archives.anglican.ca/link/official8439.

"The Anglican Church of Canada's Apology for Residential Schools." The Anglican Church of Canada. https://www.anglican.ca/tr/apology/.

"The Anglican Communion's Five Marks of Mission: An Introduction." Anglican Communion News Service, Feb 4, 2020. https://www.anglicannews.org/features/2020/02/the-anglican-communions-five-marks-of-mission-an-introduction.aspx.

Anglican Journal. "Jubilee Continues Journey of Many Steps." Sep 1, 2000. https://anglicanjournal.com/jubilee-continues-journey-of-many-steps-1052/.

"Anti-Racism." The Anglican Church of Canada, 2001. https://archives.anglican.ca/link/official7924.

Brown, Terry, and Christopher Lind, eds. *Justice as Mission: An Agenda for the Church.* Burlington, ON: Trinity, 1985.

Knowles, Norman, ed. *Seeds Scattered and Sown: Studies in the History of Canadian Anglicanism.* Toronto: Anglican Book Centre, 2008.

Lind, Christopher, and Joe Mihevc, eds. *Coalitions for Justice.* Ottawa, ON: Novalis, 1994.

MacAdam, Murray. "Shalom Justice Camp: A Recipe for Joyful Faith." *Anglican Journal*, Aug 27, 2012. https://anglicanjournal.com/shalom-justice-camp-a-recipe-for-joyful-faith-11084/.

McCullum, Hugh. *Radical Compassion: The Life and Times of Archbishop Ted Scott.* Toronto: Anglican Book Centre, 2004.

Owen, D. R. G. *Social Thought and Anglican Theology*. Toronto: Anglican Book Centre, 1980.

Anglican Church of Canada. *Preparing the Way: A Strategic Plan for the General Synod of the Anglican Church of Canada*. Toronto: General Synod Archives, 1995.

Russell, Letty M. *The Future of Partnership*. Philadelphia: Westminster, 1979.

"Why We Say 'Indigenous' Instead of 'Aboriginal.'" Animikii, Jun 17, 2020. https://animikii.com/insights/why-we-say-indigenous-instead-of-aboriginal.

6

From Colonialism through Partnership to Decolonization

An Appreciation of the Ministry of Dr. Eleanor Johnson

PETER ELLIOTT

WHY DID THE INTERNATIONAL mission work of the Anglican Church of Canada decline so rapidly and so drastically? In 1994, the Anglican Church of Canada's World Program expended $2.5 million out of a $16 million budget (16 percent of all expenditures); by 2022, Global Relations expended $300,000 out of a $9 million budget (3 percent). Staffing for international mission was reduced from three regional mission coordinators, a Volunteers in Mission coordinator, and a Mission and Justice Education coordinator, to a single Global Mission coordinator.[1] This decline happened even after the Canadian General Synod's 1995 strategic plan championed international work as a key priority. It is true that the overall income and personnel available for national church work also declined significantly, but financial considerations were not the only factor. Ultimately, it was the growing acknowledgment of the connection between Anglican Christian mission to the practices and attitudes of colonialism that led to this dramatic shift in focus and priorities for mission work in the Anglican Church of Canada.

1. I am grateful to General Synod archivist Laurel Parson who assisted in research for this article.

For decades, Anglican international mission efforts, especially among British and North American churches, were largely seen as bringing the gospel to unconverted peoples, a gospel that was inseparable from Western imperialism and British colonialism; wherever the British Empire went, the church followed. Around the world Anglican missionaries were agents not only of the gospel but also of English culture and norms. Colonialism—the policies and practices of acquiring full or partial political control over another country, occupying it with settlers, and exploiting it economically—was accompanied and supported by Church of England mission agencies such as the Church Mission Society (CMS), the Society for the Propagation of the Gospel (SPG), and by similar agencies in North America.

Dr. Eleanor (Ellie) Johnson was an anthropologist before she engaged in the work and study of mission from the mid-1980s to her retirement in 2008. As a missiologist, along with others in the field, she had long been aware of the intersection between mission and colonialism. As the lead staff person for international mission in the Anglican Church of Canada, she was committed to seeing a change in the understanding and practice of overseas mission. Through her involvement with Anglican Communion agencies, she sought to champion "partnership" rather than "paternalism" and eventually to move beyond partnership to self-determination. As a mission educator, she sought to redefine mission work, not as something the church decides to do, but as God's transformative action in the world to which we as God's people are called to participate.

It was this self-critical reflection on the very structures and processes of world mission within the Anglican Communion and ecumenically that would lead to a radical shift in Canadian Anglican involvement in international work. In particular, the Partners in Mission consultations and the Five Marks of Mission of the Anglican Communion provided tools to analyze and reframe colonial assumptions. The story of how the Anglican Church of Canada moved beyond colonial models to new understandings of partnership is a story in which the leadership of Ellie Johnson was formative. In this essay, I will explore Ellie's role as an agent of change, informed by those processes and principles of partnership.

ALL THOSE DESKS! A VERY SHORT HISTORY OF MISSION IN THE ANGLICAN CHURCH OF CANADA

"All those desks!" exclaimed Toronto's Archbishop Lewis Garnsworthy when asked to describe his impression of the national office (Church

House) in Toronto. The archbishop was struck by the row of desks in the large, open office space, which housed the personnel for the Primate's World Relief and Development Fund (PWRDF) and the Partners in Mission (PIM) department. Together they formed the section of Church House known as "World Mission," which continued until the late 1990s. There were "desks" for about twenty-five staff organized in regional groups: desks for executive staff; desks for program staff whose international work focused in Latin America, Asia and the Pacific, and Africa and the Middle East; and desks for their support staff.

Dr. Ellie Johnson first came to Church House as a mission educator in 1987 before becoming director of Partnerships in 1994 and later acting general secretary during 2005–2006 prior to retirement in 2008. She supported the effort in the early 1990s to amalgamate and coordinate the international mission of the Canadian Anglican Church by bringing together two entities within the national office: PWRDF, funded by individual donors, augmented with strong financial support from government agencies, and PIM, funded through the General Synod budget drawn from diocesan apportionment. It was a daunting task, driven by a vision of shared values and priorities that was both brave and prophetic. The consolidation of these two units continued for almost a decade, but a changing understanding of mission prompted its eventual collapse. Mission theology—sometimes referred to as missiology—was undergoing a transformation. It was evolving.

The General Synod, created in 1893, had as its primary agency the Missionary Society of the Church of England in Canada (MSCC). Unlike the independent foreign mission agencies of the Church of England, each with its own theological position, the MSCC operated on behalf of the whole Canadian church under a board of bishops, clergy, and laypeople appointed by the General Synod, and embraced both international and domestic mission activity. According to the General Synod archives, "its work included assisting missionary dioceses, Indian and Eskimo work, Columbia Coast Mission, Church Camp Missions, Jewish Missions, Japanese Missions, Immigration chaplaincies, white settlers' missions, and Indian Residential Schools. Foreign missions included church, medical, and education work in Japan, China, India, Palestine (Jerusalem), and Egypt."[2] Engagement in the work of mission was supported and assisted prayerfully and financially by the Woman's Auxiliary (WA) with branches in most every Anglican parish in Canada. Even after the "Church of England in Canada" officially became

---

2. "Missionary Society," para. 2. Indigenous Nations prefer to be called either First Nations, Metis, or Inuit. In this instance, Indian and Eskimo are left as found in the text, recognizing they are no longer appropriate.

the "Anglican Church of Canada" in 1955, the legacy of British colonialism continued to influence the church's patterns of worship and outreach.

From the late nineteenth century until the mid-twentieth century, the operative theology of mission was "over there," something that Christians from Europe and North America *did* overseas *to* other people. In Canada, the church's mission was understood in colonial terms as both "over there" (international), and "up there" (Canada's North, referring obliquely to Indigenous peoples). The purpose of this mission was to convert the heathen, ensure the salvation of their souls, and incorporate them in the church's definition of a holy life.

The Right Rev. Ian Douglas, an Episcopalian theologian and scholar of mission and world Christianity, writes,

> Conversion of "the heathen" through the spread of churches and the advance of Western "civilization" went hand in hand. The abuses (and contributions) of missionaries and the close connection between mission and imperialism in Africa, Asia, Latin America, and the Pacific are well documented. Suffice it to say that throughout the nineteenth century and for the first half of the twentieth century the Western churches had their missions, *missiones ecclesiarum* (church's missions). These missions, as dependent outposts of European and North American Christianity, usually in some "far off" part of the world, sought to extend church models and cultural worldviews of the Enlightenment.[3]

This "over there" view of mission was clearly reflected in the Order of Holy Communion of the 1959 *Book of Common Prayer*. The bidding prayers that preceded the intercession included, "Let us pray for our missionaries at home and abroad." The list of "Prayers and Thanksgivings" included prayers for the extension of the church, prayers for the conversion of the Jews, and prayers for missionary workers and missionary societies.[4] Epiphany was traditionally promoted as a season for learning about and supporting the church's missions and missionaries.

The spirituality of mission was also well captured in the 1938 *Book of Common Praise*, with a section of twenty-four hymns curated under the heading "Missionary Hymns" with titles like "From Greenland's Icy Mountains." The mission project they present was fervently upheld in its time. Hymn 281 includes the verse:

---

3. Douglas, "God's Mission," para. 9.

4. *Book of Common Prayer*, 75.

> Jewish people wandering far
> Still thine own dear children are;
> Bring them home, dear Lord, to thee,
> Safe from sin and sorrow free.[5]

Or in this geographic description of the mission field in Hymn 288:

> The lands so long enshrouded in darkness deep and drear
> Are longing for the tidings of God's love they may hear
> A cry comes o'er the mountains and floats upon the breeze,
> From tropic shores and islands, and from the Arctic Seas.
> 'Neath gleaming constellations the pole star in the north,
> From Yukon's ice-bound borders, the yearning cry comes
> forth.[6]

TOWARDS THE *MISSIO DEI*

With a growing awareness of how closely missionary enterprises were tied to the agenda and values of colonialism, consideration of the church's missions (plural, meaning projects throughout the world) began to shift to a consideration of the church's mission (singular); that is, the sense of mission as something that belonged primarily or even exclusively to the Christian church.

The decades after World War II brought significant changes in the world order: the shrinking of the British Empire and its gradual transformation into a commonwealth, and the growing movement toward independence from imperial and colonial influences in India and many African countries. It was an era that saw the establishment of institutions for world cooperation such as the United Nations, the International Red Cross, the World Council of Churches, and Young Men's and Young Women's Christian Associations. Mission organizations were becoming acutely aware of the close ties of their missionary efforts to the colonizing agenda of British and Western nations. The role of the church as the exclusive or even primary agent of God's mission in the world and creation was being called into question. Ian Douglas writes: "Increasingly the Church was seen as being an agent, at best, or extraneous, at worst, to God's intervention in the wider struggles of the world."[7]

---

5. *Book of Common Praise*, 281.

6. *Book of Common Praise*, 288.

7. Douglas, "God's Mission," para. 11.

As the World Council of Churches and the Anglican Communion became more highly organized, there was, for many, a dream of an ecumenical worldwide approach to the church's mission. However, disputes between denominations and disagreements amongst Christians blocked the implementation of a shared mission for the churches. So, in an emerging postmodern, postcolonial world, missiologists came to focus less on the church's mission and more on God's mission—the *missio Dei*—discerning how God is acting in the world.

The difference of this new understanding was that the goal of mission was not primarily to convert the heathen and extend Christian churches, but to work to bring about God's shalom—God's peace and justice in the world. The *missio Dei* assumes that God continues to be active in the world, and God's reign is a possibility to which all the baptized are called. The church, as the body of Christ, is caught up in and works for God's mission in the world—but the church is not the only way in which God works in the world. Indian theologian S. J. Samartha emphasizes,

> In a religiously plural world, Christians, together with their neighbors of other faiths, are called upon to participate in God's continuing mission in the world. Mission is God's continuing activity through the Spirit to mend the brokenness of creation, to overcome the fragmentation of humanity, and to heal the rift between humanity, nature, and God.[8]

The *missio Dei* gave impetus to the slogan "the church doesn't so much have a mission as God's mission has a church." Theologically, this is an affirmation that mission is the activity of the triune God continually at work in the world and in our lives, overflowing into our hearts so that the world can know its salvation—its healing and wholeness—that we have seen in the face of our Lord Jesus Christ. In this view, the goal of mission is not to convert the heathen, nor to be an agent of colonization, nor to grow the membership of the church: it is to enable *shalom*, the flourishing of all people and indeed all creation as beloved of God.

THE FIVE MARKS OF MISSION

One of the ways that the Anglican communion gave expression to this changing sense of mission was to develop Five Marks of Mission. The Five Marks began life as a mission statement for the church. In 1984, the report of the Anglican Consultative Council (ACC) meeting in Badagry, Nigeria,

---

8. Samartha, *One Christ—Many Religions,* 149.

included a definition of the "mission of the Church" under four headings: (1) evangelism, (2) response and initiation, (3) Christian nurture and teaching, and (4) service and transformation.[9] In a slightly different arrangement, these became the earliest version of the "marks of mission," though that phrase was not used at the time.

In 1990, at its meeting in Wales, the Anglican Consultative Council added a fifth category to this definition, saying in its official report,

> There has been a consistent view of mission repeated by the ACC, the Lambeth Conference, the Primates' Meeting, and others in recent years, which defines mission in a four-fold way. . . . We now feel that our understanding of the ecological crisis, and indeed of the threats to the unity of all creation, mean that we have to add a fifth affirmation: "to strive to safeguard the integrity of creation and sustain and renew the life of the earth."[10]

At its 2012 meeting in Auckland, New Zealand, the ACC said that these indicators, now known widely as the Five Marks of Mission, should be understood as dynamic and be reviewed regularly. At this meeting, the council revised the wording of the fourth mark, adding the phrase "to challenge violence of every kind and pursue peace and reconciliation" to the preexisting text "to seek to transform the unjust structures of society."

An introductory phrase was added: "The mission of the Church is the mission of Christ"—a tacit affirmation of the *missio Dei*. The form we now have is:

1. To proclaim the Good News of the Kingdom

2. To teach, baptise and nurture new believers

3. To respond to human need by loving service

4. To transform unjust structures of society, to challenge violence of every kind and pursue peace and reconciliation

5. To strive to safeguard the integrity of creation and sustain and renew the life of the earth[11]

It is interesting to note that while the first two marks are consistent with a traditional view of mission—as having to do with evangelism and conversion—the last three are an expression of the *missio Dei* in the world. There's nothing specifically Christian about loving service, transforming

9. Anglican Consultative Council, *Bonds of Affection*, 57–59.
10. Anglican Consultative Council, *Mission in a Broken World*, 101.
11. "Anglican Communion's Five Marks."

unjust structures, challenging violence, pursuing peace and reconciliation, or safeguarding the integrity of creation. Yet these are defined as divine activities, marks of an authentic Christian response to the gospel. And curiously the work of proclaiming good news and nurturing new Christians in the faith became increasingly relevant in North America and Europe, as secularism spread and institutional religion declined, whereas in the Global South, where the church was growing rapidly, attention to issues of inequality, justice, and ecological collapse were becoming ever more relevant.

PARTNERS IN MISSION CONSULTATIONS

In Canada and throughout the Communion, the principle of mission as a partnership of both giving and receiving among churches grew out of the formative notion of Mutual Responsibility and Interdependence (MRI) first articulated at the Toronto Anglican Congress in 1963. Partners in Mission (PIM) consultations provided a way for churches throughout the world to share their visions and priorities for mission and for churches with resources—like the Anglican Church of Canada—to listen and attend to the priorities of churches in the developing world. It was a process that sought to transform the face of mission globally, replacing paternalism with partnership. Increasingly, churches in the Global South were looking less for personnel—missionaries and Christian educators—and more for grant money to support local initiatives. The goal of PIM consultations was to ensure that resources went to support the identified initiatives local churches, not to the pet projects of the funding churches.

Thus, a crucial aspect of the Canadian church's mission strategy from the 1970s through the 1990s was active participation in Partners in Mission Consultations (PIM). Importantly, the PIM process was mutual. Not only did "resourced" churches consult with those needing resources, but, in a spirit of partnership, they invited "receiving" partners to visit their churches, to examine their mission priorities and to evaluate their effectiveness. A turning point in the life of the General Synod and its understanding of partnership was the Canadian Partners in Mission Consultation, held in Winnipeg in April 1994. Ellie and I were assigned to be staff to the planning team. International and ecumenical partners gathered for an orientation and then were assigned to join consultations about ministry areas of the General Synod of the Anglican Church of Canada.

Several partners joined together with Native Ministries (as it was then called) for a consultation made up mostly of Indigenous participants that had been planned by Indigenous Anglicans. Disclosures about abuse at residential schools were just beginning to surface; this consultation began with participants sharing painful stories of their experiences at the schools. The atmosphere was thick with emotion. Tears flowed. Indigenous lives had been deeply harmed in too many ways by a certain kind of Christian mission working hand-in-hand with the government's agenda. Something needed to change.

As discussions continued through long sessions and over meals, a vision began to emerge, supported by the partners present. A writing group was appointed who met to put the vision into words. While they wrote, the Indigenous group sat and sang hymns until late into the night. It was a remarkable time. When the writing group completed their task, they returned with a document, which, after a little more editing, was signed by everyone present. It has become a foundational document for Canadian Anglicans—Indigenous and settler alike—and is worth citing in its entirety.

A Covenant and Our Journey of Spiritual Renewal

We, the Indigenous partners in Canada of the Anglican Communion respectfully affirm our place in God's Creation and in God's Love, manifest through the Grace of Jesus Christ. In specific, we address the Anglican Canadians with whom we are in direct communion.

We have shared a journey of close to three centuries in which we have been:

- denied our place in God's Creation
- denied our rights a Children of God
- treated as less than equal, and
- subjected to abuse, culturally, physically, emotionally, sexually, and spiritually.

The result, in our communities, homes, and daily lives, has been and continues to be:

- broken homes and lives;
- sexual and family violence;
- high recidivism and incarceration rates;
- high chemical abuse;
- loss of spiritual fulfillment;
- loss of cultures, languages and traditions; and
- poor stewardship of Mother Earth.

Because the National Church's canons, structure and policies have not always responded to our needs nor heard our voice, we now claim our place and responsibility as equal partners in a new shared journey of healing, moving towards wholeness and justice.

We acknowledge that God is calling us to a prayerful dialogue towards self-determination for us, the Indigenous People, within the Anglican Communion in Canada. Through this new relationship we can better respond to the challenges facing us in a relevant and meaningful way.

As faithful people of God, guided by the Holy Spirit, we invite you, the Anglican Communion of Canada to covenant with us, the Indigenous Anglicans of Canada, in our vision of a new and enriched journey.

A Covenant

We, representatives of the Indigenous people of the Anglican Church of Canada, meeting in Winnipeg from the 23 to 26 of April, 1994, pledge ourselves to this covenant for the sake of our people and in trust of our Lord and Saviour, Jesus Christ:

Under the guidance of God's spirit we agree to do all we can to call our people into unity in a new, self-determining community within The Anglican Church of Canada.

To this end, we extend the hand of partnership to all those who will help us build a truly Anglican Indigenous Church in Canada.

May God bless this new vision and give us grace to accomplish it. Amen.[12]

It was the vision of a new relationship: a self-determining Indigenous community within the Anglican Church of Canada, accompanied by an invitation to the settler church to build a new covenant. It was an invitation to move away from the models of colonialism, and even beyond the idea of "partnership," which could be seen as "enlightened colonialism." The new relationship was neither mission, nor partnership, but a relationship between two self-determining entities. This is what the 1994 covenant sought and, since that time, has emerged within Canadian Anglicanism.

---

12. ACIP, "Covenant."

A NEW RELATIONSHIP—BEYOND COLONIAL
MISSION OR PARTNERSHIP

Over the next two decades, this covenant became foundational to the development of the self-determining Indigenous church within the Anglican Church of Canada. As her role changed within Church House, Ellie accompanied Indigenous Anglicans through this process. The understanding of partnership slowly evolved to now include accompaniment of those who had been wounded by colonial actions and attitudes of the church. Confronting racism within Canadian church and society was an essential part of this shift.

Especially as the role of the church in the tragic history of residential schools was revealed, neither the old paradigm of mission, nor the enlightened notion of partnership, would be sufficient. What was needed was relationship: Ellie stood with survivors of the residential schools as they sought to have their experiences witnessed and justice be given.

Efforts to live into the Marks of Mission found expression through the formation and development of a national Ecojustice Committee, seeking to make the essential link between care of the earth and issues of social and economic justice. The Anglican Church of Canada continued its role in international relations, but rather than sending grants and personnel overseas, it was with a view to connecting Canadian Anglicans with Anglicans around the globe in mutual relationships—through the Companion Diocese program, and through Volunteers in Mission, a program of self-funded, two-year placements of Canadian Anglicans with global mission partners. By 2022, work previously done by an entire department of World Mission was now designated as two positions: (1) Public Witness for Ecological and Social Justice, and (2) Global Relations.

By the time of her retirement in 2008, Church House had changed. The understanding of mission was transformed. The colonizing effects of mission within Canadian Anglicanism was more deeply acknowledged, and a long process of repentance had begun. While in her early years at Church House Ellie had been a reluctant manager, by the time of her retirement, her leadership, undergirded by her deep values, had made a lasting impression on the Anglican Church of Canada from coast-to-coast-to-coast.

Decolonizing Christian mission is a long, not short-term project. Indigenous wisdom suggests that seven generations will be needed to heal from intergenerational trauma caused by the residential schools and related policies and practices. While vestiges of the Canadian church's colonial heritage persist, institutional decline necessitates the difficult work of closing parish churches and reimagining ministry in new ways. Similarly, Indigenous wisdom's Seventh Generations Principle holds that decisions made today should result in a sustainable and just world seven generations into the future.[13] With the *missio Dei* guiding Anglican church efforts, intercultural, ecumenical, and indeed interfaith initiatives, can bring together people of good will to work cooperatively towards justice for the earth and human flourishing. Ellie's work as a leader in missiology both within the Anglican Communion and the Anglican Church of Canada provided the necessary intellectual framework and passion for justice that, God willing, will continue to transform the structures, policies, and practices of the church.

ELLIE JOHNSON'S IMPACT ON CHURCH HOUSE MANAGEMENT

Ellie's leadership gifts were recognized as soon as she began work as a mission educator at Church House. Within a couple of years she was appointed as associate director of World Mission with a particular emphasis on the church-to-church partnerships. After the Primate's Fund separated more formally from the World Mission department, Ellie became the director of the department, and prior to her retirement served as the interim general secretary of the Anglican Church of Canada.

While a natural and skilled leader, Ellie was a reluctant manager. She found the conflictual environment of management difficult as department heads competed over increasingly fewer financial resources to fund their priorities. Her heart was always with those who lived in the developing world who sought to minister from their meager resources. Internal conflict within the church bureaucracy must have seemed to her a privileged extravagance. As she moved through various leadership roles, she became more and more outspoken about the status of Indigenous Anglicans across the country. In many dioceses Indigenous clergy worked in non-stipendiary ministries, and their work was overseen by white bishops who enjoyed the privileges of their positions. After the church's settlement with the federal government, Ellie accompanied many former residential schools to their hearings as they sought their just financial reparations. Repeatedly, she witnessed the overt racism that existed throughout the judicial system and the church structures: she immediately made the connection between racism here and in other parts of the globe.

An apt biblical metaphor for Ellie's work is found in Luke 19:1–8: the parable of the persistent widow. Like the persistent woman in Jesus's parable, Ellie was steadfast in her advocacy for justice for the poor and the

13. "What Is the Seventh Generation."

disenfranchised. She sought to bring national church structures into alignment with the clarity of the gospel's call for justice and equity. She engaged with this focus of her work for as long as she was able, leaving it to future generations to continue being persistent for the sake of the flourishing of all people everywhere. Her work is indeed a blessing to all who follow, and her example is well worth emulating as the work for justice and equality continues.

BIBLIOGRAPHY

"The Anglican Communion's Five Marks of Mission: An Introduction." Anglican Communion News Service, Feb 4, 2020. https://www.anglicannews.org/features/2020/02/the-anglican-communions-five-marks-of-mission-an-introduction.aspx.

Anglican Consultative Council. *Bonds of Affection: Proceedings of the ACC-6, Badagry, Nigeria, 1984.* London: ACC, 1984.

———. *Mission in a Broken World: Report of ACC-8 Wales 1990.* London: Church House Publishing, 1990.

Anglican Council of Indigenous Peoples (ACIP). "A Covenant and Our Journey of Spiritual Renewal." The Anglican Church of Canada. https://www.anglican.ca/im/foundational-documents/covenant/.

The Book of Common Praise: Being the Hymn Book of the Church of England in Canada (Revised 1938). Toronto: Oxford University Press, 1939.

The Book of Common Prayer. Toronto: Anglican Book Centre, 1959.

Douglas, Ian T. "God's Mission and the Millennium Development Goals." The Archives of the Episcopal Church, Mar 19, 2007. https://episcopalarchives.org/cgi-bin/ENS/ENSpress_release.pl?pr_number=031907-03.

"Missionary Society of the Church of England in Canada (MSCC) Fonds—1877-2011." Anglican Church of Canada. https://www.anglican.ca/archives/holdings/fonds/missionary-society-of-the-church-of-england-in-canada-mscc-fonds/.

Samartha, S. J. *One Christ—Many Religions: Towards a Revised Christology.* Maryknoll, NY: Orbis, 1995.

"What Is the Seventh Generation Principle?" Indigenous Corporate Training Inc., May 30, 2020. https://www.ictinc.ca/blog/seventh-generation-principle.

7

From Partnership to Friendship

How a Canadian Anglican Priest became a Bishop in the South Pacific

TERRY BROWN

IN THE ALMOST SIXTY years between the 1963 Toronto Anglican Congress and the 2022 Lambeth Conference, enormous changes have taken place in the Anglican Communion. While there were earlier pan-Anglican conferences (London, England, 1908; Minneapolis, 1954), the 1963 Anglican Congress was a nodal point in the globalization of the Anglican Communion, largely for good, as it shaped the direction the Communion would go in the next half century. Its adopted manifesto, "Mutual Responsibility and Interdependence in the Body of Christ," condemned old paternalistic mission relationships and espoused radical sharing of personnel and financial resources around the globe with deep commitment to mutual respect, listening, and equality. The concluding section of the manifesto declared, in boldface in the original document,

> We are aware that such a program as we propose, if it is seen in its true size and accepted, will mean the death of much that is familiar about our churches now. It will mean radical change in our priorities—even leading us to share with others at least as much as we spend on ourselves. It means the death of old isolations and inherited attitudes. It means a willingness to forego many desirable things, in every church.

> In substance, what we are really asking is the rebirth of the
> Anglican Communion, which means the death of many old
> things but—infinitely more—the birth of entirely new relation-
> ships. We regard this as the essential task before the churches of
> the Anglican Communion now.[1]

"Mutual Responsibility and Interdependence" (abbreviated "MRI")
quickly began to shape seriously Anglican Church of Canada mission
policy. Likewise, MRI, which quickly developed into "Partners in Mission"
(abbreviated "PIM"), enabled Ellie to be appointed Mission Education coordinator of the Anglican Church of Canada in 1987 and move on to a variety
of significant positions in the national office and that continued to model
both MRI and PIM.

Almost directly, the 1963 Anglican Congress and MRI shaped my own
theology of global mission. I came to Canada in September 1971 from the
USA to study theology at Trinity College, Toronto, where my church history
professor was Cyril Powles, later my doctoral dissertation supervisor and,
with his wife Marjorie, a good mentor and friend. I believe the conference
caused Cyril and Marjorie to continue to question whether they should still
be in Japan. (Cyril's father had been an early Canadian missionary to Japan,
returning after World War II as an assistant bishop. Cyril was born in Japan
and he, with Marjorie, returned to Japan as Canadian Anglican missionaries after the war.) In the late sixties, Cyril wrote a series of articles in the
Japan Christian Quarterly, espousing a "moratorium on missionaries" for
Japan, to enable the Indigenous church to develop without undue Western
influence and power. Convinced of this view, they returned permanently to
Toronto in 1970, where Cyril took up the Trinity professorship.

At Trinity, I took Cyril's "Third World Christianity" course, which was
designed to understand global Christianity from the perspective of Indigenous Christians rather than missionaries and which included a Marxist
critique of colonialism and the missionary movement. As I had spent eighteen months in Japan in the US Army and knew some Japanese, at one point
I asked Cyril about going to teach in Japan. He discouraged me, suggesting
it was not the right time for Westerners to return to the Japanese church.
Though back in Canada, Cyril and Marjorie continued to be involved in the
Anglican Church of Canada's World Mission program and in the late seventies Cyril published a controversial World Mission booklet, *Towards a Theology of Mission for Today*, incorporating many of the insights of his Third

---

1. Brown, "Mutual Responsibility and Interdependence," paras. 32–33; the manifesto is available online. For a good critical overview of the congress, see the special
issue of *The Witness*, "Reports on the Anglican Congress," also available online.

World Christianity course.[2] His questioning of the biblical authenticity of the Great Commission (Matt 28: 16–20) angered some. The overall theme of the pamphlet was, in many respects, MRI, now converted into partnership.

The 1963 Anglican Congress proposed a massive global process of assessment and action around the personnel and financial needs of every province and diocese in the Anglican Communion. The second (Dublin, 1973) and third (Trinidad, 1976) meetings of the Anglican Consultative Council (ACC) (a kind of executive council of the Communion, with episcopal, clerical, and/or lay representation from every province of the Communion), set up the Partners in Mission process to systematically enable these conversations. A global PIM officer was appointed, based in the ACC office in London. (Fr. Martin Mbwana, a gifted and energetic Tanzanian priest, performed this function in my time at Church House.) Typically, an Anglican province (or equivalent) would call a PIM consultation, inviting its overseas and ecumenical partners, new and old, to discuss the province's PIM priorities, for future exchange of personnel, financial support, and, sometimes, advocacy. The ACC PIM officer coordinated and attended these consultations. Participants were to be both lay and clerical and the actual PIM consultation was usually preceded by exposure visits by foreign partners around the hosting province.

By the 1978 Lambeth Conference, the global PIM process was well underway, but strains were already beginning to show. The eight sections of LC-1978 Resolution 15, "Partners in Mission," strongly affirmed the PIM process but also pointed out the failings: lack of interest in the theology of mission over against its implementation, lack of any internal provincial PIM experience, lack of ecumenical involvement, PIM invitations to only those who "share a natural or racial affinity" and a corresponding lack of interest in the insights of other cultures, lack of pre-consultation exposure visits, lack of engagement with important secular issues, and lack of follow-up. Perhaps the most damning concern was articulated in section 7: "PIM has helped us to develop the concept of sharing rather than of some giving and others receiving. Yet there is an ever-present danger of lapsing into the 'shopping list' way of thinking. At the same time we are sure that consultations should always contain the opportunity for the frank stating of specific needs."[3]

---

2. Powles, *Towards a Theology of Mission*. The booklet itself is undated but notes on its title page, "This paper was developed and adapted through consultation with the World Mission and World Relief and Development committees of the Anglican Church [of Canada]."

3. "Lambeth Conference," 10.

I provide this background on MRI and PIM because by the time I was appointed by the Anglican Church of Canada World Mission program in 1975 (a few months after my ordination as a priest in the Diocese of Fredericton) as lecturer in Theology at Bishop Patteson Theological Centre (BPTC) in the Church of the Province of Melanesia, *mutual partnership* was the reigning Canadian Anglican theology of mission, to which I then subscribed and still do. My appointment was for three years only, following the length of terms of my two Canadian predecessors, Paul Moore and Jim Draper. We were all appointed to assist the Church of Melanesia (COM), as it is commonly called, to develop Indigenous leadership by training clergy and laity at the provincial theological college.

While I was hired and paid by the Anglican Church of Canada, I was working under Indigenous supervision, including Norman Palmer, the province's first Indigenous archbishop, and Harry Tevi, the Indigenous BPTC warden (principal), a priest from the New Hebrides (now Vanuatu), the COM's first degree-graduate of Pacific Theological College (PTC) in Suva, Fiji. I was warmly welcomed; I enjoyed teaching a wide variety of theological subjects (all was diploma level), learned Solomon Islands *pijin*, supervised and drove the trucks, assisted in ordering library books, and be-friended the students, often going home with them on holidays. (Not long after my arrival, the COM held its first PIM consultation and the Canadian delegates visited me.) Since the first Canadian appointment, the number of expatriate staff was decreasing and the number of Indigenous staff increasing. I stayed on for a second three-year term, eventually becoming deputy warden.

BPTC itself had been shaped by changing views of mission and included a monthly college meeting in which students freely brought up whatever topic they wished, often berating staff for failures such as inedible food or bad driving. One could only sit and listen quietly and try to respond. I enjoyed the egalitarian and affectionate qualities of Melanesian societies, reading much anthropology and history, and returned to Canada with some reluctance in May 1981. I wished to pursue graduate studies and, theologically, I was convinced that I must leave.

In the next four years (1981–1985), I pursued graduate studies at Trinity College and Toronto School of Theology, eventually writing my doctoral dissertation on the US Anglo-Catholic Marxist theologian F. Hastings Smyth (1888–1960) and the religious community he founded in 1939, the Society of the Catholic Commonwealth, to which Cyril and Marjorie and many friends in Canada and beyond had belonged. Foreshadowing Latin American liberation theology, the SCC encouraged Marxist analysis of global situations of oppression including apartheid South Africa. Although the SCC collapsed in 1966, SCC values, including solidarity with workers and victims of human rights abuses, continued in its former members' ministries and writings, including Cyril's *Towards a Theology of Mission for Today.*

Although returned from the Solomons, I continued to be engaged in Church of Melanesia friendships and issues, making a three-month visit back to the Solomons and Vanuatu in 1983, followed by further visits at least every two years until I was elected bishop. I also began hosting Solomon Islands and Vanuatu visitors (usually my former students) for short visits. Some of the stories I heard were alarming in their accounts of Indigenous episcopal authoritarianism. These concerns were summed up in a chapter, "Neo-Colonialism in the Third World Church," that I wrote in the Festschrift for Cyril and Marjorie Powles that my fellow Trinity graduate student, Chris Lind, and I edited and published in 1985 *Justice as Mission: An Agenda for the Church.*[4]

As my graduate studies neared completion, it became clear that no academic position was available so I applied for the position of East Asia Mission and Development coordinator in the World Mission program of the Anglican Church of Canada, replacing Rhea Whitehead, who had moved to a similar position in the United Church of Canada. I was accepted and was soon plunged into the world of Anglican Church of Canada global mission partnerships. Initially the job description included only East Asia, with other staff looking after South Asia and the South Pacific as small parts of their job descriptions, but with both mission partnership and Primate's World Relief and Development Fund (PWRDF) responsibilities. I also had responsibility for coordinating overseas personnel appointments globally, in coordination with the appropriate regional World Mission staff. The structure was unwieldy, especially as it meant coordinating with two national committees, the World Mission Subcommittee and PWRDF, who had very different mandates and expectations. It also meant working under both the World Mission and PWRDF directors, who were often in conflict. The two committees had totally different procedures for preparation of project proposals to be submitted to them and often related to very different (and sometimes conflicting) partners in the same country. Restructuring of World Mission and PWRDF soon became necessary.

It was about this time that Ellie Johnson joined the staff as Partners in Mission Education coordinator, working with her development counterpart, Sue Stevens, PWRDF Development Education coordinator. The director of World Mission, John Barton, whom Ellie eventually succeeded, ostensibly

---

4. Brown and Lind, *Justice as Mission,* 7–16.

oversaw the whole operation, thus only he had to attend both Partners in Mission and PWRDF national committees. Ellie's mission education predecessor, Celia Hannant, who had already begun attending international Anglican meetings trying to define the Anglican understanding of mission, moved on to become the new Volunteer in Mission coordinator. Ellie entered a world of ecclesiastical restructuring (increasingly, also downsizing), a skill she would later develop and use extensively, in both Anglican and ecumenical structures.

As Asia/Pacific mission coordinator, I was responsible for co-coordination of Anglican and ecumenical mission partnership relations with the entire Asia/Pacific region, including support of theological education, exchange of personnel, overseas students, PIM consultations, human rights and justice advocacy (for Asia, done partly through the Canada/Asia Working Group ecumenical coalition), development of new autonomous ecclesiastical provinces, companion diocese relationships, PIM funding, south-south appointments, accompanying the primate on visits to the region, and, in support of Ellie, work on interpretation of the priorities of the region to the Anglican Church of Canada.

My two regional mission colleagues—the late Canon John Rye, Africa and the Middle East regional mission coordinator, a returned long-term Anglican Church of Canada missionary in Ghana where he declined an episcopate, and Fr. David Hamid, Latin America and Caribbean mission coordinator, currently assistant bishop of the Church of England Diocese of Europe—and I became lifelong friends. We worked closely and were dubbed the "Three Musketeers." The three of us worked with Ellie and she sometimes visited our regions. With the retirement of John Barton, as director of World Mission, she became our (very supportive) boss. She was extraordinarily respectful and solicitous of our work and was especially helpful in annual job appraisals of how we were spending our work time, always allowing enough time for rest.

A couple of mission partnership issues stand out from that time, one of which especially concerned Ellie and her work as mission education coordinator. Her task was to interpret mission in terms of mutual partnership to Canadian Anglican dioceses and parishes, many of whom still had very traditional understandings of global mission as evangelism of non-Christians, or who had rejected that model completely in favor of, for example, support-church or secular development organizations such as PWRDF or Oxfam, those having little interest in *any* theology of mission, partnership, or otherwise. As the PIM process often seemed to take place on the international or national level only, far from the local parish, an effort had to be made to "personalize" mission that had significance to local parishes. One approach was the "project book," which described various attractive mission or development projects to which parishes might subscribe. However, this approach risked over-monetizing PIM, with attractive projects receiving funds and others (though perhaps more important) receiving none. A variety of programs were developed: companion diocese relationships with visits in both directions; the Volunteer in Mission program in which a parish supported one of its members to work overseas; visits to parishes from overseas partners and Canadian overseas personnel, telling of their work; the overseas internship program for Canadian theological students and—in cooperation with PWRDF—letter-writing campaigns; and other human rights and justice advocacy programs.

A second issue, which predated Ellie's appointment, was the eventual ascendancy of PWRDF over Partners in Mission in the national program of the Anglican Church of Canada. There were many reasons for this shift. It was hard for PIM to shake off the negative image of mission as supporting ignorant and arrogant paternalistic missionaries; critical secular-minded Canadian Anglicans often preferred to support integral human development as represented by PWRDF. PWRDF was also able to access significant Canadian government funding through the Canadian International Development Agency (CIDA) but only if their overseas partners' development projects did not support overtly religious activities such as theological education or evangelism. This requirement also caused overseas partner churches to establish their own autonomous development organizations to access overseas government funds more easily. PWRDF staffing numbers grew, sometimes attracting staff with much more interest in integral human development than the Anglican church with its theological partnerships and programs, especially if they were opposed to political liberation movements, such as the pro-Pinochet Diocese of Chile. This skewing of mission towards development produced inequalities in the overseas churches we were supporting. John Rye often told the tale of the diocesan development worker in his Land Rover passing the catechist on his bicycle, leaving the latter in the dust.

What seemed like a divorce was finalized when PWRDF, to protect itself from financial liability coming out of the Indian residential schools crisis, incorporated itself as a legal entity separate from General Synod in 2000. General Synod's PIM program still had the Missionary Society of the Canadian Church (MSCC) as its legal entity and could not escape financial liability for its involvement in the Indian residential schools tragedy. In some places, such as South Korea, overseas partners became more self-sufficient, and PIM funding properly shifted to supporting Canadian Indigenous ministry. In other cases, important overseas mission funding was simply dropped. At the same time, diocesan and national budgets were contracting as the number of Canadian Anglicans declined and parishes (and even one diocese) closed. As a mission educator, Ellie increasingly had an uphill task.

Some, but not all, of this writing was on the wall as I approached eleven years as Asia/Pacific mission coordinator in late 1995. When John Barton retired as director of World Mission a few years earlier, I considered applying for the position but was tired of mission bureaucracy and wanted to do something more exciting. The Asia/Pacific position, with its constant overseas travel, was beginning to strain my personal life, preventing or fragmenting friendships. I supported and welcomed Ellie's appointment as director and appreciated her conscientious supervision and constant encouragement. I was, however, not sure about my next step. I imagined some sort of position in the Church of Melanesia as a clergy continuing education officer, though I did not want to return to BPTC. In mid-1995, on a visit to Vanuatu, I was asked by Charles Maon, the Diocese of Vanuatu diocesan secretary, if I would consider standing for election as first bishop of the new Diocese of Banks and Torres being carved out of the Diocese of Vanuatu. The new diocese was very small, very remote with limited communications and I had never lived in Vanuatu before. I felt that I would not be able to cope with the isolation and immediately declined.

However, later in the year, when I visited the COM provincial office in Honiara, the provincial secretary Nick Ma'aramo, a Malaitan, asked if I would consider putting my name forward for bishop of Malaita. The diocese's third bishop (all three were Malaitans) had resigned over financial issues, but then rescinded his resignation, causing a legal crisis that was only finally settled by the High Court of Solomon Islands, which declared that he was no longer the bishop and evicted him from the bishop's house. The diocese was badly divided between those who supported and opposed the bishop, and many argued that a neutral bishop from outside the diocese was the best hope for calming the diocese, the largest in the Church of Melanesia. He assured me that I would have a very strong chance of being elected. I did not give a firm answer but said I would give the matter serious consideration.

I returned to Canada and consulted with Anglican Church of Canada colleagues, including the primate Archbishop Michael Peers; Ellie, as director of World Mission; my "Musketeer" colleagues, John Rye and David Hamid; Cyril and Marjorie Powles; and others. All were encouraging. I had often complained about expatriate bishops in the Global South and all my work as a theological lecturer and mission coordinator had been in support of the development of Indigenous leadership. To take on an episcopal role in the Solomons seemed counterintuitive. On the other hand, decades of PIM theology and practice had leveled the playing field. My potential episcopal colleagues, all Indigenous, had been trained at Pacific Theological College, St. John's Theological College, Auckland, and Yale Divinity School. Most had been theological educators. One had been a bishop in Papua New Guinea. The Primate, Archbishop Ellison Pogo, was an intelligent and strong leader and a good friend; he had often complained to me about his predecessors and their authoritarian ways.

Likewise, Malaita, one of the last of the Solomons' islands to be colonized and evangelized, was full of vigorous and confident people (some would add, overaggressive) and they would not let themselves be oppressed by me. I had traveled often in Malaita and liked the people. If I was elected, I would be employed entirely under local auspices, including a very large drop in stipend (unlike my 1975 BPTC appointment) with no special provisions made for me because I was an expatriate. Having long developed a mission theology of *kenosis* (self-emptying, Phil 2:7), that was fine by me. Having met and dealt with many bishops over the previous twenty years (and listened to complaints about them), I had strong ideas about what to do and not do as a diocesan bishop in the Global South.

Finally, I decided that if they wanted me, they could have me, and submitted my consent and curriculum vitae. On January 25, 1996, the Feast of the Conversion of St. Paul, the combined electoral board of the province and diocese, meeting at St. Paul's, Auki, elected me the fourth bishop of Malaita unanimously on the first ballot; as required, their election was immediately ratified by the COM Council of Bishops. I received the results in a half-expected phone call from Archbishop Ellison in the late evening the day before in Toronto. I was initially stunned as I had never seriously considered being a bishop but announced the news the next day and began to prepare for travel to and residence in the Solomons. I experienced the election as a moment of liberation and a wonderful new opportunity to build the church in Malaita with Malaita Anglicans, some of whom I had known for twenty years and whose children bore my name.

My consecration as bishop on Pentecost Sunday, 1996, was a festive event.[5] The principal consecrator was the COM primate Archbishop Ellison Pogo, assisted by all the COM diocesan bishops and many of the retired bishops, including Archbishop Norman Palmer. All three former bishops of Malaita took part. Overseas bishops included Stewart Payne, archbishop of western Newfoundland, representing the Anglican Church of Canada (the only white face amongst the bishops); Albert Ramento, the obispo máximo (supreme bishop) of the Philippine Independent Church, murdered a few

5. The picture of Ellie which fronts this book is from that very event.

years later for his support of human rights in the Philippines, now counted a martyr; Bundo Kim, OSB., the reclusive monk-primate of the Anglican Church of Korea; James Ayong, the bishop of Aipo Rongo in PNG, who had been an overseas partner on the Anglican Church of Canada PIM Committee and who later became an outstanding primate of the Anglican Church of PNG; Jabez Bryce, bishop (later archbishop) of Polynesia, whom I had first met in 1975, soon after his consecration, as I first travelled to the Solomons; and Whakahuihui Vercoe, the venerable Māori bishop of Aotearoa. Canadian guests were Ellie, Cyril Powles, Canon John Rye, John Vandenberg (PWRDF Asia/Pacific coordinator), Peter Orme (incumbent of St. Anne's, Toronto, where I had been honorary assistant), and two Volunteer in Mission appointees who were already in the country, Br. John Blyth and Pauline Bradbrook. The COM paid for my parents' travel costs. The congregation numbered several thousand and the day was filled with feasting and dancing, ending with a large party at the bishop's house. In a couple of days, all had departed, and I was on my own. Ellie, among others, immensely enjoyed the event. She got to know my parents and was a friendly support to them.

The story of my twelve years as bishop of Malaita (1996–2008) belongs in a different place but Partners in Mission theology clearly shaped my praxis. In the large bishop's house, I extended hospitality to all and sundry. I visited the most remote villages in the diocese, some of which had not been visited by a bishop since the 1940s, if ever. I supported the continued development of Airahu Rural Training Centre, offering both technical and theological training. Four religious communities (two for men, two for women) grew, as well as the Fauabu Rural Health Centre, a historic Diocese of Melanesia hospital dating from the 1930s. The diocese grew: I consecrated many church buildings, ordained dozens of deacons and priests and confirmed over eleven thousand confirmation candidates. Lay Christian education programs ran regularly in the parishes, with many specialized programs for women, youth, chiefs, catechists, and others. We continued to minister through the difficult "ethnic tension" crisis of 1999–2002, where skills and insights about human rights abuses, violence, and armed conflict, which I had learned from the churches of the Philippines, Sri Lanka, and Burma, became very useful.[6]

As I approached sixty, following the COM canon, I submitted to diocesan synod the question of extending my appointment to age sixty-five (the final maximum retirement age), suggesting that I was open to the extension but wished it to be less than five years, as I was sure that Indigenous

6. For an account of those years, including my subsequent work with the Solomon Islands Truth and Reconciliation Commission, see Brown, "Solomon Islands 'Ethnic Tension' Conflict."

episcopal candidates were coming along. The diocesan synod extended my retirement to my sixty-fourth birthday, and on August 18, 2008, I retired as bishop of Malaita. I continued for four more years in Honiara as a volunteer archivist for the COM under contract with the COM Council of Bishops, another story.

In November 2012, I returned permanently to Canada, to a parish priest appointment in Hamilton, Ontario, in the Diocese of Niagara. I considered staying on permanently in the Solomons but reading correspondence in the COM archives about the difficulty retired missionaries who stayed on too long caused to the church, I decided it was best to leave. By now, living in the Solomons had become very expensive and I could not afford it. I also still abided by the insight of the great missiologist, Roland Allen, a prophet of Partners in Mission theology, that mission required not just presence but also departure.

On the global Anglican scene, the Partners in Mission process became cumbersome and came to an end. Evangelicals always felt that it short-changed evangelism. Thus, the 1988 Lambeth Conference moved away from PIM and declared the 1990s the "Decade of Evangelism." But in the decade before, a series of international Anglican working groups, in which Ellie took part, worked hard on developing a more sophisticated Anglican missiology: the Advisory Group on Mission Issues and Strategy (MISAG 1), 1981–1984; MISAG 2, 1987–1992; and the Anglican Communion Standing Committee on Mission (MISSIO), 1993–present.[7] Each working group was authorized by and reported to meetings of the Anglican Consultative Council.

To make a very long story short, one significant document and one significant insight emerged from these consultations and ACC amendments: The Five Marks of Mission and the strong emphasis, reflected in MISSIO's title—that mission is first God's Mission (*missio Dei*) before it is ours—demonstrate how we engage in Christian mission in joining in God's mission in Jesus Christ, wherever it is, whether within secular society or the church.

Missio Dei theology is not without its problems and its own ambiguous history, and the term "missional church" runs the risk of being used so frequently that it is meaningless.[8] All this international Anglican discussion of missiology I avoided by becoming bishop of Malaita. Instead, I took part in the Anglican primates-mandated Theological Education for the Anglican Communion (TEAC), setting benchmarks for Anglican theological

7. MISAG 1, 2, and MISSIO can be found on the Anglican Communion website. https://www.anglicancommunion.org/.

8. Engelsviken, "*Missio Dei.*"

education of bishops, priests, vocational deacons, and licensed lay workers across the Communion. However, Ellie, to her immense credit, was fully involved.

As I compare the earlier MRI and PIM models of mission with current Marks of Mission and *missio Dei* models, I sometimes fear the latter are too abstract and programmatic and lack relationality. Certainly, the issues addressed in the latter, especially social justice, human rights, and environmental concerns, are important, if not life-threatening, and need the attention. But partnership, a perfectly good translation of the biblical Greek *koinonia* (usually translated "communion" or "fellowship") places friendship and relationality as first and basic. People need to be respected and loved as persons; and work for social justice or the environment accompanied by chronic loneliness and alienation is not good for the soul or for the church. Parishioners are not helped by being told that *missio Dei* is only "out there" in the world and not in their midst, in their relationships of friendship and mutual support. The Anglican Communion is an enormously complex, and variegated reality and theological reflection often best starts in the most local context. Even before I became a bishop, I realized that personhood in Oceania (and I suspect in many other Indigenous societies around the world) is relational and deeply social, and that Western theologies of individual commitment and behavior imposed indiscriminately on all are often not appropriate and, indeed, can be destructive. Partnership, *koinonia*, establishes relationship and friendship as a foundation of mission and I am sorry to see it disappear from much of Anglican missiology today.[9] The "Calls" of the 2022 Lambeth Conference are a theological smorgasbord, for good or for ill.[10] The danger is adopting one call as primary and ignoring the others.

These days, it is impossible to predict one's legacy and I cannot say how my Malaita episcopate will be regarded in years to come. Perhaps some will deem it the last gasp of colonialism or neocolonialism in the Church of Melanesia, or, despite my best efforts, still an exercise in paternalism. Perhaps some will find fault with my adaptation to Oceanic boundaries or lack of them, so different than Anglo-Saxon ones. However, I still have hopes that I did well. A few years ago, I was surprised to discover that for some, my name had become a Malaita *pijin* verb meaning to be generous; for example, *teribroun litelbit*, "hey, be a little bit generous." That gave me hope that I had done less harm than good, and I remain thankful for my twelve years as bishop of Malaita, by far the most joyful years of my life.

9 Brown, "Personhood as a Tool."

10. "Lambeth Calls."

BIBLIOGRAPHY

"The Anglican Communion's Five Marks of Mission: An Introduction." Anglican Communion News Service, Feb 4, 2020. https://www.anglicannews.org/features/2020/02/the-anglican-communions-five-marks-of-mission-an-introduction.aspx.

Brown, Terry, ed. "Mutual Responsibility and Interdependence in the Body of Christ: Toronto Anglican Congress, 1963." Project Canterbury, 2009. http://anglicanhistory.org/canada/toronto_mutual1963.html.

————. "Personhood as a Tool to Reflect upon Communion." *Anglican Theological Review* 88 (2006) 163–79.

————. "The Solomon Islands 'Ethnic Tension' Conflict and the Solomon Islands Truth and Reconciliation Process: A Personal Reflection." In *Flowers in the Wall: Truth and Reconciliation in Timor-Leste, Indonesia, and Melanesia,* edited by David Webster, 279–92. Calgary, AB: University of Calgary Press, 2017.

Brown, Terry, and Christopher Lind, eds. *Justice as Mission: An Agenda for the Church.* Burlington, ON: Trinity, 1985.

Engelsviken, Tormod. "*Missio Dei*: The Understanding and Misunderstanding of the Theological Concept in European Churches and Missiology." *International Review of Mission* 92 (2003) 481–97.

"Lambeth Calls." Lambeth Conference, 2022. https://www.lambethconference.org/wp-content/uploads/2022/07/Lambeth-Calls-July-2022.pdf.

"The Lambeth Conference: Resolutions Archive from 1978." Anglican Communion, 2005. https://www.anglicancommunion.org/media/127746/1978.pdf.

Powles, Cyril. *Towards a Theology of Mission for Today.* Toronto: Anglican Church of Canada, 1980.

The Witness. "Reports on the Anglican Congress." Sep 5, 1963. https://www.episcopalarchives.org/e-archives/the_witness/pdf/1963_Watermarked/Witness_19630905.pdf.

8

The Living Legacy of Dr. Eleanor Johnson in the Anglican Church of Canada and Anglican Communion Today

ANDREA MANN

I FIRST MET DR. Eleanor Johnson one Sunday morning at St. Jude's Anglican Church, Oakville, in the late 1980s. Ellie had been invited by our priest, Canon Ian Dingwall, to preach about the church's ministry with Anglicans around the world. I knew little of the church's international work and world, though was aware of some aspects—through parish prayers, special Sunday School activities, and fundraising—of the companion diocese relationship at the time, between the Diocese of Niagara and the Diocese of Seychelles in the Province of the Indian Ocean.

I was unaware that this was the beginning of a friendship and collegiality that would last more than three decades, with Anglicans and others in more than fifty countries of the Anglican Communion, in many wonderful experiences of accompaniment and action in the gospel. It was an adventure that started, a few years later, with a two year sojourn as a Volunteer in Mission in Sri Lanka from 1994 to 1996, and continued in 1997 when I was hired onto the Partnerships team, directed by Ellie, as the regional mission coordinator for Asia and the Pacific.

During Ellie's fourteen-year tenure as director of the General Synod's Partnerships department, policy and programs flourished.[1] Her work ethic and high standards of professional conduct, brilliant sense of humour, interest in people, passion for justice, and faith in God's mission, the *missio Deo*, were inspiration for her twelve-member staff team, working on international mission, social and ecological justice, and Indigenous ministries.

Much has rightly been said about Ellie's conviction and compassion in the church's early years of acknowledging and accepting responsibility for the direct and generational impacts of the Indian residential school system upon Indigenous children and their families and communities. Indigenous leaders have noted with wide appreciation the crucial importance of her work with a survivors' group for the Indian Residential Schools Settlement Agreement and her involvement in a pilot project for alternate dispute resolution—initial steps toward the healing and reconciliation journey that continues. Similarly, Ellie's leadership in developing the church's prophetic witness on gender justice, economic and environmental justice, and peace and reconciliation was instrumental in Anglican and other ecumenical efforts toward ensuring services and justice for the most marginalized.

Ellie's conviction for transformative change in the attitudes and structures of the Anglican Church of Canada was also evident in her lifelong learning and being with global peoples and communities in their contexts and cultures. Her professional studies and training as an anthropologist and her Christian faith inspired her international mission staff to approach the world and our work in it with curiosity, intelligence, friendship, and faith—ready to follow the leading of the Spirit in and through the other, trusting in the God who has gone before us. Those who learned from Ellie's leadership and followed her example of "relationships first" with the peoples of the Anglican Communion can attest to the wisdom of being as prepared as one can be for global encounters, then to let go so that true partnership might emerge from discerning and setting priorities in the spirit of "mutual responsibility and interdependence."

Ellie was active and highly respected in her international work with the Mission and Evangelism Commissions and related groups of the Anglican Communion in the 1980s and 1990s. Her participation from 1984 to 1990 in the Mission Issues and Strategic Advisory Group 2 (MISAG 2), and later as a member of the Standing Commission for Mission of the Anglican Communion (MISSIO) from 1993 to 2000, contributed much to the values

1. The Partnerships department was formed as a result of the restructuring of General Synod in 1996, bringing together the work of the Ecojustice Committee, the Partners in Mission Committee, as well as Indigenous Ministries and the Anglican Council of Indigenous Peoples.

and recommendations presented by these groups—to Anglican Consultative Council meetings in 1990 (ACC8) and in 1999 (ACC11), to directors of
mission in the Anglican Communion Office, and to mission and evangelism
in the Anglican Communion until today.

A TRANSFORMING JOURNEY

Foremost among the documents produced by these commissions for the
wider Communion was the 1999 MISSIO Report, *Anglicans in Mission: A
Transforming Journey.* Those who read this report more than two decades
later will hear Ellie's clear voice and enthusiasm for the mission of God and
the church, for justice, and for bringing local and global together. Anyone
reading these texts will recognize Ellie's influence that continues to be relevant and instructive for the church of the early twenty-first century.

Among the many stories, discussions, and recommendations in the
1999 MISSIO report, three connect directly to Ellie's contributions to the
renewal of mission theology and practice that continues to be relevant and
instructive to this day.

The first is her case study, "A Journey of Repentance: The Anglican
Church of Canada's Struggle for Transformation," acknowledging the
church's cultural arrogance and complicity with the government of Canada
in assimilating Indigenous peoples through the operation of twenty-six Anglican Indian residential schools in the nineteenth and twentieth centuries.
Ellie described the church's association with colonization as the "dark side"
of the missionary endeavour: from the sixteenth to the twentieth centuries,
the church aligned itself with its political masters in the expansion of Europe's empires, devastating millions of Indigenous peoples, cultures, and
spiritualities worldwide. She concluded,

> Mission is indeed about proclaiming the Good News of God's
> love through Jesus Christ, but it is also about affirming that all of
> humankind is created in God's image, with no group having the
> right to re-create others according to its own limited vision. So
> where the missionary project has a shameful and arrogant his-
> tory, mission today must be about humility, repentance, justice
> and reparation.[2]

Second, Ellie sent an unequivocal message to the Canadian settler
church in the late 1990s, that mission today must be undertaken with humility, repentance, justice, and reparation, when she stated that "racism/

2. Johnson and Clark, *Anglicans in Mission*, 45.

ethnic superiority is also one of the underlying causes of the failure of many of our current attempts throughout the Anglican Communion to establish partnership relationships based on respect, mutual responsibility and interdependence."[3] If Ellie were with us today she would wholeheartedly endorse and have something to say about the emerging and urgent work of decolonizing international mission partnerships. And third, Ellie's voice can be heard in the MISSIO report as it goes on to call the Communion back to the original vision of Partners in Mission as an ongoing process of mutuality and interdependence.[4] "Mutual responsibility and interdependence," or MRI as it was known, was the heart and soul of the manifesto of the Anglican Congress held in Toronto in 1963.

Within the Anglican Communion, Partners in Mission (PIM) grew out of MRI as an attempt to foster a deeper understanding and practice of partnership. The Partners in Mission process provided a structure for each province or church to set its own priorities, not on its own, but in consultation with other Communion provinces as active partners. In 1993, thirty years after "Mutual Responsibility and Interdependence in the Body of Christ," the Anglican Consultative Council adopted Ten Principles of Partnership as an elaboration of the PIM process and a reiteration of the core principle of MRI.

Ellie's commitment to MRI had a lasting influence on the missiology and practice of Partnerships staff then and Global Relations now. In time, however, the Communion's Partners in Mission Round Table, a multilateral structure for bringing together provinces of the Anglican Communion for consultation and decision on mission projects, was to give way and be replaced by new ways of working in respectful bilateral relationships nurtured by the Ten Principles of Partnership. What had begun as a commitment to mutuality and interdependence in the gospel had become what has been described as a "shopping exercise" whereby the majority-world provinces of the Communion presented their needs to the minority-world provinces for funding consideration. The inherent imbalance of privilege and power around such tables inevitably created one-way giving and receiving, leaving little opportunity for true mutuality and interdependence.

3. Johnson and Clark, *Anglicans in Mission*, 47.
4. MISAG 2, *Towards Dynamic Mission*, 24–30.

PRINCIPLES OF PARTNERSHIP IN THE TWENTY-FIRST CENTURY

There are many examples in the work of the Partnerships staff team from 2000 to the end of Ellie's directorship, and to the present, that express how the Anglican Church of Canada has tried to be true to MRI and the Ten Principles of Partnership in its relationships with the Communion for God's mission. Ellie ensured that these values were instilled throughout the orientation and training of staff, committee members and volunteers, mission personnel, and international theological student interns. Regional Mission Coordination staff teams sought to establish and sustain a person-to-person, relationships-first approach with international Anglican and ecumenical partners—through regular correspondence, regional travel, in-depth visits involving various local leaders, participation in worship, and local immersion within a partner's jurisdiction to learn how church ministries changed peoples' lives through education, health care, church planting, and more. We shared our reports on such visits with our partners and with Canadian church structures and members—a record of so much more than project expenditures and receipts. Block grants were the standard way of sending financial support for the partner's distribution to national mission priorities. It was a given that the Partners in Mission Standing Committee would include at least one partner from the Communion in the majority world, with time on the agenda for regular reflection and discussion on issues of mutual concern and challenge, difference and diversity, and ways of working.

Another aspect of Ellie's legacy in the missional work of the Anglican Communion can be found in the fourth of the Five Marks of Mission, which now reads, "To seek to transform unjust structures of society, to challenge violence of every kind and to pursue peace and reconciliation." The 1999 MISSIO report commended the Five Marks of Mission to each province and diocese of the Communion, challenging them to develop or revise their understanding of mission faithful to Scripture. The report provided background and context to the Five Marks with suggestions for ways to continue "along the road towards being mission-centered."[5]

With Ellie's leadership, and that of successive Partnerships Committees and staff, the Anglican Church of Canada took up MISSIO's challenge, and in November 2007 the Council of General Synod passed a resolution that endorsed "the recommendation of the Partners in Mission and Ecojustice Committee that the Anglican Consultative Council consider adding a sixth Mark of Mission to its current list, that relates to peace, conflict

---

5. Johnson and Clark, *Anglicans in Mission*, 20–21.

transformation, and reconciliation, and the General Secretary communicate this recommendation and endorsement to the Anglican Consultative Council."[6]

The 2009 Anglican Consultative Council meeting in Kingston, Jamaica, agreed in principle to a sixth mark. However, instead of adding an additional mark, the 2012 Anglican Consultative Council meeting in Auckland, New Zealand, decided to amend the fourth mark to include references to peace, conflict transformation, and reconciliation. For more than a decade, this fourth mark in its 2012 iteration has been a powerful witness of global Anglicanism, alongside ecumenical organizations, faith groups, and social movements, for "speaking truth to power," acting for transformational social change, and adding the voice of millions of Anglicans in their pursuit of peace with justice and reconciliation.

2011–2013: A KAIROS MOMENT

In the fifteen years following Ellie's retirement in 2008 as director of Partnerships, much has changed. By 2011, the structure and capacity of the department had been reduced from a multi-program unit of eleven staff to a team of three with responsibility for the church's national and international mission and justice priorities. The loss of human, material, and financial resources was felt deeply by church members and staff, by local and global partners alike. Given the projected decline of financial support from dioceses, what future role could General Synod have in these areas of ministry? How could the remaining Partnerships staff continue to serve effectively? Many were asking, in anger and grief, whether this was the end of the work of the national church in international mission and ecojustice.

Over the next two years, from 2011 to 2013, my work as the continuing coordinator of the church's international Partners in Mission ministry would in part address those questions, asking, "What would Ellie do?" The work involved many hours of meeting and conversation with Canadian Anglicans concerned with the life and witness of the Anglican Communion—through companion diocese relationships, theological student exchanges, the networks of the Anglican Communion, and more. In light of the strategic priorities set out for General Synod in "Vision 2019," we asked ourselves what was essential to bring forward from the past into the present, what priorities and best practices were the most important for our relationship with Anglicans and Episcopalians globally and with the worldwide church.[7]

---

6. "Partners in Mission."

7. Vision 2019 Task Force, "Dream the Church/Vision 2019."

We asked ourselves, "Who is Partners in Mission?" and "What structures would work for the church now?"

The message from church members was clear: *The participation of General Synod in the life and ministry of the Anglican Communion, locally and globally, is a core, indelible aspect of the Anglican Church of Canada's corporate DNA as church. We are partners in mission with others. We look forward in faith to many years of continued partnership in mission within the Communion, "mutually encouraged by each other's faith" (Rom 1:12). These relationships express our commitment to being a partner in God's mission for the whole world, and our deep need for community in Christ.*

Likewise, that two year period was a time of holding discussions with historic bilateral partners in the Communion, with international ecumenical partners, and with the Anglican Communion Office. It was a time of gathering and studying reports, papers, statements, and resolutions, addressing the changes and challenges of the global context for mission, looking for signposts of partnership with other General Synod ministries, and with other provinces of the Communion and Anglican mission agencies.

The messages from global partners were also clear: *We are aware of the changes occurring in the northern, western church, of declining numbers of church members, and of diminishing levels of funding for local, national and global church ministry. We are aware of the challenges these changes impose, and of the many needs your people have. Funding is one small part of our relationship. We will manage and grow with what we have. Please, however, continue to visit, to exchange prayer and news with us. Be there on the other end of an email to answer a question, send a greeting, receive proposals, and accompany us in our need for life, and peace, and justice. Please continue to be with us, as we will be with you, as disciples of Jesus in the mission of God.*

The year of 2013 was a *kairos* time: the voice of God could be heard and felt in the words and the passion of Canadian Anglicans and Communion partners urging us, the remnant Partners in Mission staff, to find ways of walking together in the "new normal," as partners and friends in Christ. It was a time of endings and new beginnings as we made hard choices to pare down the breadth of the previous work of Partners in Mission—more than thirty-five partners in fifty countries coordinated by three separate mission "desks"—while creating deeper relationships with fewer partners in each global region, coordinated by one desk. This was an opportunity, as Ellie had urged a decade before, to reestablish partner relationships based on respect, mutuality, and interdependence, to carefully examine what had failed in the past, and ask why.

FROM PARTNERS IN MISSION TO GLOBAL RELATIONS

Of the three foundational MRI principles—mutuality, responsibility, interdependence—mutuality provided the greatest impetus for developing a single, integrated Global Relations ministry. Mutuality was the lens through which staff, volunteers, and partners could examine the past, review the present, and complete the difficult work of identifying relationships and priorities that would continue or not. It was a hinge moment between Partners in Mission and Global Relations, a change in approach or at least an awareness that something different was needed from us if our relationships were to be genuine and meaningful and lead to good results. This is not to say that the previous work of Partners in Mission, and the World Mission program before that, was directive or disinterested in sharing the news and priorities and needs of the Canadian Anglican Church with global partners. Indeed, those with whom we still collaborate and serve appreciate with gratitude the commitment of Partnerships personnel over the decades—to storytelling, to respectful relationships, to listening and making changes in systems in order to affirm the authority and responsibility of partners.

Rather, the change we needed to make was to know our own local context better, to be freshly aware of the mission priorities of the Canadian church and its needs for companionship and solidarity, to be better prepared to make connections between local and global, and to commit resources that would strengthen companionship and solidarity for ministry in which we and others would act more effectively together. The Canadian church needed a national hub, a platform with the capacity not only to continue with key bilateral relationships, but also to strengthen local leadership for global partnerships, while sharing stories and news of the global Anglican family to which we belong.

With the encouragement of Canadian Anglicans and global partners, the newly named Global Relations ministry began to shift focus toward building relationships and deepening our understanding of others, toward supporting important and sometimes difficult conversations between the Canadian church and the wider Communion. One such example of this was the decade of Consultation of Anglican Bishops in Dialogue, a "fluid group of bishops from eight African Provinces, The Anglican Church of Canada, The Church of England, The Scottish Episcopal Church, and The Episcopal Church,"[8] who met annually between February 2010 and February 2020. Imbued with the African *Indaba* spirit of the 2008 Lambeth Conference,

---

8. "To Be One."

and the encouragement of a small, voluntary fringe gathering at Lambeth of twenty African and Canadian bishops, the Consultation of Anglican Bishops in Dialogue began in 2010 under the leadership of Archbishop Colin Johnson, Diocese of Toronto, and the Rev. Canon Dr. Kawuki Mukasa.

As interest and participation in the consultation grew—more than sixty bishops would eventually participate in the decade of dialog—Canon Kawuki Mukasa was hired by the General Synod's Faith, Worship, and Ministry department, in part to broaden and deepen this dialogue for Canadian and Communion bishops. When it became clear that Global Relations staff could also play a role, we did so, becoming the planning and administrative office of the consultation from 2014 to 2020.

Global Relations staff began to seek other opportunities for alliances with national ministries, ecumenical organizations, and other provincial and Communion justice networks and international partners—engaging in issues such as the eradication of human trafficking and slavery, the protection of the rights of human rights defenders, and the pursuit of peace and reconciliation. With others, Global Relations supported the prophetic call of Canadian Anglican Church leaders to speak to government on matters of international and national concern.

COMPANIONSHIP IN THE COMMUNION

A related shift in the work of Global Relations over the past fifteen years has been to develop structures that support church members for active companionship with provinces and dioceses of the Anglican Communion. The Canadian Companions of Jerusalem, established in 2011, is one such example that lifts up Ellie's teaching: that local is global and global is local. The two are inextricably linked, essential to forming relationships for mission. The Canadian Companions of Jerusalem is a "national, voluntary body of members of the Anglican Church of Canada drawn together in common concern and support for the well-being of the Church in the land of Christ's birth, life, death, and resurrection."[9] The Companions of Jerusalem, with the administrative support of Global Relations and other General Synod ministries, have developed the church's annual Jerusalem and Holy Land Sunday, which we celebrate together with the Evangelical Lutheran Church in Canada. A broad range of worship resources are available and renewed yearly for local parish participation. The Companions support the specific ministry needs of the Episcopal Diocese of Jerusalem with funds raised through Companions fees, donations, and Jerusalem and Holy Land Sunday

9. "Companions of Jerusalem," para. 1.

offerings. The 2023 Pilgrimage of Learning and Discovery for twenty young adult Canadian Anglicans in the biblical lands in the season of Easter was another Companions of Jerusalem initiative.

Moreover, in the Anglican Church of Canada today, there are fourteen companion diocese relationships that link Canadian dioceses with other dioceses in Canada and in the Anglican Communion—to encourage and pray for one another, learn and share each other's joys and concerns, and participate in face-to-face, spiritual, and material exchanges. Covenanted diocesan companionships are good examples of how prayer, people, visits, and material resources enable and sustain relationships over time for local mission with Anglicans in other parts of the world or other regions in Canada. This long standing initiative of the Anglican Communion has, since the era of the World Mission and Partnerships departments to the present, brought thousands of Canadian and global Anglicans together for friendship, learning, worship, and service.[10]

The Global Relations team assists dioceses who are seeking to begin or strengthen companion relationships by suggesting potential contacts in the Anglican Communion, offering resources for worship and covenants, and providing information about joint ministry agreements. We also assist with opportunities for learning about intercultural faith experiences, leading parish mission and pilgrimage groups, and how best to send funds abroad.

CONCLUSION

Ellie Johnson awoke each day with an indefatigable readiness to share a word with Canadian Anglicans about the marvelous, inspiring, and deeply faithful people who are part of the global Anglican family, to encourage Canadian parishes and dioceses to meet others in the worldwide Communion—in print, online, on pilgrimage, on vacation in global destinations, and in any way possible.

Much has changed since Ellie's retirement in 2008, in particular in the program once known as Partners in Mission, which Ellie guided and inspired for fourteen years. It is true that the structures and resources to support a program like Partners in Mission are no longer there, and the role and purpose of General Synod's international mission partnerships are no longer the same. Yet it is also true that the current Global Relations ministry has its own distinctive role and purpose: to enable the Anglican Church of Canada to become more authentically mutual in our relationships within the Communion and the ecumenical church—bringing greater awareness

10. See "Companion Diocese Relationships."

of our own mission priorities, a greater capacity for local mission in response to global realities, and stronger partnerships with other churches and allies in Canada.

A final word: I am so deeply grateful, Ellie, for who you were and how you encouraged and challenged all of us to be the best we could be, in working for the new day that was breaking upon the global Anglican church, and in our awakening to the egregious sins and crimes of racism and imperialism, embedded in our missiology, against the dignity and integrity of human beings and creation.

Your proclamation in myriad ways of the good news of Jesus Christ and God's abundant life for all has continued to resonate in my seeking and in the church's search today for serving the *missio Dei* with humility, repentance, justice, and reparation.

The stories you taught and told of the Communion's involvement in mission-centered ministry continue to be relevant to the evolving work of the General Synod's global relationships and the Communion's councils and networks as they endeavor to include all voices, perspectives, dreams, aspirations, and gifts of the Spirit.

Your loving response to the needs of staff and their families, of church members and Communion partners, by being with them and for them, your huge smile and infectious laughter, your good counsel, ferocious compassion, and commitment to justice have brought us to wholeness and new life. We are welcome still in so many places throughout the Communion on the strength of your example as a friend and servant leader. We are still welcome and trusted to respond to the Communion's needs as we are able.

You would be pleased indeed to hear and experience how the false dichotomy between mission and justice has begun to fade away over the past decade. In particular, the fourth mark of mission, which bears your signature vision, is integral to the Anglican understanding and work of mission and ministry in Canada and the Communion.

Lastly, you would be delighted and inspired by the ways in which the seeds and green shoots you tended in the work of the Partners in Mission Committee and the Ecojustice Committee—to strive to safeguard the integrity of creation and sustain and renew the life of the earth—have grown and born fruit through the cycles of the church's learning and witness in service to all of creation.

BIBLIOGRAPHY

"Companions of Jerusalem." The Anglican Church of Canada. https://www.anglican.ca/gr/provinces/jerusalem/companions/.

"Companion Diocese Relationships." The Anglican Church of Canada. https://www.anglican.ca/gr/global-local-mission/ccdp/.

Johnson, Eleanor, and John Clark, eds. *Anglicans in Mission: A Transforming Journey; Report of MISSIO, the Mission Commission of the Anglican Communion.* London: SPCK, 2000.

MISAG 2 (Mission Issues and Strategy Advisory Group 2). *Towards Dynamic Mission: Renewing the Church for Mission.* London: Anglican Consultative Council, 1993.

"Partners in Mission and Ecojustice Committee #009-01-07-11: Marks of Mission." The Anglican Church of Canada, 2007. https://archives.anglican.ca/link/official9485.

"To Be One: Consultation of Anglican Bishops in Dialogue." The Anglican Church of Canada. https://www.anglican.ca/gr/bishopsconsultation/.

Vision 2019 Task Force. "Dream the Church/Vision 2019: A Plan for the Anglican Church of Canada." The Anglican Church of Canada. https://archive.anglican.ca/gs2010/wp-content/uploads/019-GS2010-Vision-2019-Report-and-Appendices.pdf.

III. INDIGENOUS VOICES AND STORIES OF SOLIDARITY

9

Ellie Johnson and the Residential Schools Settlement Agreements

NANCY HURN

AMONGST HER MANY ROLES at the General Synod of the Anglican Church of Canada over the years—as education officer in 1988, then as director of Partnerships from 1994 to 2006, and finally as (acting) general secretary prior to her retirement in 2007—the footprint of Ellie Johnson remains deep and wide. Coupled with her significant Anglican Communion and ecumenical work, and through her coordinating role with various diocesan staff and bishops across Canada, she was pivotally involved with Indigenous persons and communities who sought justice for survivors and all those adversely affected by our church's legacy in the Indian residential schools (IRS). Since the early 1400s, European colonial expansion westward across North America brought settlers into contact with existing Indigenous communities. Centuries later as Anglican missionaries entered western Canada, and as contact with colonial explorers and settlers increased, the specter of racism was never absent. Like so many of us, Ellie discovered racism in action—at times blatantly obvious, and at other times more subtle, though prevalent. Her vision of the goals of missionary work itself changed over the years. This essay will attempt to convey not only some of the detail of her own healing and reconciliation journey, along with the journey of our church, and most importantly the journey required of residential school survivors, of their descendants, and of Indigenous people across the land increasingly called "Turtle Island."

Ellie was often asked to describe the changing relationship between early missionaries and people living on reserves and in Indigenous communities. Since the early 1920s, hoping to improve educational opportunities and overall quality of life for Indigenous families and children, the church colluded in a national, colonial assimilation strategy. Church leaders took little time to question the effects of collaboration, or the colonization process itself. Such ignorance fostered a culture and practice of abuse throughout over thirty Anglican schools from Quebec to British Columbia. Even in those places where some benefit from school experience can be asserted, the process of eviction from homes, of separation from language and culture, and the teaching that British settler culture is superior to all other cultural communities is nothing short of evil.

At a synod of the Diocese of Toronto in 1988, Ellie joined Archbishop Terry Finlay to explain the changes in the approach to mission work at the national level of the Anglican Church. Historically, mission agencies were primarily concerned with the conversion of souls. While a clear witness to the salvific power and presence of the risen Lord in the experience and lives of adherents, "mission" historically and in the present moment has been and remains multifaceted. For Ellie, mission requires the pursuit and welcoming of justice. Most Indigenous recipients of the gospel received the story of grace, yet often were denied the experience and effects of justice. The archbishop and Ellie supported each other on their journey to seek truth, reconciliation, and healing on behalf of the Anglican Church of Canada and for the survivors of the schools. The archbishop later raised significant funds for the survivor compensation fund and was appointed primate's envoy on residential schools and truth and reconciliation following his retirement as archbishop of Toronto.

Dreadfully slowly, over many years, policies were created hoping to develop a "partnership of equals" between Indigenous people and settlers, though action and outcomes did not always reflect the equality which was sought. Such an ambitious partnership eventually became the underlying goal of the Truth and Reconciliation Commission (TRC). Prior to the TRC, however, a number of significant historical events occurred, each requiring a particular response from the church.

Starting with the Indian Residential Schools Settlement Agreement (IRSSA), an agreement negotiated by representatives in the churches and in government emerged through negotiations. Ellie was not involved in the negotiations proper, but she was centrally involved in responding to the consequences of such negotiations. An online government of Canada web page describes these negotiations in these words:

The implementation of the IRSSA began on September 19, 2007. The Settlement Agreement represents the consensus reached between legal counsel for former students, legal counsel for the Churches, the Assembly of First Nations, other Indigenous organizations and the Government of Canada. The implementation of this historic agreement brings a fair and lasting resolution to the legacy of Indian Residential Schools. The Settlement Agreement includes five different elements to address the legacy of Indian Residential Schools: a Common Experience Payment (CEP) for all eligible former students of Indian Residential Schools; an Independent Assessment Process (IAP) for claims of sexual or serious physical abuse; measures to support healing such as the Indian Residential Schools Resolution Health Support Program; an endowment to the Aboriginal Healing Foundation commemorative activities; and finally the establishment of a Truth and Reconciliation Commission (TRC).[1]

ANGLICAN APOLOGY

Alongside this response from government, the Anglican Church of Canada found its own way forward. Published in 1969, *The Hendry Report* identified the needs of Indigenous Anglican People for self-determination within the decision-making body of the church.[2] The report bridges two of "four distinct policy phases that coincide with specific time periods: 1) end of assimilative policies (1946–1969), 2) Aboriginal Rights support (1970–1989), 3) acceptance of the residential school legacy (1990–1999), and 4) response to litigation and the development of the 2007 Indian Residential School Settlement Agreement."[3] As acceptance and understanding of residential school legacy grew, certain actions were essential, firstly an apology. The opportunity arrived as Canadian Anglican Indigenous leaders gathered at National Native Convocation (later renamed the First Sacred Circle) at Minaki, Ontario, Friday, August 6, 1993.

The terms of the 1993 apology made by the primate, Archbishop Michael Peers, to the Indigenous people who attended assured that the church would truthfully acknowledge its historic collusion in administering the schools. Indigenous coordinator, the Rev Laverne Jacobs, helped craft the apology and Vi Smith gave the acceptance response of behalf of the elders and participants present that day. Ellie worked diligently and

1. "Indian Residential Schools Settlement Agreement," §1.

2. Hendry, *Beyond Traplines.*

3. Beninger, "Indigenous Policies," ii.

compassionately to live out this apology made on behalf of all bishops and members of the Anglican Church of Canada. The apology was translated into eleven Indigenous languages and was given as follows:

> Together here with you I have listened as you have told your stories of the residential schools.
>
> I have heard the voices that have spoken of pain and hurt experienced in the schools, and of the scars which endure to this day.
>
> I have felt shame and humiliation as I have heard of suffering inflicted by my people, and as I think of the part our church played in that suffering.
>
> I am deeply conscious of the sacredness of the stories that you have told and I hold in the highest honour those who have told them.
>
> I have heard with admiration the stories of people and communities who have worked at healing, and I am aware of how much healing is needed.
>
> I also know that I am in need of healing, and my own people are in need of healing, and our church is in need of healing. Without that healing, we will continue the same attitudes that have done such damage in the past.
>
> I also know that healing takes a long time, both for people and for communities.
>
> I also know that it is God who heals, and that God can begin to heal when we open ourselves, our wounds, our failures and our shame to God. I want to take one step along that path here and now.
>
> I accept and I confess before God and you, our failures in the residential schools. We failed you. We failed ourselves. We failed God.
>
> I am sorry, more than I can say, that we were part of a system which took you and your children from home and family.
>
> I am sorry, more than I can say, that we tried to remake you in our image, taking from you your language and the signs of your identity.
>
> I am sorry, more than I can say, that in our schools so many were abused physically, sexually, culturally, and emotionally.

On behalf of the Anglican Church of Canada, I present our apology.

I do this at the desire of those in the Church like the National Executive Council, who know some of your stories and have asked me to apologize.

I do this in the name of many who do not know these stories.

And I do this even though there are those in the church who cannot accept the fact that these things were done in our name.

As soon as I am home, I shall tell all the bishops what I have said and ask them to co-operate with me and with the National Executive Council in helping this healing at the local level. Some bishops have already begun this work.

I know how often you have heard words which have been empty because they have not been accompanied by actions. I pledge to you my best efforts, and the efforts of our church at the national level, to walk with you along the path of God's healing . . .

Thank you for listening to me.

+ Michael, Archbishop and Primate, August 6, 1993.[4]

NEXT STEPS

In 1992 the General Synod Healing and Reconciliation Fund was established to fund healing programs for many Indigenous communities. Developed and implemented by an independent board, with church and government representatives, Ellie and the healing fund manager encouraged deeper relationships with First Nations, Metis, and Inuit peoples.

At an ecumenical meeting of church leaders, in January 1999, Donna Bomberry, coordinator for Anglican Native Ministries reported that "as one who works with native people inside the Anglican church, their main interest is in healing and reconciliation. The apology by the Primate encouraged real hope. . . . The importance of self-determination might help to alleviate any backlash in the future. . . . We need to build on that relationship. . . . Adversarial approaches will not do it." Michael Peers responded at this same meeting: "We have to be able to tell our story with authenticity and our First Nations' peoples must tell it," to which Ellie added, "We must try to walk through this together. There is something quite profound about those who

4. Peers, "Apology."

have been victims and are struggling to hold onto their faith. Walking with them through the valley is very moving."[5]

A NEW AGAPE

In 2001, General Synod adopted "A New Agape," a plan agreed on between the Anglican Council of Indigenous Peoples (ACIP) and the church, to enrich Indigenous relationships and seek five key goals: self-determination, justice, healing, historical reparation, and walking in partnership.[6] The preamble reads, "The Anglican Church of Canada is committed to a new relationship with the Indigenous (or Aboriginal) Peoples of Canada. This new relationship is based on a partnership which focuses on the cultural, spiritual, social, and economic independence of Indigenous communities. To give expression to this new relationship, The Anglican Church of Canada will work primarily with Indigenous Anglicans for a truly Anglican Indigenous Church in Canada. It is an important step in the overall quest for self-governance."[7]

From 2001 onward, various dialogues occurred as the need to resolve conflicts emerging from court decisions across the country continued to grow. Claims against the government and Anglican, Roman Catholic, Presbyterian, and United Church of Canada entities increased at an alarming rate—the inefficiencies of the judicial system made resolution inequitable and very slow. The financial implications for the Anglican Church of Canada were made very clear as the claims were resolved, as the legal and compensatory costs rose. A complex, wide-ranging, and increasingly difficult process required a broadscale administrative approach.

On November 20, 2002, an agreement between the Anglican Church of Canada and the government of Canada became necessary to prevent the bankruptcy of the church. It consisted of two parts, including a legal settlement covering compensation cost and exploratory dialogues to help assess damage and resolve conflicts. An agreement was made that ensured the 100 percent of compensation costs would be split—with 70 percent covered by the government and 30 percent covered by the Anglican Church—with an overall cap not to exceed $25 million. (It is worth mentioning that most of this money came from the dioceses. Such significant buy-in was one of the

5. Johnson, "Canadian Journey of Repentance." Draft version in Johnson folder in Anglican Archives.

6. Indigenous Ministries, "New Agape.

7. Indigenous Ministries, "New Agape," para. 1.

highlights of the Anglican response, all pledged within three winter months, in many cases through the calling of special synods.)

The agreement included clauses to ensure that a humane and rigorous Alternate Dispute Resolution (ADR) process would be used to establish individual compensation, and that a programmatic approach would later be taken by both the government and church to respond to the loss of language and culture. At this time, representatives of the government of Canada were decidedly averse to paying compensation for the loss of language and culture.

EXPLORATORY DIALOGUES

Leading up to the signing of the Anglican Agreement, Ellie Johnson was assigned the role of exploring the terms of the ADR process. Seeking to improve relationships among the residential school survivors, ADR money could be directed to survivor compensation and less to lawyers and court costs. In this effort, a series of eight exploratory dialogues were held across Canada during the period September 1998 to May 1999. These dialogues brought together residential school survivors, Indigenous leaders, and healers, along with church and government officials. The dialogues each took place over two days and the principles, lessons, and values brought forward in the discussions led to the creation of a set of Guiding Principles (1999) and established a pilot dispute resolution process. With the goal of "working together to build restoration and reconciliation" the principles sought to build relationships through mutual respect and understanding. Conversations were to be community-appropriate, with special provision of support for those disclosing abuse. They were to be holistic and spiritual thus acknowledging the broad impact of the schools. Participation was voluntary with the right to return to legal process guaranteed.

Fair results would include: "a) Disclosure with safety, b) Validation with sensitivity, c) Remedies with flexibility, d) Commemoration with respect, and e) Healing, closure, reconciliation, and renewal." In sum, "these principles are part of a searching process. They must always be used as guides, not rules—which must be respected, but not rigidly applied. . . . We walk in the courageous footsteps of those who first brought to our consciousness and conscience the abuse that survivors experienced at native residential schools. In drafting these Guiding Principles, we have before us the faces, and have drawn together the voices, and woven together the words, of those who told their stories in the Exploratory Dialogues across Canada."[8]

8. Johnson, "Personal Notes."

Ellie explained her own engagement in the dialogues through an article in the Anglican Communion magazine:

> My own involvement has been to attend a series of consultations to explore alternatives to litigation. I am one of those who has listened to and received the stories of anger, pain and suffering on behalf of the Anglican Church. This experience has called into question for me the entire missionary project and the way in which we as Christians approach other people in our efforts to proclaim the Gospel. Mission may indeed be about proclaiming God's love through Jesus Christ, but it is also about affirming that all of humankind is created in God's image, with no group having the right to re-create others in its own limited vision. So, where the missionary project has a shameful and arrogant history, mission today must be about humility, repentance, justice, and reparation. And with God's grace, we may eventually achieve reconciliation.[9]

The human connection Ellie so often exemplified is represented in obtaining the input from those harmed in the residential schools. During the third dialogue held in Regina, Saskatchewan in November 1998, Ellie noted, "[Bishop] Tom Morgan read the Primate's apology, and as at the Calgary Dialogue, it was a very moving moment. . . . Our apology is by far the best, and having it read out by a bishop of the church has enormous symbolic significance. The Rev. Arthur Anderson (Diocese of Qu'Appelle) spoke about the new relationship developing between the Indigenous and non-Indigenous members of our church, and he read the Covenant Statement (1994). This too had quite an impact."[10] Ellie's participation in these events, and her leadership style, ensured that those with the most knowledge and authenticity would be given the opportunity to make their concerns or comments known. She followed the content of the Primate's apology as she sought the truth to be shared by those who were most experienced.

On the night before the 2003 agreement was signed, there were very strong objections raised by the Indigenous staff and members of the Anglican Council of Indigenous Peoples (ACIP), that compensation from loss of language and culture was *not* to be included in the agreement. Anglican Church leaders chose to sign the agreement anyway, and a serious disagreement ensued. According to Ellie, this was a very difficult time; however, she learned a great deal through the process, as did the primate and archdeacon Jim Boyles. As the ADR was implemented, the deficiencies of the agreement

9. Johnson, "Canadian Journey of Repentance."
10. Johnson, "Personal Notes."

became clear. Many concerns and complaints were raised by the early claimants. The guiding principles developed for the ADR process were unsatisfactory, and a new process to address the loss of language and culture and a more specific and consistent grading of the abuses needed to be defined for compensation purposes.

In a presentation given at her home parish of St. Simon's, Oakville, Ellie revealed her concerns about the situation at that time:

> Within the church, relations between Indigenous and non-Indigenous Anglicans have been severely strained, with a feeling that much of the progress of the past decade towards right relations has been lost. The formal signing of the Settlement Agreement happened last March, with the Anglican Council of Indigenous Peoples immediately speaking out against this action in a public press release. In the months since then, I have felt deep discouragement, almost despair, unable to see how to go forward, but trying not to lose faith. Then a month ago, God's Spirit worked in a mysterious way.
>
> The Anglican Council of Indigenous Peoples had a leadership conference in Winnipeg. This conference included leaders from both the Indigenous and non-Indigenous parts of the Church. I was privileged to be among those invited, but went in with some trepidation, fearing the worst-case scenario, which would have been a decision by angry Indigenous Anglicans to separate and establish their own church. Instead, by the grace of God, Indigenous church leaders decided to stay within our church, and to move forward in establishing separate governance structures within our church for Indigenous members, in accordance with resolutions approved by General Synod in 1995.[11]

Right relations would once again be put into a better place with the graciousness of the Indigenous peoples.

The revised Indian Residential School Settlement Agreement was evolving to include the government of Canada and the four mainstream denominations that ran the schools, including Anglican, Presbyterian, and United churches and the Roman Catholic Entities. In May 2005, there was a major shift in the alignment of the parties who *aligned themselves with the survivors* with a goal toward healing. At that time the federal government appointed the Honorable Frank Iacobucci to bring together the Assembly of First Nations, churches, and legal counsel for the survivors to obtain agreement on a fair and equitable response to the residential school legacy.

11. Presentation to St. Simon's, Oakville, Ontario, Nov 16, 2003.

As general secretary, Archdeacon Jim Boyles represented the Anglican Church of Canada and conducted the main financial negotiations. Under the revised agreement, the final contribution of the Anglican church was reduced from $25 million to $16 million dollars which allowed some additional funds to be made available for the Anglican Healing fund. Some dioceses received a refund to use locally for healing and reconciliation work. Based on this agreement, a release was to be signed ensuring the former students would not bring further legal action against the churches regarding their experiences in the residential schools.

There were now two parts to the compensation payment, the Common Experience Payment (CEP) and the Independent Assessment Process (IAP). Ellie Johnson, representing the Anglican Church, continued with the amendments to the agreement which were based on an improved IAP. To reach agreement on compensation for the experiential impact on the survivors, a CEP was set up to cover the wrongs that were common to everyone. It included removal of children from their families, including substandard accommodation, and poor education, the loss of language, and loss of culture. In addition, students were then compensated based on the number of years they could prove they attended a residential school.

The second part of the agreement in principle was fiercely pursued by the Assembly of First Nations (AFN) and the Anglican, United, and Presbyterian churches in Canada. There were important advancements made by the IAP that included additional awards given for physical and sexual abuse. The issue of student-on-student abuse became important to the revisions, especially as it related to female students. Much of the progress that was made during this transition reflected Ellie's concern for Indigenous people and her approach to the human elements of mission work.

Full agreement and signing of the Indian Residential School Settlement Agreement by all thirty dioceses, and the General Synod itself, needed to occur. As acting general secretary, Ellie needed to ensure this was done in a timely manner. This was a monumental task, as she consulted with the bishops and chancellors of each Anglican entity. Many church officials were still not convinced that the church should be held accountable for these historical wrongs.

An article in the *Anglican Journal* dated March 1, 2006, noted,

> Ms. Johnson said that the accord would also include, as an appendix, the composition, mandate and plans of a truth and reconciliation committee. The agreement in principle released last November had stated that a "truth and reconciliation process" would involve a "national truth-telling project to set the historic

record straight" and would provide opportunities for a local, community-based "truth-telling program" that will be spread over five years to enable former students to tell their stories. . . . Ms. Johnson said the Anglican Church of Canada is willing to send copies of records in its archives to this proposed [research] centre.[12]

Through the evolution of Ellie's time working with and advocating for Indigenous people as part of the truth and reconciliation process, her understanding of racism grew and changed over time. Hearing firsthand the experiences of the survivors, Ellie came to understand how systemic racism was part of the fundamental reasoning for both government and church role in administering the residential school system.

During the many international visits Ellie made throughout the Communion to explain the impact of the residential school legacy on the survivors and the mission work of the church, she spoke about *acknowledging the truth*. The path of healing and reconciliation in Canada was led by the anti-apartheid movement in South Africa, the Irish Catholic mother and baby homes, and Indigenous concerns raised in Australia and New Zealand. Ellie spoke about her experiences at a World Council of Churches meeting, at a Global Episcopal meeting, and at an International Anglican Standing Commission on Mission and Evangelism (IASCOME) meeting, where she detailed the terms of the settlement agreement and the history of the residential schools.[13]

In a local presentation at St John's Anglican Church in Ancaster, Ontario Ellie said,

> I do believe that we are in the midst of an important "moment of truth" in Canadian history. We are trying to build a nation based on justice and respect for cultural and racial diversity. But until we make restitution for our foundational sins of racism and injustice against the original inhabitants of our land, these efforts are seen as hypocrisy. And the world is definitely watching us, especially those parts of the world struggling with their own issues of poverty, ethnic conflict, and local legacies of colonialism.[14]

12. Sison, "Bishops Endorse Revised Accord," para. 3.

13. Rosenthal and Erdey, *Communion in Mission*, 122.

14. Presentation to St John's Ancaster, Ontario, Oct 21, 2001.

THE APOLOGY FOR SPIRITUAL HARM

As the healing and reconciliation process continues to unfold across our church, with Ellie's words feeding my own conscience, I find it helpful to recall the "Apology for Spiritual Harm" offered by then primate Archbishop Fred Hiltz on the floor of General Synod in Vancouver in 2019. There is insufficient space in this essay to include the full text so a short extract must suffice:

> For a number of years, since the Indigenous Covenant of 1994, there has been a call for an apology for spiritual abuse endured by Indigenous Peoples through the era of colonial expansion across the Land, and particularly through the era of the Indian Residential Schools.
>
> In the Apology to survivors of the Residential Schools delivered on August 6, 1993, Archbishop Michael Peers expressed his remorse on behalf of the Anglican Church of Canada that "we tried to remake you in our own image."
>
> Today, I offer this apology for our cultural and spiritual arrogance toward all Indigenous Peoples—First Nations, Inuit and Métis—and the harm we inflicted on you. I do this at the desire of many across the Church, at the call of the Anglican Council of Indigenous Peoples, and at the request and with the authority of the Council of the General Synod.[15]

Each of these apologies (1993, 2019) were such important offerings, so long overdue, so very necessary as part of a process which continues to this day. It is unfortunate that in 2019, Ellie was not able to express her opinion or support for this later apology. I am certain however that she would have been pleased to add her own enthusiastic voice.

Ellie Johnson was at the center of a team of faithful justice seekers who over many years—as Indigenous and non-Indigenous Anglicans—have collaboratively brought our church—and ourselves with it—to a much better place, a place where healing, justice, and reconciliation have become a dominant theme and constant practice, a reality while imperfect and still evolving that remains a goal worthy of pursuit. In comments included in *Communion in Mission*, she wrote, "The Spirit will guide us if we do not harden our hearts. Reconciliation is our vocation—since Christ came to show us the way to be reconciled with God and with each other. We continue to make mistakes and our steps falter but we cannot turn away or give

---

15. Hiltz, "Apology for Spiritual Harm," paras. 1–3.

up. Our only choice is to go forward, in trust and hope."[16] This we shall do, together.

BIBLIOGRAPHY

Beninger, Carling C. "The Anglican Church of Canada: Indigenous Policies, 1946–2011." Masters thesis, Trent University, 2011. ProQuest. https://www.collectionscanada.gc.ca/obj/thesescanada/vol2/002/MR81125.PDF?is_thesis=1&oclc_number=881138037.

Brown, Terry, and Christopher Lind, eds. *Justice as Mission: An Agenda for the Church.* Burlington, ON: Trinity, 1985.

Hendry, Charles. *Beyond Traplines: Does the Church Really Care? Towards an Assessment of the Work of the Anglican Church of Canada and Canada's Native Peoples.* 2nd rev. ed. Toronto, ON: Anglican Book Centre, 1998. Orig. pub. 1967.

Hiltz, Fred. "An Apology for Spiritual Harm." The Anglican Church of Canada, Jul 12, 2019. https://www.anglican.ca/news/an-apology-for-spiritual-harm/30024511/.

"Indian Residential Schools Settlement Agreement." Government of Canada. https://www.rcaanc-cirnac.gc.ca/eng/1100100015576/1571581687074#sect1.

Indigenous Ministries. "A New Agape: Plan of Anglican Work in Support of a New Partnership between Indigenous and Non-Indigenous Anglicans." The Anglican Church of Canada. https://www.anglican.ca/im/foundational-documents/anewagape/.

Johnson, Ellie. "A Canadian Journey of Repentance." *Anglican World Magazine*, Jul 1999.

———, ed. "Foreword." In *Welcoming the Stranger: Mission as Transformation*, 7–10. Toronto, ON: Anglican Book Centre, 2007.

———. "Personal Notes: Third Exploratory Dialogue." Anglican Church of Canada, Nov 1998, Anglican Church of Canada Archives, Regina, Canada.

"Meeting of Church Leaders on Residential Schools." Anglican Church of Canada, Jan 8, 1999, Anglican Church of Canada Archives.

Peers, Michael. "The Apology—English." The Anglican Church of Canada. https://www.anglican.ca/tr/apology/english/.

Rosenthal, James M., and Susan T. Erdey, eds. *Communion in Mission: Final Report of the Inter-Anglican Standing Commission on Mission and Evangelism.* New York: Church Publishing, 2006.

Sison, Marites N. "Bishops Endorse Revised Accord." *Anglican Journal*, Mar 1, 2006. https://anglicanjournal.com/bishops-endorse-revised-accord-3093/.

16. Rosenthal and Erdey, *Communion in Mission*, 122.

10

Ellie in the Storm
A Reminiscence

ESTHER WESLEY

The following interview has been edited for clarity and context.

ONE OF THE THINGS I have to say about Ellie is her ministry in the area of Indigenous ministries, especially in the area of residential schools. Changes have happened through many people's work. I think during the time Ellie worked at Church House, that was the toughest part for her. I think she faced the toughest part of the residential schools aftermath at the beginning of the Anglican Church of Canada's engagement with survivors.

Initially, we faced a lot of anger together. I know that at times she was afraid. It's not something that anybody can belittle, being afraid. It was scary attending some meetings with survivors who were bitterly disappointed about some parts of the Residential School Settlement process and agreement. I have to say it was scary, for me and for Ellie. Ellie would invite me to attend meetings with her so we could support one another during those rough times. It was rough! To come to a meeting full of survivors and to say you are part of the church, the church that had abused you and those you know who had also been abused. That was no easy task. It was really difficult to go through.

So Ellie just came to meet. I really did admire her, to pick up her strength and be able to say, "I work for the church" and then wait until people stopped yelling at us before we went on. People would talk about their communities, the changes that have happened. By the time I finished my work it became so much easier, because you know your real work can start after people talk about reconciliation. Ellie did a lot of work in reconciliation, simply by being there. Just by being there, by showing up, representing the church—whether the church cared or not—and I have to say, that many times the church didn't care—but Ellie did.

I really admired her for the healing and reconciling part of her work. I wasn't involved in any of her other work, but the reconciling work, of all the stuff that she did, I would have to say that this was the most important part. Many times she would say, "I don't want to go to these meetings with survivors because I'm going to be yelled at." Then she and I would sit down and talk and eventually decide that "we'll go, and see what happens." Sometimes we'd laugh and say, "See, we came out alive!" Things have come a long way since those early years; by the time I left the work, things had become much easier, much calmer.

Ellie and I saw so many changes. If you want to talk about miracles, well we saw those miracles; we saw those changes. By that time when Fred Hiltz became primate, we saw those changes in the friendships—in the beginning, people were so, so angry at the church, just so angry. By the time Primate Fred came on board, there was amazing support for healing and reconciliation—from the very same people who were so angry. This was really a miracle.

Of course, racism was everywhere. There were a lot of accusations of racism; it still exists today. At the very beginning Ellie and I had talked about how to deal with this. Then the World Conference on Anti-Racism in Durban, South Africa was set to commence. One day I was sitting in my little cubicle. Ellie came and said, "There's a conference and I want you to go." I said, "I'm new here," and Ellie said, "That's why I want you to go." I had absolutely no clue what this was all about. So from there the anti-racism work began. Part of that work is managed by the Canadian Ecumenical Anti-Racism Network (CEARN). The work is still going on and I am still part of it—nobody was ever named to replace me. That was another rough area of work, talking about racism to church leaders. There were many times I was actually afraid of the things that we faced in that work in our church. That work also was and can still be pretty rough.

Another thing about Ellie, for me personally in the anti-racism work: I saw Ellie change, I really did see her change. At first, she wasn't quite sure about the impact of racism on racialized people. And the reason why I say that is when I came back from Durban, I had shown her the statement made by the World Council of Churches (WCC), that racism is a sin. She asked,

"Who said that, and why did they say it?" We had a good discussion on that, and I then found Ellie really changed—she changed the way she looked at the ministry she was involved in. She came to see how racism, how racist attitudes, and how racist words impacted people. So many people say the word "racism" but still don't know what it means or what it looks like. Eventually she began to understand that racialized people talk about racism from the impact of racism on their life. It's not just a word. After that she really committed to the anti-racism work.

She was a great listener. She really calmed me down, many times. I am so glad to have known her and to have worked with her. The work isn't over, but things are better now because of her. Thanks Ellie.

11

Come Short of Breaking Camp
Reentering the Land in the Diocese of Islands and Inlets

LOGAN MCMENAMIE

I AM ORIGINALLY FROM Scotland. I spent my formative years on the west coast of Scotland and was a member of the Congregational Church of Scotland. In school and in church we learned about the "great missionary" days of the church. I was certainly affected by the story of the great missionary movements and the heroes of the faith, of those taking the gospel to the heathen in various parts of the world. Our hymns spoke about "heathen" lands from afar; our Scriptures spoke of heathens abroad. As you will see, my understanding of Indigenous culture and traditions changed as I came to appreciate the richness of various Indigenous beliefs and practices.

One of the great stories was that of David Livingstone, Scottish explorer, abolitionist, and physician. He was a national hero. Like many other schoolboys, I was taken on a trip to Blantyre, his birthplace, where we heard stories of his encounter with David Stanley, along with his faithful servants, James Chuma and Abdullah Susi, who buried his heart and carried his body to the coast. Then we heard of his fight with the lion—such excitement, particularly when we viewed his severed arm bone. All this with his "rags to riches" story, his involvement in the anti–slave trade movement, and his quest for imperial reform was inspirational. However, he was also a colonial explorer who, along with the gospel, brought the best of the British empire and commerce. I attended Sunday school and the Boys' Brigade where these stories of brave missionaries were reinforced. I dreamed of being a missionary.

As I matured, however, questions arose for me about the church, faith, and the Creator[1]; I became an agnostic. In 1970 I met a young woman (Marcia, who later became my wife) who was on a world tour that began in my hometown of Greenock, Scotland. Marcia had grown up a Baptist in Victoria, British Columbia (BC), Canada. While we were dating she asked me about my ambitions. I said I wanted to be a missionary. She divulged how that made her Baptist heart glad. Unfortunately, I spoiled the moment—I revealed that I did not believe in the Creator. Over the years however, I met some different people who helped me enter into a relationship with the Creator. Those people were from a variety of denominations, but after a while I joined the Anglican Church where I was subsequently confirmed and eventually sought ordination, a journey that has led me to become a priest and a bishop in the church.

In this chapter, I want to illustrate a journey-in-partnership, introduce readers to some of the people who understood the value of relationships found in partnerships, and to explain how those relationships helped people be drawn closer to each other and to the Creator. Partnership is about listening and understanding that the Creator is at work in the world, and to demonstrate how discovering the Creator in the culture, language, and traditions of others can occur. To do this we need to reenter the lands where we have assumed others are lesser than us and in need of our culture, traditions, and commerce.

Partnership was a major component in the "Sacred Journey," the vision quest I led through the Anglican Diocese of British Columbia (now the Diocese of Islands and Inlets) in 2015. It was only through partnership that this event could take place. Familiar names in the diocese, Wayne Stewart, Marvin Underhill, Imelda Secker, and Alex Nelson, were one logistical team who planned and organized the events and the journey. The other team were the chiefs and elders who met with me, listened, shared their wisdom, and taught me protocol. All were essential partners in the journey.

My journey in understanding partnership began when Barry Jenks was the diocesan bishop (1992–2002) when I began to serve as priest at the parish of St. George the Martyr in Cadboro Bay, Victoria, British Columbia, in 1993. Barry had served as a volunteer in mission (VIM) as part of our Anglican Church of Canada, Partners in Mission (PIM) program. As

---

1. "Creator" is capitalized throughout given its identification with the divine, i.e., "God."

bishop, he initiated an annual mission conference. It was at one of these conferences that I first met Ellie Johnson, director of Partnerships with the Anglican Church of Canada. Our paths crossed again when I was elected to the Council of General Synod (COGS) in 1996. Ellie was both passionate and compassionate about the work of partnership.

It was during this time that I was introduced to a new idea of mission: the idea and theology that said we were in a process of mutual learning. Mission was a two-directional work—both parties gave and received—this was not the understanding I grew up with, where the white church shaped the non-white recipients with its own wisdom and experience. Partnership said we did not have all the answers and we had much to learn from the culture, faith, and experience of those we worked with in other countries. It was from this revised understanding of our partnership work, nationally and internationally, that we learned what was needed. It certainly was not about us coming as the wise ones.

My initial relationship with the First Nations communities on Vancouver Island began during my work with Bishop Barry. It was the beginning of the truth-telling that was taking place with respect to our church's legacy with the Indian residential schools. Barry invited me to be part of a group of clergy and laypeople who were meeting in healing circles with members of the Indigenous community; some were survivors and others descendants of survivors. Their stories of abuse, of deprivation of language and culture, were horrific.

Years later when I was dean of Victoria's Christ Church Cathedral I asked then retired Bishop John Hannen to come on staff to help me. John had been the bishop of Caledonia, a diocese with a large Indigenous population. He had come to our diocese upon retirement to work with the Indigenous urban community in the Greater Victoria area. John's ministry was legend in the church, both provincially and nationally. His relationship with the Nisga'a people of the Nass Valley in British Columbia ultimately had a huge effect on the Anglican Church of Canada in its journey with Indigenous peoples. This partnership provided a solid witness to the church and to government, as the Nisga'a negotiated land claims and eventually created their own constitution and claimed their right to government.

John invited me to consider taking over the work of urban First Nations at the cathedral as he assisted me in other ways. It was during this time that I began to build a relationship with a number of Indigenous leaders, including Chief Bobby Joseph (Hereditary Chief of the Gwawaenuk people); Frank and Alex Nelson (Musgamagw Dzawada'enuxw First Nations in Kingcome Inlet), and Jill Harris (formerly Chief of the Penelakut band). My first meeting with Alex began a friendship that continues to this day. He is for me an elder, a mentor, a spiritual leader, an advisor, and a friend. At our first meeting in a coffee shop he said to me "we are not going to dance at your gatherings anymore." (In other words, our dancing is not cultural entertainment.) However, Alex was instrumental in our first major piece of work at Christ Church Cathedral with the urban First Nations. Kingcome, along with Wakeman, Hope Town, and Gilford (all on the mainland of British Columbia) are part of our diocese. In 2012, these communities were transferred from the Diocese of New Westminster because they were connected with 'Yālis (Alert Bay) and St. Michael's Residential School—families of the residential school survivors lived in both places.

In 2010 the Kingcome River flooded the community and the village had to be evacuated. 'Yālis was the place to which folk were evacuated. The urban First Nations group decided to hold a fundraiser to help the communities. Support also came from the urban Nishg'a (from Vancouver) and various other urban First Nations communities on Vancouver Island. Alex was very much part of the leadership; he was our important connection with both Kingcome and 'Yālis. We raised $30,000 to send to the elders at Kingcome to help the community reestablish itself. This was a major connection for the cathedral and a good learning in partnership with the Indigenous community on the island. It was at that point in time that the cathedral began to understand its role, not as one to *direct* this funding, but equally to *listen* to our partners, and to *trust* them as to how this money was to be best used.

Jill Harris is a former chief of the Penelakut band, and also a postulant for ordination in the Diocese of British Columbia. She had been very involved in a diocesan group named Aboriginal Neighbours, which had carried out some very good work in building relationships and fostering healing between Indigenous and settler communities. It was from Jill that I first learned the term "reverse missionary." She spoke about her call to be a reverse missionary to the church. Jill saw firsthand the effects of the church's missionary movement where residential schools attempted to destroy her culture. She understood that this church needed to hear a gospel rooted in First Nations' understanding of the Creator. Jill understood her call was to bring the church into a new understanding of the work of mission being discovered in partnership.

Now is a good time to name the First Nations communities on Vancouver Island, including the surrounding islands, and the mainland of British Columbia that make up the diocese. When the churches came to set up the residential schools, the Indigenous population was divided into Roman Catholics, United Church adherents (formerly Presbyterians), and Anglicans. The Coast Salish communities were Roman Catholic, the

Nuu-chah-nulth United, and the Kwakwaka'wakw Anglican. These denominations ran five residential schools on Vancouver Island and surrounding islands: Ahousat and Alberni (Presbyterian/United Church), Christie and Kuper Islands (Roman Catholic), and ʻYãlis (Anglican).

So what would this reverse missionary work look like? I believe it begins with honesty about the past and speaking the truth about the Anglican church's place and role in colonialism. We, along with the government of Canada, participated in an evil system that was responsible for a cultural genocide. It would mean the church would need to look at what reconciliation meant to us, an honesty about our past and our place in it. We could not deny it by saying that this happened before us, so we were not responsible. *It was us!* An apology for the actions was required without seeking forgiveness—forgiveness was not ours to request. A recognition that we would need to go on the journey of reconciliation was essential. Reconciliation not being an end but a journey; reconciliation not coming to an agreement, but a newfound living-well with our differences; a decolonization of the church.

Fast forward a few years; I was now the Anglican bishop of the Diocese of Islands and Inlets (formerly the Diocese of British Columbia). By then I had heard and learned much about the Anglican missionary movement, how along with a European theology we brought trade and commerce at the expense of the Indigenous community—we forcefully converted, and we stole the land.[2]

I had spoken about the church's relationship with the Indigenous community in questions posed to episcopal candidates prior to the diocesan episcopal election in 2013. I said it was time for us to begin a new relationship with the Indigenous peoples alongside whom we live and work. I had committed myself and the diocese to work with and learn from the Indigenous communities on whose traditional territories we lived, worked, prayed, and played. To determine how this new relationship and partnership could be brought about, I reflected on the following questions: (1) How could we come into a new relationship with the Indigenous communities? (2) How could we learn from their traditions, teachings, language, and culture? (3) What do their traditions have to say to us? I had long taught about those who brought the gospel to the Celtic lands (Ireland, Scotland, Wales, Isle of Man, Cornwall, and Brittany). Something very different happened in the relationship between the First Peoples of those lands and the Christians who first engaged them. While many of those stories are based on fancy rather than fact, it seems to me that whatever else happened in that first engagement there was a mutual learning.

2. Anglican Church of Canada, "Doctrine of Discovery."

Those who first brought that gospel to those lands saw something important in the traditional teachings of those original inhabitants. In seeing that, they incorporated some of those teachings into their understanding of Christianity. In a similar manner, those First Peoples saw something in Christian teachings that *did not abolish the old ways but fulfilled them.* I was sure that entry into a new relationship with the First Peoples residing on or around Vancouver Island would involve listening, in heeding their teaching, and seeing things in a new way. In learning from them, we would become a better church and a better people. At the installation of a bishop in the church an anthem, typically a "royal" anthem is sung. I had decided that this was not going to happen. I asked Alex Nelson if he and his family would drum and sing me in at this time. While Alex had previously indicated that they would no longer dance and sing at our ceremonies, time had passed, and I was now in a strong and close relationship with Alex. His subsequent involvement in my installation arose from this relationship.

Not long after I became bishop, I attended a gathering at the University of Victoria at which Waziyatawin, a Dakota professor, activist, and author from Pezihutazizi Otunwe (Yellow Medicine Village) in southwestern Minnesota, spoke about her book *What Does Justice Look Like?*[3] A settler asked her, "What would you like us to do now that we are here and settled?" Basically, what would make you happy? After a period of silence Waziyatawin responded, "I would like you all to go back to where you came from." After a further period of silence she continued, "I know that is not going to happen so what I would like you to do is to just come short of breaking camp."

"Just come short of breaking camp?" I wondered what that meant for me and the diocese. We are not going home, but perhaps in some way we could reenter the land, only this time not as a colonial church bringing the Creator to those with no appreciation for the Divine, but as a church that was looking for a partnership involving mutual learning. What would it mean for us as Anglicans to reenter this particular land, what we thought was our land, realizing that it is not our mission but the Creator's mission which we are called to discover. How do we honor the fact that the Creator was already in the land, in the people, in the language, and in the culture and tradition of the Indigenous people? Christopher Duraisingh[4] said that the colonial church had come as if they were carrying the Creator on their back. We had to understand that before we came, the Creator was already present in the people and in the land.

3. Waziyatawin, *What Does Justice Look Like?*

4. "Christopher Duraisingh is Otis Charles Visiting Professor in Applied Theology and faculty emeritus at the Episcopal Divinity School, Cambridge, Massachusetts." Duraisingh, From "Church Shaped Mission," 1.

I was invited in 2015 to attend the symbolic demolition of St. Michael's Residential School on ʻYālis. We gathered in front of the school with some four hundred survivors and their families. We did not know who was going to be called to speak on behalf of the Anglican Church. Alex Nelson was the master of ceremonies for the event. As he called me to speak, he stumbled over my last name as many do. However, that gave me an opportunity to introduce myself and to give my own apology, which follows.

My name is Logan. I am bishop of these islands. We have one community on the mainland, Kingcome. [I now know the communities also include Wakeman, Hope Town, and Gilford.] I am honored and humbled to have been invited onto your traditional lands and I am honored that I have the opportunity to speak to you today.

I honor all the survivors who are here today and thank you for your courage and fortitude. I came here today to do three things: to truth-tell, to look for healing, and to continue on the road of reconciliation. I want to open my heart to you today. When you look at my heart you will see a part of it which is dark and sad, because we as Anglicans came here as part of a colonial power. We arrived on this land and failed to see that the Creator was present in the land, the sea, and the sky. We failed to see the Creator in you, in your customs, in your traditions, in your language, and in the old ways.

We took your children away from you and placed them in schools like this one. In these schools these children experienced physical, sexual, emotional, psychological, and cultural abuse.

On behalf of the Anglican Church of Canada and my diocese I am very, very sorry. We failed you, we failed ourselves, and we failed the Creator.

We gather today because of a promise. And if you would look at the other side of my heart, you would see it is full of hope. It is the hope I see in your eyes, and in the eyes of your children and grandchildren. I see this hope as I hear the Creator in your language, and as I see the Creator in your customs and traditions and in the old ways. I see this hope in the land, the sea, and the sky. I said that I have come to truth-tell, to look for healing, and to continue on the road of reconciliation. I see the promise of healing for you and for us; our healing is intrinsically connected with your healing.

I commit my diocese to stand and journey with you on this road. You will lead, and it will be at your invitation that we will join you. I commit that we will stand with you at any time and any place. I said at the beginning that my name is Logan. I get

that name from my grandmother; it is our clan. Our crest has a
heart on it and it has three nails in it. It speaks of a time gone by,
and of the courage of our ancestors. It says on the crest, "This is
the glory of my ancestors."

For me and my family the three nails will from this day
on stand as truth telling, healing, and reconciliation. Today is a
historic day. There is so much promise coming from the Creator.
We will commit ourselves to continue on this journey. It is my
prayer that my grandchildren and great-grandchildren and your
grandchildren and great-grandchildren will look back on this
day and say, "This was the courage of my ancestors." *Gila' Kesla*.

Archbishop Michael Peers had already given an apology on behalf the
Anglican Church of Canada at the National Native Convocation in Minaki,
Ontario, on Friday, August 6, 1993. We had made a giant poster of this apology for the 2015 demolition. It was ten feet by thirty feet, and was attached
to the side of the school. There were piles of rocks on the ground. The rocks
formed part of the healing process, because at the end of the ceremony at-
tendees threw rocks at the side of the school building and at the poster of
the apology. For me it was the beginning of a relationship with the Kwa
kwaka'wakw, especially the 'Namgis and the Musgamagw Dzawada'enusw.

It was now time for the diocese to take up the work of truth-telling,
healing, and reconciliation. I started to plan what this might look like. As
I was planning a way to symbolically "come just short of breaking camp" 1
came across a paper "What Was John the Baptist Doing?"[5] by Colin Brown
of Fuller Theological Seminary. In the paper he speaks about John's baptism
and what exactly John was doing. As the Jews had different purification
rites, he surmises that John's action must be more than a rite of purification. Colin's thesis is that John was inviting the people to leave the land and
cross the Jordan River and symbolically reenter the land again as a renewed
people of the Creator. For Jesus, who our theology informs us had no sin,
this baptism was not a right of cleansing but a participation event in leadership. Jesus was taking on the role of the "new Joshua" (Josh 3–4) crossing the
Jordon again, leading the nation into a renewed relationship with the land
and its people. He was leading a reentry into the land. For me this was the
first step in my symbolic leaving in order to reenter into the land on behalf
of the diocese. The question now was this: How would this look and what
shape should it take?

5. Brown, "John the Baptist."

Enter Steven Charleston and his book *The Four Vision Quests of Jesus.*[6] In his book he associates the transfiguration, the wilderness experience, the garden, and the cross to Indigenous action and understanding of the vision or spirit quest. In an Indigenous vision or spirit quest, Charleston describes how the chief goes on a journey on behalf of the community. He goes alone . . . but with the community symbolically traveling with him. The chief would go on a three-day retreat into the wilderness with only a blanket. The chief would seek a vision on behalf of the community and go without food and water for four nights. It is from this that the basis of the Sacred Journey took shape.

I would travel on behalf of the diocese and symbolically reenter the land one community at a time. The plan started to come together. I would go first to 'Yālis, the home of our closest relatives the Kwakwaka'wakw. I would go into the bush on a vision quest and then enter the land and ask for permission to reenter and stay. I would walk the 470 kilometers (we actually walked over 550 kilometers) from 'Yālis to Victoria, British Columbia, with the journey ending on Easter Sunday at Christ Church Cathedral in Victoria, British Columbia. There was some thought that the journey should begin in Victoria, however the symbolism of coming to the Cathedral with teachings and culture from the Indigenous community was a more powerful and appropriate gesture.

But there had to be a journey *before* the Sacred Journey. This meant a meeting with all the Indigenous communities I would pass through on my way south. The route down had been planned by my friend Wayne Stewart. Each day was paced out and each stop marked. He had made plans with all the parishes I would pass through. There would be events and gatherings as we journeyed down, which would enable us to meet with folk, to answer questions, to tell stories, and have folk join us in the walk.

Before all this could happen we set up meetings with First Nations communities. We met with their chief and representatives who were survivors or family members of survivors of the residential school system. Each meeting began with truth-telling. There was a need for honesty on our part. We acknowledged our part in colonialism, our involvement in the residential schools; we acknowledged our part in the abuse of the children . . . and we apologized. We explained the purpose of the Sacred Journey and extended an invitation to community members to walk the road of reconciliation with us. These meeting were tense and labored; there was a rawness to these meetings; the hurt and pain was strongly felt.

---

6. Charleston, *Four Vision Quests of Jesus.*

There were four basic responses from Indigenous leaders on the first journey: (1) yes, we will meet you and be part of this act of reconciliation; (2) we do not need to do this but you are welcome to continue to live here; (3) we will need to speak to the elders and get back to you (a polite way of saying *no*); and (4) an indifference (which *was* a no) with a concern that we would be bringing up painful and hurtful issues with the survivors of residential schools. We respected and honored all of these responses.

Next I went to meet with my doctor to see if I was fit enough for this journey. He confirmed I could walk the distance but advised that the fast without food and water for four days was not a good idea. I had, and still have, two elders who advised me. One was Dr. Martin Brokenleg, an Indigenous scholar and spiritual director. The other was Alex Nelson. Martin suggested that it was possible to modify the vision quest to suit the situation and that a fast from sun up to sundown would be appropriate. I met with Alex to determine what this vision quest might look like. He arranged to meet me on 'Yālis territory to set up the vision quest and the ceremonial re-entering of the land. Chief Bobby Joseph was to be the master of ceremonies.

When the time came to begin the journey Alex met me at sunup at a park in the center of 'Yālis. He walked with me through the paths and guided me on the best route to take. His teachings set me up for the day: listen for the Creator in creation—look beyond the obvious. We found a tree that had been hollowed out; he invited me to go in and spend some time inside creation, and listen. He invited me to listen for the singing of the trees and to look for spirit guides. He instructed me, as I walked in this place, to see beyond the obvious—to see, feel, and sense the Creator in creation, to be open to creation and therefore open to the Creator.

I spent that day walking, sitting, standing, and listening for the Creator in creation. As I walked around the paths I was inspired to stop at different places to learn from each experience. The singing of the trees, the hollowed-out tree, and the tree that had fallen exposing its roots all gave me a different experience. It opened me up to a theology that was not prescriptive but one of discovery in the present—a theology that grew out of relationship, environment, and experience—one that was found in the everyday life of a people and place. It was not one that was imposed from away but one that grew out of everyday events and occurrences, from the animals, the birds, and the fish. When we came we imposed upon people a theology from away that did not have that connection with the everyday, with the land, and with the animals.

The next day the Sacred Journey began at the big house in 'Yālis. I was given a Kwakwala speaking chief who took me outside the big house. We knocked on the door and were asked why we sought entrance. My chief explained the reason. As I looked at the faces of the chiefs who inquired, I could see what I was to see in every community I entered. Some were supportive of my request, some were indifferent, some were opposed. However, we entered and became part of the feast of traditional and cultural events, and as non-Indigenous people we entered into a new relationship and journey.

Inevitably some of the best teachings happened in an unplanned way. As we left by ferry the next day I was sitting with Bobby Joseph, Buggs Dawson, and Alex Nelson. The conversation was rich. Buggs said to me, "Bishop, as you walk down the island, remember each step is for a child in residential school." Again, I was prompted to "look beyond the obvious, to see beyond the trees, the plants, the animals, the hills, and the mountains and see the Creator in the centre of the creation."

My grandmother's family came from Argyle in Scotland. They were Gaelic-speaking people. In 2021 I went with my daughter Meghan and my friend Wayne Stewart to Cape Breton in Nova Scotia. Our goal was to hike the ninety-two kilometer Camino Nova Scotia—Slighe nan Gàidheal (The Gael's Trail)—on the east coast of the island. Pilgrimage is a physical expression of partnership. At the end of the pilgrimage we met with young Gaelic-speaking people who taught us language, story, and song, along with how to introduce oneself in Gaelic and to understand that language comes with a worldview. This understanding of language and worldview is a huge component of partnership. As we hear the language of another culture it is important to understand that it comes to us with a different understanding of the way the world is engaged and understood. This experience reminded me of something the National Geographic explorer Wade Davis said: "Indigenous people are not failed examples of white western ways of thinking and believing."[7] Learning the language is an important part of reentering the land. There are more than thirty-four Indigenous languages spoken in British Columbia. On Vancouver Island and the surrounding Gulf Islands the languages are Kwakwala (Kwakwaka'wakw), Halq'eméylem, Lekwungen, and SENĆOŦEN. The removal of language was one of the main weapons of colonialism.

In a parish in the Comox Valley, there is a lovely couple who immigrated from Wales. They settled in the valley as teachers in the public school system; they were members of the Anglican Church. On the journey, they came and walked with me through the valley. They both speak Welsh and have kept up their language through the years. As we were walking, they said to me, "Do you know that those who did this to First Nations say they

7. Davis, "Worldwide Web of Belief."

did not know what they were doing? They say they did not know that they suppressed them by intentionally removing their language from them. They knew what they were doing because they bloody well did it to us before they came here. It has long been a tool of colonialism. In Wales we had to wear a board with 'WELSH NOT' written on it if we spoke Welsh. In the Gaelic-speaking communities of Scotland they were given a wooden spoon if they spoke Gaelic. At the end of the day both resulted in corporal punishment. They knew what they were doing!"

In this journey it was of paramount importance that the church show humility. We set some protocols that were important. We decided there should be no government involvement and no press. Some suggested I be led in with bagpipes because of my Scottish heritage. I declined as they had unfortunately been used in the colonization of many other people. We would follow a monastic rule of study, work, prayer, hospitality, and stability. For the most part, the journey would take place in silence so we could build on the invitation to look beyond the obvious and look for the Creator in creation.

We began and ended each day in prayer. At the beginning of the day we would remind ourselves to look beyond the obvious and watch for spirit guides who would show us the Creator. Each evening we would ask the question: "Where did you experience the Creator today?" We used a book by John Philip Newell *Praying with the Earth: A Prayerbook for Peace*.[8] The prayers seemed to jump off the pages for us. A short Scripture from the Psalms, the Qur'an, and a Gospel formed part of our daily meditation. Traveling down the island we connected with many Indigenous communities in a number of ways. Some members of these communities met us on the edge of their territory and walked in with us—Qualicum, Chief Michael Recalma; Snuneymuxw, Elder William Good; Snaw-Naw-As, Patti Edwards; Penelakut, Chief Joan Brown; Songhees, Elder Butch Dick; Tseycum, Chief Harvey Underwood. Other nations said they could not come to meet because they were busy with harvest, while others said they could not come to meet but gave us permission to "enter and continue to live" on their territories.

The Sacred Journey enabled the diocese to begin a new relationship with the Indigenous communities where parishes are located. The heart of the diocese was now opened for congregations to learn from Indigenous people and grow in relationship with them. I am so very grateful to all the Indigenous communities for their trust, openness, and honesty. I am so very grateful to Alex Nelson who began the Sacred Journey with me in 'Yālis and

8. Newell, *Praying with the Earth*.

who was at the cathedral on Easter Sunday to welcome me at the end of the journey.

We would be amiss if we thought that the symbolic reentering of the land was limited to the physical land where we live, work, play, and worship. It is important to acknowledge the traditional territories on which we find ourselves. It is important to recognize and name this land as stolen. This recognition, however, must include a commitment to action and the work of reconciliation. If we are speaking just short of breaking camp then we must be speaking about a dismantling or a deconstruction of our colonial practices. Reentering the land includes changing our structures, institutions, our governance, and the way we think. Reentering the land is not a one-time event—it is a journey that we must commit ourselves to taking every day. The Sacred Journey of reentering the land is a metaphor for every journey we need to take—a journey into who we were, and who we are now—as a parish, as a diocese, and as a community of faith. Reentering the land involves physical, psychological, and spiritual pain for us and those we meet. There are no easy or pain-free journeys. These are journeys worth taking.

It is understood that the culture and ritual of the big house restores a balance to all things. Relationships that are changing, that have become askew with the Creator, with others, and with nature, are healed and restored. The Sacred Journey was a gesture to restore a balance; as we continue to reenter the land. We are called to restore balance in all of our relationships.

We are part of a system that stole a people's land, culture, language, and traditions. We cannot alter that history, though we can probe its roots and causes. As we recall the work and witness of Ellie Johnson we know that education is key to moving the healing and reconciliation process forward. The journey is not over—in so many ways, it has only just begun. *Gilakasa'la.*

BIBLIOGRAPHY

The Anglican Church of Canada. "Doctrine of Discovery: Stolen Lands, Strong Hearts." YouTube, Apr 11, 2019. https://www.youtube.com/watch?v=mQwkB1hn5E8.

Brown, Colin. "What Was John the Baptist Doing?" *Bulletin For Biblical Research* 7 (1997) 37–50.

Charleston, Steven. *The Four Vision Quests of Jesus*. New York: Morehouse, 2015.

Davis, Wade. "The Worldwide Web of Belief and Ritual." Feb 2008. TED video, 18:59. https://www.ted.com/talks/wade_davis_the_worldwide_web_of_belief_and_ritual?language=en.

Duraisingh, Christopher. "From Church-Shaped Mission to Mission-Shaped Church." In *Anglican Theological Review* 92.1 (2010) 7–28.

Newell, John Phillip. *Praying with the Earth: A Prayerbook for Peace*. Grand Rapids: Eerdmans, 2022.

"The Story of the Sacred Journey: A Penitential Walk toward Reconciliation." Diocese of Islands and Inlets. https://www.bc.anglican.ca/diocesan-ministries/reconciliation-beyond/pages/sacred-journey.

Waziyatawin. *What Does Justice Look Like? The Struggle for Liberation in Dakota Homeland*. St. Paul, MN: Living Justice, 2008.

12

Companions on the Journey
A Conversation

ALEX AND NELLA NELSON

What follows is a transcription of an interview between Bishop Logan McMenamie and Alex and Nella Nelson. While Bishop Logan has described his own reentry experience above, it is important to hear from those who experienced the sacred journey as Indigenous supporters.

[ALEX] I'm glad we are doing what we are doing, looking back at the reentering process. The memory bank is random. Now in this process of going back, Nella and I have some thoughts and reactions. Nella has been a teacher all her life where she wrote reports—I'm not so good at reports. She'll help us out.

[LOGAN *asks*] Alex and Nella, what do you remember about the project?

[NELLA] When I first read your report on the process (of reentering the land), one of the things that is important in your opening paragraph is your use of the word "heathen." You pull it back at the end of the document thankfully. For us, as we grew up on the other end of the spectrum, we were certainly affected by the phrase heathen and heathen lands. In various parts of the world, the gospel was to be given "to the heathens."

I have another story to tell. My great-great-grandmother, Jane Constance Cook (1870–1941), was an Indigenous activist in the Anglican Church. We have her book: *Standing Up for the Ga'axstal'*.[1] As someone living at the crossroads of customary ways and the drastic changes that colonial power brought to the people on the coast, Ga'axstal'as navigated both worlds. She was part of a high-ranked, Kwakwaka'wakw family and also an ardent Christian who was a leader in the Anglican Womens' Association in 'Yālis" (Alert Bay).

My family is the Cook family at Alert Bay. We grew up in the Anglican Church. This is the lens through which I view life. With reference to the "heathen," and at the end of the document, the perceptions you were taught—I wonder, how did your mind switch? How did you discover the need to change terminology? "Heathen" was no longer appropriate for you once you understood our processes and ceremonies. As our bishop, you weren't simply standing at the pulpit and talking. We got to see what you were saying.

[ALEX *jumps in*] I really have a problem with the term "heathen." What does that mean to listeners? It sounds so agnostic. I had my back up to begin with when you first used the word. The more we talked about it, this wasn't about heathenness in a defined way. The interpretation of another race (its beliefs, culture, and language) . . . with reference to the prayers, and to the Bible . . . these are teachings that have traveled the world and get repeated over and over again. We need to be careful with our words.

I told our bishop (Logan) when we first started, this project, this process is becoming so awesome. It adds to the importance of what we're doing—with healing and reconciliation—and what you're also doing. You have stimulated so many good things in my mind, that I had to go back and say, "How are we describing this heathen?" In my own interpretation it's a totally negative term. In my own heart how do I understand that? Your experience, however, changed so much over the years. Now we can start pulling people together, in healing and reconciliation, as it's called. We can learn how to understand each other in a good and proper way. Yes, you were in my bad books at the start—you are back in my positive books again [*laughter*].

So one day our bishop invites us to go to Christ Church Cathedral in Victoria. I have my older brother Frank, our traditional chief, with me. We were invited to go there to interpret some verses from the Bible—how we saw it, how we might use it, or to redescribe it. We attended as good parishioners—hey, we were early! The bell was ringing on and on . . . Frank and I were sitting in the pew. It was quiet, and we heard the organ playing. That

---

1. Robertson, *Standing Up with Ga'axsta'las*.

quality of beautiful music took us back to our memories. We remembered some of those organ-playing days in Kingcome Inlet, and who played them in our little church.

There's an added story that comes with this. There was an elder in our village who every Sunday would start walking at one end of the village where he lived, in order to get to church, but nobody would start the service without him. I guess he arrived on "Indian Time" [*smile*]. He would enter the church—and we are talking about entering and reentering after all. Once he came, the bell would ring again, to let us know that things are happening in the church—as we sat in the cathedral we remembered these things. Between Frank and myself, we also remember Dad asking us to be a lay reader. We didn't know what a lay reader was, but we would start to speak from the pulpit, and make reference to the Bible. When we did this we started to understand Dad's role in the church.

In the midst of all this, and thinking philosophically, I started to validate my belonging to the church. Our elders were the ones that decided to build our church. So when our elders speak, our village speaks, so that little church became our big house. (Frank and I are still sitting in our cathedral pew—ideas go in and out of my head.) As part of that church is this alright? Is this OK? Dad is a lay reader. Frank and I were sitting there, with the other parishioners—hey, we were early—such an awesome moment, to be there, in the quiet, sitting silent, entering another phase in our lives. We sat there in silence, in obedience, because "the Bible tells us so!" [*laughter*].

That's how you tell your story—you speak of your belonging, of your sense, of your heart, and it starts to unfold—and in this case it helps me interpret that there's something in this big house. We have witnessed similarities between what we do and what we look like. We carry the high principles of life, honesty, trust, integrity.

We have regalia, it's our identity. This is who we are and who we've become. Then, I saw our bishop in his regalia. There's reasons for that. Then there's the singing. We sing songs that tell of our history in our culture. In the cathedral, there's the hymns which I read slowly so I can process the deeper understanding of the hymns. Singing . . . there's a common relationship between singing and the sentiment that the songs convey.

In my Residential Schools Reconciliation presentations, I use an image of the totem pole on the one hand and the church on the other hand. There's a rainbow that encompasses both. I give thanks to the Creator for introducing those two worlds to me, worlds that come together. We are doing the same things, believing the same things.

[*Asked for her thoughts on the sacred journey,* NELLA *replied*] I knew Alex was involved with the journey from Alert Bay to Victoria, at the same time as all the Truth and Reconciliation (TRC) hearings and events were happening. It is interesting because I speak more about Alert Bay. There is a faith there, in that other little church where they meet weekly. [Sitting in that church] they sing the hymns in my own language. I remember my great granny. I see an element of reconciliation even for those not born into the church. There was and is awareness there. Anytime someone reaches out and does a process it's really important for our people. In that little church, there is a sense of faith and belonging. Concerning reentering the land, the church is willing to step back and be willing to do this, to want to do it, and to profile it—that's good. There's still a lot of people who react negatively who went to residential schools. They are saying how fast we go back to singing the hymns in our language, to comfort our souls, and with our drumming too, it's a tighter weave at home.

I am so grateful that you took my father's funeral. People felt that when they came in for our service, the church was a place of belonging. People said you role-modeled to us what you could do. My Dad was an alcoholic, but we were all brought up in the church. I played piano, and he wanted me to be the organist when my auntie could not continue. I tried once but I am not an organist. That service you took [for my father] was a coming home for some people. What you did in your process was to reactivate some processes of thought and acknowledgement, as you became a role model for others.

[ALEX *takes up the story*] I remember our first meeting at a Victoria coffee shop. In your report you quoted me saying, "We are not going to dance anymore" at your ceremonies. I need to correct that to "we are not going to *start* the dancing anymore." [To start the dancing is a specific role and responsibility.]

[NELLA] Ceremony is important to us. Recognize that when we do ceremony, it helps us to rebalance ourselves—we did latch onto to ceremony as it related to what we did as well. The function of ceremony and ritual is to create a balance, even in our big house. When we start to do dances it's about the rebalancing in our ceremony.

[ALEX] Nella had the vision of having me marry her in church, in Alert Bay. At the conclusion of your walk, when you arrived in Victoria, we knew you were going to go to the cathedral. As you were walking by Royal Athletic Park where a big soccer tournament was taking place, I knew someone in charge. I told him about why the walk was happening. Could I make an announcement at that time? I asked. "By all means," he said. At that moment, the Creator brought things together. My announcement helped them to recognize something was happening outside that soccer game. Creator brings so many things together in a marvellous way.

[NELLA] How do we bring the two worlds together? I remember Dr. Albert Marshall, a Nova Scotia elder who talked about "two-eyed seeing." You see the world—Western and Indigenous—you take the strength of both.

[*Asked about the response of other Vancouver Island First Nations and his role in explaining the walk to others,* ALEX *replied*] I spoke with other First Nations in passing. I explained my understanding of the process. I never really got any response.

[NELLA] Logan, thinking again about hymns and "heathen lands." You started to recognize an imbalance. You saw that balance is recreated through an understanding of ritual. Ritual is an understanding that there is a process.

[ALEX] I think back to the 2015 demolition of St. Michael's Residential School in Alert Bay. I wonder what that meant to the witnesses who attended. At one point some threw bricks at the school, but some kept the brick as a reminder of the event. I think about the Witness Blanket. [It's made of pieces from former residential schools across Canada. It's An installation built by Hayalthkin'geme (Carey Newman)].[2] This is a part of reconstruction. I would love to get our people together to talk about rebuilding ourselves, remembering what happened, and how we put ourselves back together, doing the work of reconstruction—and then we celebrate. At the survivors' event, a young lady was taking pictures—her name was Carmen. The pictures could not be shared as she was from a different nation. I saw them however, especially some made in the big house, which was filled with hundreds of orbs, circles of light, all over the big house. The energy and light showed up in the big house as people were working on moving forward.

[ALEX] Our grandson said before the digger hit the school wall, "Watch my Grampa—he's gonna cry." I couldn't help it—I understand what happened to us in that era. So going forward, how do we use this experience as part of closure? Well, we "shut that door!" I work with ISPARK, a sports organization. They videoed that "holy" night. I spoke about that night at a different event. After the presentation, a guy comes up to me saying, "I have video of that."

"What should we call it?" I said.

"Shut that door!" he said. Thinking about all these events, over many years, I look at all these moving parts, and you pulled it together, as you reentered our land.

[NELLA] Some people are still finding it hard to hear the stories. There's a lot of new legal settlements now—the TB hospitals, then the next wave, boarding homes—it's a busy time for remembering.

---

2. "Carey Newman"; see also https://witnessblanket.ca/.

[*To Logan's question, "How do you be a witness today?"* NELLA *replied*]
The one thing that is critical to my culture is that all of the work that we do, it literally doesn't have value unless you have witnesses. People have a responsibility to continue to share the story of what they saw, to be able to correct stories that other people have heard; the stories and the history don't live without witnesses. Hence the value of the Witness Blanket project. Your sermons don't exist without witnesses, listeners become the carriers of your message. At potlatches sometimes people will be paid fifty cents to become witnesses. In our potlatches you leave with a gift, not because you sat there all night, but because you now have a responsibility to share back home.

BIBLIOGRAPHY

"Carey Newman." University of Victoria. https://www.uvic.ca/finearts/ahvs/people/faculty/profiles/cnewman.php.

Robertson, Leslie A., and the Kwagu'l Gixsam Clan. *Standing Up with Ga'axsta'las: Jane Constance Cook and the Politics of Memory, Church, and Custom.* Vancouver, BC: UBC, 2013.

Ellie with John Rye, Terry Brown, David Hamid, and Barbara Jenks

Ellie with Primate Michael Peers and Donna Bomberry

Ellie with Primate Fred Hiltz

Ellie Johnson and Hulene Montgomery—Hulene led PWRDF, and Ellie led World Mission

IV. MISSION AND ECOJUSTICE

Reflections and Analysis

13

The Promise of Place

Shaping a Local Anglican Response to Global Realities

JESSE ZINK

As PART OF HER work for the General Synod, Ellie Johnson represented the Anglican Church of Canada on two successive mission commissions of the Anglican Communion: first MISSIO,[1] which met from 1993 to 1999, and then the Inter-Anglican Standing Commission on Mission and Evangelism (IASCOME) from 2001 to 2005. It is instructive now to reread these reports and see how the concerns they raise and their approach to mission are very much of their moment at the turn of the twentieth century into the twenty-first. In the introduction to the final report from IASCOME, for instance, the commission's chairman, Bishop Sebastian Bakare of Manicaland, reflected on the way in which Anglicans now live in a "global village" that requires finding new ways "to participate meaningfully in God's Mission."[2]

In its reflections on mission and evangelism, IASCOME, he writes, kept in mind the dynamic relationship between "the local as well as worldwide context challenging the mission and evangelism of the church." That context is marked by new realities, that he lists as "HIV and AIDS; conflicts and wars; unfair distribution of resources; religious conflicts; misuse of power and authority; challenges in the context of human sexuality; corruption;

---

1. Mission Commission of the Anglican Communion.
2. Rosenthal and Erdey, *Communion in Mission*, 197.

human rights and gender equality; abject poverty, to mention but a few."[3] The introduction is indicative of the entire report. There is a strong emphasis on mission as being of God, the *missio Dei*. The relationship between local and global is repeatedly stressed: global issues are made known in local contexts to which all churches are called to respond. There is a repeated stress on globalization and the idea of a "global village," reflecting the recognition that the world was increasingly connected and interpenetrating. Some of the "new realities" that Bakare lists are still with us, if they were ever actually "new." Others have fallen off the church's radar screen.

With the end of IASCOME, the Communion lost a worldwide body that brought Anglicans together from different contexts for missiological reflection. While various informal commissions and networks have met since the end of IASCOME, the Communion appears to lack the finances or the will to convene another similar group. In this chapter, I seek to put myself in the mind of an Anglican mission commission and ask what are the key realities of a world approaching the second quarter of the twenty-first century. With these realities in mind, I explore possible missiological responses. Since I write as an individual and not as a member of a commission, the chapter is meant to be exploratory and suggestive, not comprehensive and authoritative. But I think the exercise of surveying the world from the perspective of mission, which past Anglican mission commissions have done and of which Ellie Johnson was such an important part, remains a key task for Anglicans today.

In what follows, I first outline what I take to be three key "realities" (to adopt Bishop Bakare's language) of a shared global context—human migration, climate change, and global capitalism—that do not appear on the IASCOME list and cannot but shape the local and global life of the church. I then draw on current trends in Anglican thinking, highlighting in particular the contribution of Indigenous thinking, that pay attention to place and Land. This new emphasis, I then suggest, offers a useful missiological lens for structuring the church's response to these realities, and I highlight two examples of ways in which attentiveness to place and Land helps can help shape local, contextual ministry that responds to the global context.[4]

---

3. Rosenthal and Erdey, *Communion in Mission*, 197.

4. I deliberately capitalize Land as a way of indicating its significance to Indigenous peoples. It functions in much the way that other proper nouns do in the English language and so merits capitalization.

NEW REALITIES: MIGRATION, CLIMATE, CAPITALISM

Human migration in the twenty-first century takes many forms: bankers, lawyers, consultants, and other professionals; students seeking education; temporary workers sending remittances home to support family members. Human migration also includes the category of people who have no choice in their movement, such as refugees and asylum seekers fleeing violence or the threat of persecution at home. Border areas of the world have at various points in recent years received intense media attention that crystallizes (not always helpfully) the reality of this movement. These border areas have also become increasingly dangerous and deadly to the people seeking to cross them.

Human migration is not new but several aspects of the current situation are. The first is the sheer scale of movement. Given the diversity of forms of movement, firm numbers are difficult to come by, but it seems clear that there are more people on the move than ever before. The United Nations High Commissioner for Refugees reports that there are nearly ninety-five million "people of concern" in the world, up from sixty-four million in 2015. This group includes internally displaced people, who flee their home but not their country of nationality and so are not formally classed as refugees; asylum seekers; and refugees who are afforded specific protections under international law.[5]

A further novel element is the way countries of the world lack clear agreement about how to respond to this movement. International agreements that are meant to govern the response to refugees and asylum seekers were crafted in a much different period from our own. These agreements seem less and less relevant as the nature and relative ease of migration changes, media coverage of human migration blurs important distinctions, and populist political leaders wield immigration as a cudgel against their opponents. Canada is increasingly rare in the welcome it offers to many categories of migrants. Encountering people on the move from many different parts of the world will remain a key part of the mission context in Canada for many years to come.

Climate change is a second major reality shaping local and global contexts. The urgency of the crisis has been evident as new phrases like "atmospheric river" or "heat dome" have entered the lexicon. Weather events that were once thought of as once-in-a-century or once-in-a-millennium occurrences have been happening with startling frequency. The amount of carbon

---

5. United Nations High Commissioner for Refugees, *Global Report.*

already in the atmosphere means that these impacts will only worsen in coming decades. Climate change is a result of many factors, but at its root Christians can understand it as the result of a disordered relationship with God's creation. The modern Western approach to the natural world sees resources to be exploited, rather than a creation with which we exist harmoniously. In this context, it is no surprise that climate change is also attended by a biodiversity crisis. We are living through the midst of a sixth great extinction in which human activity is leading to the extirpation and elimination of a great diversity of the plant, animal, and other life with which God has given us to live in relationship.[6] Climate change is so encompassing, a matter that response is required on all levels and across a range of domains, including politics, culture, and economics. But it also requires a spiritual response. The continual human push to harvest resources and move into new areas of habitation bespeaks a disordered human desire for continual accumulation, in a word, for "more." But in a world of finite resources, the drive for more leads to harmful outcomes and an imbalanced life.

The final reality I identify is entrenched forms of global capitalism, sometimes referred to as neoliberalism.[7] The end of the Cold War and the putative "end of history" brought with it the apparent triumph of Western capitalism, which rapidly spread into new parts of the world. In the years since, the reach of multinational global corporations has only expanded and deepened. The values of the market economy have expanded into new realms for which they are not suited, forming and deforming our societies in ways many people are only beginning to grapple with.[8] Reaction and opposition to neoliberal capitalism has come on many fronts, including religious. Both Justin Welby, the archbishop of Canterbury, and Pope Francis have written at length about the dangers of this form of economic structure. Francis wrote about the "idol" of money and "the dictatorship of an impersonal economy lacking a truly human purpose" in his first lengthy teaching document as pope.[9]

Welby has written a book *Dethroning Mammon* that calls attention to the way in which "Mammon draws our gaze away from things that are more worthy of our attention, but have not been given the badge of a comparable monetary value."[10] Global capitalism is a pervasive and entrenched power. Indeed, as both Welby's and Francis's comments make clear, it acts at times

6. Kolbert, *Sixth Extinction.*

7. Clapp, *Naming Neoliberalism.*

8. Sandel, *What Money Can't Buy.*

9. Francis, "Evangelii Gaudium," para. 55.

10. Welby, *Dethroning Mammon*, 40.

as a god. While it has spread wealth around the globe in countless new ways, it has also deepened inequality within and between countries and left us with distorted values and actions.

These "new realities" are challenging not simply in their scale but also their interrelatedness. Climate change, for instance, is increasingly a factor in the movement of people. In parts of the world in which climate change is disrupting the balance of life, one option is movement to a more stable place. Such movement does not fit neatly into existing categories of migration and poses substantial questions to the global community. Meanwhile, the drive for profit, for "more," that is characteristic of capitalism is incompatible with a finite natural world.

The more that global capitalism holds sway, the more we will be forced to reckon with a relationship with the community of creation that is disordered and out of balance. The way in which global capitalism distorts our values makes it easier to ignore the suffering of one another. It is for these reasons that Pope Francis, for instance, has linked capitalism to a "globalization of indifference" and highlighted in particular the suffering of migrants.[11] Begin to pull on one string and it becomes clear how tangled they all are. There is no one "right" way to respond, and since these global realities are felt differently in different local contexts, responses will vary. Many Christians in many traditions and at all levels of the church are already devising innovative and creative responses. What Christians need above all is a manner of living and way of being that is rooted in the Christian faith and offers a wholesale alternative and challenge to the dehumanizing nature of these realities.

PLACE AND LAND

I was once asked to offer reflections on Anglican theology at a time of human migration.[12] As I prepared that material, I found myself repeatedly returning to the idea of place and specific locations. At a time of human migration—displacement—I began to realize how important it is that there are welcoming places for people to arrive. An emphasis on place has long been characteristic of the Anglican tradition, a characteristic shared with other forms of Christianity as well. The Benedictine monastic tradition prizes stability or attachment to a single community in a particular place.

11. Francis has used "globalization of indifference" in many of his public remarks. It also appears in "Evangelii Gaudium," para. 54; "Laudato si'," para. 52; and "Fratelli Tutti," para. 30.

12. Zink, "Anglican Theology," 31–47.

The Church of England to this day remains structured around parishes, which are first of all geographic entities. Place is meant to structure ministry. Traditions like the beating of the bounds on rogation days, in which the community walks the boundaries of the parish, offer a liturgical expression of this reality and commitment. In Canada, such parishes are now largely vestigial, but the commitment to geography and place remains: our church is structured by dioceses, which understand themselves to be responsible for mission and ministry in a particular locale or region. In rooting themselves in place, Christians are simply heeding the command of Jesus who called us to love our neighbor; that is, the one who is near to us.

In a globalized and interconnected world, a commitment to local places might seem retrograde. Indeed, the realities of a global world that I have sketched out in the first part of this chapter remind us that we are nearer to many more people than ever before. It is true that advances in travel and communications technologies have acted to weaken links between human communities and place. But local realities continue to be determinative. I understood this in a new way during the COVID-19 pandemic. The pandemic was inherently a global reality but the news and information I valued most was local: What were case counts in my city and province? When would schools reopen? What were the gathering restrictions in the place where I live? In a global world, local places continue to matter.

It is a welcome trend, therefore, that some voices in Anglican theology have begun to revisit the significance of place for the life of the church.[13] This line of thinking reminds us that humans are made to be rooted people, who are grounded in embodied communities tied to particular locations. It is from these locations that our communities derive meaning. If this is the case, then Anglicans are called to be part of that process of making meaning and forming communities in particular places: "If members of Christian communities could learn to be good neighbours to one another and to larger communities of which they are a part, they would have something infinitely worthwhile to offer to the world. And it would be the very best form of evangelization."[14] The ministry of a Christian community in a suburban place might be different from the witness of such a community in a downtown neighborhood, which would be different from the mission of a church in rural Canada. But each of those communities is called to invest in the unique place where they find themselves and create a community.

---

13. Inge, *Christian Theology of Place*; Rumsey, *Parish*; Sheldrake, *Spaces for the Sacred*.

14. Inge, *Christian Theology of Place*, 136.

It is likely that there are many other people—Christian or otherwise—who may also wish to join in the work of place-making. Here it is valuable to remember that Christians offer unique aspects of meaning to place construction. Notably, there is an eschatological element to Christian community formation. The Christian tradition and Scripture teach that particular places can point us towards the goal of God's action in history and the new Jerusalem where God will dwell with God's people. Scripture provides beautiful images of God's new creation of sacred places. Ezekiel, for instance, receives a vision of a river, full of fish: "On the banks, on both sides of the river, there will grow all kinds of trees for food. . . . Their fruit will be for food, and their leaves for healing" (Ezek 47:12). The work of place construction is done not out of a sense that these places hold ultimate value or meaning but because they "give spatio-temporal expression to the 'new place' in the midst of the old—a task that, crucially, involves the demotion of past and present places from their claim to ultimacy, which is the very root of territorial idolatry."[15] Christians are called to create places that anticipate God's healing and renewal that will come from a particular place created and made holy by God's dwelling with God's people.

A caution is in order. Human history tells us we have a natural tendency towards claiming ownership and control of places. This is true for churches no less than for any other human institution. It is wise to remember, therefore, that we continue to live in a global world. The forces that create widespread human migration, for instance, are not lessening. Our places will constantly be welcoming new people. Forming community and meaning in particular places, therefore, cannot be understood as an exclusionary call. Rather, the Christian call to place-making is a call to create permeable places that find meaning in their rootedness while also remaining open to the flows of new ideas, resources, and people that arrive in that place.

Place is important, but we cannot end our reflection there, particularly at a time when the Anglican Church of Canada is considering the place of Indigenous people in the church and remains committed to reconciliation. A central part of the witness of Indigenous peoples has been the importance of Land in constituting identity, grounding the relationship with the Creator God, and expressing relationship with the world and other people. There is not space here to provide a full-scale depiction of Indigenous understandings of the Land, which can vary among Indigenous peoples and are best learned by spending time with Indigenous peoples on the Land itself. I want to highlight a handful of aspects concerning the relationship with the Land that may usefully enrich a place-based understanding of the Christian faith.

15. Rumsey, *Parish*, 171.

My own experience with Indigenous peoples is with the Iñupiaq of western Alaska and the Cree of James Bay. What is clear in observing and participating in their Land relationship is that there is no sense of owner-ship of the Land. One (white) observer of Cree life near James Bay in the 1960s received this reply when he asked who owned a lake they were canoe-ing across: "That's a White man's question! The land belongs to no one; we belong to it. We eat what it gives us, until the day it eats us."[16] Similarly, in *Braiding Sweetgrass*, Robin Wall Kimmerer offers what might be called the parable of the wild strawberries to share how the Land is understood as a gift. As a child she picked these every year for her father's birthday. They shaped her view of the world and the Land as a gift that came to her through no action of her own: "You cannot earn it, or call it to you, or even deserve it. And yet it appears. . . . Gifts exist in a realm of humility and mystery."[17] Understanding these strawberries as a gift, she practiced self-restraint and tried not to take too much. She contrasts the gift economy with a capitalist economy of private property, in which self-restraint is not a virtue; rather the accumulation of more is. Kimmerer asks how we can come to understand the Land and the earth as a gift again and "make our relations with the world sacred again?"[18] This emphasis on Land as gift is a helpful complement to Anglican place-based thinking, which is less likely to consider questions of ownership and private property in its construction of places.

The indigenous relationship with the Land carries with it aspects of both rootedness and journey. As the Cree theologian Ray Aldred writes, "the Cree idea of living is . . . about journey. But equally, it's about being properly connected while on that journey. When journeying on this land, the heart of Cree spirituality is that we are related to this land. We're also now related to each other."[19] In other words, there is a dynamic relationship between the Land and the movement that takes place through the Land. It is not surprising that through his work Aldred invites non-indigenous Canadians to remember the reality of treaty and work towards a shared dwelling in the Land. We are journeying together on Land that throughout most of Canada is now shared through treaty and we are called to work towards relationship with all life—human and non-human alike—with whom we share the Land. That shared dwelling and shared relationship will be specific: depending on where we live on the Land, the animals, plants, and human relations we

---

16. Soucy, *Waswanapi*, 37.

17. Kimmerer, *Braiding Sweetgrass*, 23–24.

18. Kimmerer, *Braiding Sweetgrass*, 31.

19. Aldred and Anderson, *Our Home and Treaty Land*, 158.

have will be different, writes Aldred. But all of us are called to a wholeness of relationship that is rooted in a shared journey across the Land.

Land and place are, I believe, distinct but related concepts; there is ample space available to explore this relatedness further, as a grounding not only for reconciliation between indigenous and non-indigenous members of the church, but also an orientation for Christian mission. Both place and Land call us to the creation of distinct and unique communities marked by whole relationships, each tied to the part of Creation in which they are located. Place reminds us that humans are involved in constructing these communities. Land reminds us of the givenness of the Creation and how we as human creatures are always responding to God's creative goodness. Above all, the relationship with the place and Land is one of thanksgiving. As Aldred writes, "Thanksgiving is how we maintain a good relation with the land, where the Creator has placed us."[20]

Christian life and witness are rooted in the Eucharist, an act of thanksgiving not only for creation but for the action of Christ in embodying the love of God. From communities grounded in place and on the Land, Christian life begins in thanksgiving and overflows to others. But at a time of climate crisis, our relationship with the world around us cannot be simply one of thanksgiving. Aldred writes, "To be Indigenous is always to be from a specific place and yet also in a sense to be *for* that place. Spirituality, therefore, means situating ourselves in a specific land, people, narrative, and tradition."[21] When our Christian communities are so situated, we cannot help but be advocates for the Land which forms us.

PLACE AND LAND IN RESPONSE TO "NEW REALITIES"

In this chapter, I have sought to describe several global realities and then point towards a set of ideas concerning place and Land that provide one way of grounding a Christian response to these realities. I have seen these ideas put into practice in many parts of the church, including and especially in Indigenous Christian communities. In conclusion, I want to highlight two examples of Christian responses that exemplify what I have sought to describe.

In recent years, many church communities have come to understand the value of the property that they own. This has often involved selling part of this property to realize capital to continue to fund the congregation's

20. Aldred and Anderson, *Our Home and Treaty Land*, 147.
21. Aldred and Anderson, *Our Home and Treaty Land*, 85.

operations. But some congregations have looked at their property less in terms of finances and more in terms of place and Land. One trend has been the proliferation of church-based gardens and other agricultural projects. The experience of those who have been involved in such projects demonstrates the missional significance of place and possibility that comes from being rooted, literally, in the Land.

In his overview of these projects, Brian Sellers-Petersen writes that church-based gardens are tools for evangelism and discipleship while also strengthening the relationship with the whole community of creation: "Vegetables and herbs present a hospitable environment for productive visitors such as butterflies, bees, and earthworms. . . . It is part of our environmental stewardship. As we cultivate the soil, we care for the earth and promote discipleship."[22] One church in Chicago, for instance, laid out its garden in the same style as its sanctuary, with raised beds in place of pews and a pond in place of a baptismal font. It shares the produce through its food bank ministry, exemplifying the nature of a gift: it receives from the Land and shares with others. The garden has also deepened relationship with the local community: "The openness and attractiveness of the garden often draws interest from passersby. As a place of service and learning, the garden connects volunteer groups from nearby schools. . . . As a public symbol of community engagement, the garden bears witness to the parish's core value of radical hospitality."[23] It is not only in the United States that church gardens are proliferating.

I have heard similar testimonials from congregations involved in such work in the Diocese of Montreal. As a community gardener myself, I know the way in which gardens can be a place for intercultural sharing as people from around the world grow plants familiar to them from their home and bring them alive in a new place. By connecting a Christian community with the place in which it finds itself and the Land on which it is located, gardens help these communities work towards right relationship with the whole created order, build an economy based on gift and thanksgiving, and create places of welcome for all who pass by.

My second example is less earthy, but no less significant. One of the challenges of mission discourse in the church is that it has often separated mission (understood as what the church does outside its building) with the worship life of the church (understood as what happens on Sunday morning). Yet given the importance of worship to Christian life and especially

---

22. Sellers-Petersen, *Harvesting Abundance*, 10.

23. Sellers-Peterson, *Harvesting Abundance*, 54. The church referenced is St. Paul and the Redeemer on the South Side of Chicago.

to the Anglican tradition, this division makes little sense. There are many ways in which our worship can be more closely connected to mission but here I want to draw attention to the offertory, the moment in a eucharistic service when bread, wine, and money are brought forward and offered to God on the altar. In the Anglican tradition, the words often associated with this come from 1 Chr 29: "All things come of thee, O Lord, and of thine own have we given thee." The full context of that passage is instructive. King David is about to die and hand everything over to Solomon. He prays:

> But who am I, and what is my people, that we should be able to make this freewill-offering? For all things come from you, and of your own have we given you. For we are aliens and transients before you, as were all our ancestors; our days on the earth are like a shadow, and there is no hope. O Lord our God, all this abundance that we have provided for building you a house for your holy name comes from your hand and is all your own. (1 Chr 29:14–16)

Both the familiar, abbreviated version and the longer passage highlight several significant points. First, as humans we are dependent on God's creation. We are but one part of a larger community of creation that God has created and set us in the midst of. There is no indication that we have any special place in this community other than what God has blessed us with. Second, we are impermanent dwellers in this place. David describes himself and his predecessors as "aliens and transients." This idea will be picked up in later Christian thought to describe followers of Jesus (1 Pet 1:1, 17). At the same time, however, David is announcing his desire, fulfilled by Solomon, to hallow a particular place by building a temple as a dwelling for the Lord. It is possible to be both connected to a particular place and understand oneself as a migrant. Finally, the offertory reminds us of our reliance on one another and on God. We cannot offer our gifts to God on our own. We need someone to collect the money and bake the bread and make the wine.

The offertory, therefore, reminds each Christian of our status as a migrant before God and helps us seek God's pilgrim way, in the same way that so many people around the world are on the move today. It also connects each Christian to a particular place. The offertory is also a reminder of the nature of God's gift, that it is God who gives all of Creation from which the congregation receives what is necessary to return thanks to God. Finally, the offertory is a reminder of our dependence on others, on God's creation, and above all on God. Before I can celebrate the Eucharist, I need to acknowledge and be reminded of the web of relationships of which I am a part and which find their origin in God.

If we are serious about what the offertory means, then Christians are called to be people who take "place" seriously. The bread and wine comes from some place specific on the earth. Let's ask where. More broadly, we can ask the questions about ourselves as well. We are embodied and are in a specific place as well. Where are we? What is this place? How is this land related to our lives? Who has been on this land before us? Who is newly arrived on this land with us now? At their best, the practice of land acknowledgements in Christian congregations point us towards these questions. But I think we have some way to go in realizing the full value of these acknowledgements. It is in deepening our connection to our place—a direction in which we are pointed by the very act of offering our gifts before God every Sunday—that we can frame a response to the realities of the world today.

CONCLUSION

Coming at the turn of the twentieth century, the IASCOME report offered an important reminder of the way local and global realities are connected to one another. That remains profoundly true today. Human migration is a global issue but becomes known to many people when newcomers arrive in their community. Climate change is by its nature global but people understand its impacts best when they notice shortening winters or lengthy summer heat waves in their own communities. Our economic system is global and interconnected, but the way in which it distorts our values and deforms our communities is best understood in the lives of individuals and communities around the world.

The challenge for Christians today is the same as the one Ellie Johnson and the other authors of the IASCOME report identified: move forward in the reconciling mission of God. What I have sought to do in this chapter is highlight one overlooked part of our theological inheritance and reclaim the significance of place. The time is also ripe for non-indigenous Anglicans to receive wisdom and learning from our indigenous siblings in Christ and deepen our relationship with the Land as a constitutive part of our identity. I do not claim that this is the only way for Christians to respond to the times in which we live. But I do think that in these relationships—with one another, with our places and Land, and above all with God in Christ—we will find the sources of a way of life that challenges and transforms the societies around us with the good news of God made known in Jesus Christ.

BIBLIOGRAPHY

Aldred, Raymond, and Matthew Anderson. *Our Home and Treaty Land.* Kelowna, BC: Wood Lake, 2022.

Clapp, Rodney. *Naming Neoliberalism: Exposing the Spirit of Our Age.* Minneapolis: Fortress, 2021.

Francis, Pope. "Encyclical Letter Fratelli Tutti of the Holy Hather Francis on Fraternity and Social Friendship." The Holy See, 2020. https://www.vatican.va/content/francesco/en/encyclicals/documents/papa-francesco_20201003_enciclica-fratelli-tutti.html.

———. "Encyclical Letter Laudato si' of the Holy Father Francis, on Care for our Common Home." The Holy See, 2015. https://www.vatican.va/content/francesco/en/encyclicals/documents/papa-francesco_20150524_enciclica-laudato-si.html.

———. "Apostolic Exhortation Evangelii Gaudium of the Holy Father Francis to the Bishops, Clergy, Consecrated Persons and the Lay Faithful on the Proclamation of the Gospel in Today's World." The Holy See, Nov 24, 2013. https://www.vatican.va/content/francesco/en/apost_exhortations/documents/papa-francesco_esortazione-ap_20131124_evangelii-gaudium.html.

Inge, John. *A Christian Theology of Place.* London: Routledge, 2003.

Johnson, Eleanor, and John Clark, eds. *Anglicans in Mission: A Transforming Journey; Report of MISSIO, the Mission Commission of the Anglican Communion.* London: SPCK, 2000.

Kimmerer, Robin Wall. *Braiding Sweetgrass: Indigenous Wisdom, Scientific Knowledge, and the Teachings of Plants.* Minneapolis: Milkweed Editions, 2013.

Kolbert, Elizabeth. *The Sixth Extinction: An Unnatural History.* New York: Henry Holt, 2014.

Rosenthal, James M., and Susan T. Erdey, eds. *Communion in Mission: Final Report of the Inter-Anglican Standing Commission on Mission and Evangelism.* New York: Church Publishing, 2006.

Rumsey, Andrew. *Parish: An Anglican Theology of Place.* Norwich: SCM, 2017.

Sandel, Michael. *What Money Can't Buy: The Moral Limits of Markets.* New York: Farrar, Straus, and Giroux, 2012.

Sellers-Petersen, Brian. *Harvesting Abundance: Local Initiatives of Food and Faith.* New York: Church Publishing, 2017.

Sheldrake, Philip. *Spaces for the Sacred: Place, Memory, and Identity.* Baltimore: Johns Hopkins University Press, 2001.

Soucy, Jean-Yves. *Waswanapi.* Translated by Peter McCambridge. Montreal: Baraka, 2020.

United Nations High Commissioner for Refugees. *Global Report, 2021.* UNHCR, The UN Refugee Agency, 2022. https://reporting.unhcr.org/globalreport2021/pdf.

Welby, Justin. *Dethroning Mammon: Making Money Serve Grace.* London: Bloomsbury, 2016.

Zink, Jesse. "Anglican Theology in the Midst of a Migration Crisis." *Journal of Anglican Studies* 17 (2019) 31–47.

14

The Climate Crisis and the Church

A Landscape for Theological Education

SYLVIA KEESMAAT

This article was originally presented as one of a number of symposium addresses sponsored by Trinity College, Toronto, each grappling with both the needs of clergy and congregations in relation to "creation care" and how theological education could support those needs. It was subsequently published in The Toronto Journal of Theology *volume 38, number 2 (2022), pages 206–13. It is reprinted here under copyright with permission from University of Toronto Press https://utpjournals. press and the author.*

THIS PAPER EXPLORES THE needs of clergy and congregations in relation to the climate crisis, with a special focus on how seminary curriculum could support new and current clergy as they provide leadership in relation to the climate crisis. I will approach this topic from two different contexts.

On the one hand, I am one of the volunteer cochairs of the Bishop's Committee on Creation Care for the Diocese of Toronto. In that capacity I work with clergy and laypeople in the diocese on resources for our churches related to the climate crisis, ecological and racial justice, and decolonization.

On the other hand, I am also a biblical scholar who has taught both academic and lay courses on creation in the biblical story and climate catastrophe. I will address, therefore, both the needs of the churches, and the needs of the students with whom I have interacted over the years as a teacher in both academic and nonacademic contexts.

Let me begin by saying that I am in agreement with those who emphasize that the climate crisis, the collapse of biodiversity that surrounds us, and the increasingly catastrophic results of our warming planet are the defining issues of our time. This topic, therefore, extends far beyond anything encapsulated in the phrase *creation care*. We are at a crisis moment.

Our clergy and the congregations that they lead know that we are in crisis. And, as hard as I think this might be for scholars such as ourselves to hear, they are not looking for intellectual resources to help them understand the situation we find ourselves in, nor are they looking for the kind of personal, individual actions that have failed to halt the trajectory of carbon capitalism and the continued injustices of colonialism and racism. The most basic need that they share with me is fundamentally pastoral and spiritual. Our faith communities are permeated by something that is often called climate grief or climate anxiety, but which could also be called a deep foreboding about what the future holds for them, for their children, for their communities, and for the earth.

I would suggest that their primary need in such a context is, first and foremost, resources and practices for grappling with climate grief and climate anxiety. They are in need of strategies for acknowledging their grief, narratives for creating a context in which it can be understood, and supports for bearing their grief. What might such resources look like and how can we possibly provide them? I have five suggestions.

PLACE FOR LAMENT

In the first place we need to reclaim our story, the biblical story, as a vigorous, dynamic narrative that gives meaning both to our grief and to our hope. There are many ways that this happens.

One way is to reclaim the biblical tradition of lament as a way of framing and understanding our grief. The biblical story reveals that the Creator knows the place of grief well. God is grieved over the violence on the earth in the time of Noah. God mourned the stubborn hearts of a people who were not able to remember the God who had released them from slavery. God lamented the devastation the people caused on the land and in the lives of the poor.

Interestingly, we haven't always been aware of this grief when we've read the text. On more than one occasion, the translators of the Septuagint rendered the Hebrew word for grief as *anger*, since grief was seen as an inappropriate emotion for a God (e.g., Ps 78:40; Isa 63:10). Anger was, somehow, more appropriate. The reasons for this are fascinating, but too complicated to explore in this context. However, such translations have impacted our theology to the present day. This is most evident in our views of penal substitutionary atonement with its emphasis on Jesus's death as necessary to appease an angry God. Oddly enough, as Terence Fretheim has argued, the biblical witness consistently paints another picture: throughout the Hebrew Bible the Godward side of judgment is always grief. Such grief is repeatedly linked to God's love throughout the prophets. Because of God's love for this wayward people, their faithlessness results in grief and sorrow for God, even as the people face the consequences of their actions (Hos 11:1–9).[1]

In such a context, Jesus died not because God was angry, but because of God's grief, rooted in love. Romans 5:8 says, "God proves God's love for us, that while we were still sinners Christ died for us." And everyone who watches baseball knows that it was because God so *loved* the world, that God gave God's only son (John 3:16).

It is because of such love that Jesus grieved that Jerusalem didn't know how to live in peace (Luke 19:41–44). It is because of such love that the Spirit grieves and groans with a broken creation (Rom 8:26). It is because love goes all the way down that lament lives at the heart of God and at the heart of the biblical story.[2]

But such lament is not only found in the heart of God. The biblical story also bears witness to the lament of the creatures and the land in Hos 4:1–3 and Rom 8:18–26: creation is grieving over all that we have inflicted on the earth. So perhaps living in lament is actually the place that we are meant to be right now. There are four reasons, I think, for this:[3]

First, to live in lament is to truly image God. God laments the brokenness of humanity, and the destruction of creation. God grieves the brokenness of the places we should be rooted in and the brokenness of our community. God grieves the loss of the beautiful creatures. To lament these things is to image God.

Second, to lament is to know that this is not the way the story was supposed to end; it is to live in the tragic gap between what is, and what could be. We had hoped for a different ending to the story, just as God had hoped for a different ending to the story (see, for example, Jer 3:19–20). We had

---

1. A detailed discussion of these and other passages are found in Fretheim, *Suffering of God*, 107–26.

2. For more on this see Keesmaat and Walsh, *Romans Disarmed*, 372–73.

3. The following paragraphs are dependent on Keesmaat and Walsh, *Romans Disarmed*, 154–61.

hoped to always be rooted in our place. And we lament that the story is not turning out how either we or God had hoped. That is the tragic gap that we find ourselves in, and in that space lament is born.

Third, to lament is to admit that we are a people of love, for we grieve the loss of what we love. Love and grief are two sides of the same coin. For some people this is nothing new: Indigenous peoples who have been forced off their land by colonialism; Black farmers taken off their land, and then forced off their land again and again; and refugees who have been compelled to leave the places they love. These are communities acquainted with grief.

For others the loss of our place occurs with an increasing realization of the depth of the climate crisis. Either way, the places we loved are gone. And we grieve their loss.

Fourth, to grieve is to acknowledge, perhaps, that we are complicit, that we have lost what we love through our own actions, our own addictions, and our own need for security. And this grief may be the hardest to bear, for we are at a loss about how to change, how to uncouple our imagination from the narratives that our culture tells, the narratives that assure us that our comfort is more important than the life of other creatures.

We are all hungry for repentance but unsure about what it looks like. Cohen wasn't far off when he sang, "When they said, 'Repent,' I wonder what they meant."[4] As a result, we grieve our own inability to change.

So maybe we need to enable our communities to give voice to lament, to learn how to dwell in that lament, to remember what it is that we have lost. Maybe we need to recapture the ancient practice of allowing lament and grief, to become the insistent prayer that we bring before the throne of God day in and day out.

In doing this we are in good biblical tradition for there are more psalms of lament than any other kind of psalm. And, when we dare to voice our lament, just like the psalmists, we are daring to admit that we don't have it all under control. The psalms of lament are ancient Israel's way of saying, "God, we know that this is all in your hands, and we know that you can do something about it, so enough already, when are you going to fix this?" Or, in the words of the psalmists: "How long, O Lord, will you turn the other way?" (Ps 13:1–2).[5]

All to say, perhaps we need to remind our communities that lament is a *faithful* response to the destruction that surrounds us. And in doing

4. Cohen, "Future," 370.

5. See also Pss 35:17; 79:5; 82:2; 89:46; 90:13; 94:3; 119:84. Walter Brueggemann explores the importance of lament in ensuring that questions of justice are consistently placed before God in his "The Costly Loss of Lament."

so, perhaps we will create safe communities in which to share, grieve, and attend to our pain, as a necessary part of imagining a new future.

THE BIBLE AND CLIMATE CATASTROPHE

We also need to recognize that the biblical story speaks of climate catastrophe in more than one place: What is the story of Noah if not the story of a climate catastrophe (Gen 6–9)? What is Jeremiah's description of creation coming undone if not ecological destruction (Jer 4:23–28; 9:10–11)? What is Hosea's description of the perishing of wild animals, the birds of the air and the fish of the sea, if not an extinction (Hos 4:1–3)? What do these stories have to teach us about faithfulness in the face of climate change?

There is far more going on in these texts than I can possibly cover here. Let me just raise one implication from each passage: Noah was a farmer who knew the importance of genetic diversity. Noah and his family nurtured a ridiculously small gene pool through the deluge. Did they think this would be enough to renew life on the earth? As a farmer myself, I suspect that they had their doubts. One bull and one cow cannot create a healthy breeding herd. And yet, this foundational story of our faith credits this ridiculously small act of shelter and nurture as the basis for the renewal of life. What if we began in a very literal way to create places of shelter, places where biodiversity could flourish, no matter how small? What if we engaged in rewilding all of the spaces that we had influence over? What if we took seriously the call to create an ark in the face of the coming deluge?

Jeremiah described the destruction of the land as the total breakdown of creation (Jer 4:23–28; 9:10–11),[6] yet called those in exile to plant gardens, nurture offspring, and seek the flourishing of those enemies that surrounded them. In short, he called those who had been torn from their homes to learn the rhythms for planting and harvesting of their new land. He called them to create a multiage, multiethnic community that was rooted in their place (Jer 29:4–7). Now, Jeremiah's letter to the exiles is a complicated passage: some of us reading it are indeed those who have been forced into exile, refugees from the places we love. But others of us reading this passage are those who created the exile, those who have displaced others from their land. To both of us this passage calls us at a basic level to learn what it is to be attentive to the land where we now live together, to explore a resilient, diverse community together, working for the healing of the place we find ourselves. The possibilities for doing that will need to address the foundational dynamics of racism and colonization. This is deeply intersectional work.

6. For more on this see Davis, *Scripture, Culture, Agriculture*, 10–14.

Zacchaeus wanted to follow Jesus, so he returned all that he had taken from his neighbors. This would have meant that Zacchaeus returned all of the *land* that he had taken when his neighbors fell into debt. The story of Zacchaeus is essentially a story of reparation (Luke 19:1–10). What does this have to do with the climate crisis? Grief over the destruction of creation is tearing us apart. For some, this grief is because our land is being increasingly destroyed. For others, those in the Indigenous community, the Black community, the Japanese community, this grief is rooted in the way that land has repeatedly been taken and the way that communities have been torn from the land. The land grieves, the creatures grieve, the people grieve. Only when land is returned to the care of those who have affection for it can healing come. Only when reparations are made real, will salvation come to our home.[7]

GRAPPLING WITH COLONIALISM

As some of the above passages indicate, it is becoming increasingly evident that our destruction of creation is closely connected to colonialism and our commodification of not only the land but also Black and brown bodies. In Canada and the United States this is an area that is being increasingly explored in environmental conversations in both the Indigenous and BIPOC communities.[8]

Our communities and clergy need safe spaces where those who have benefited from colonialism and racism, as well as those who have been the victims of colonialism and racism, can together experience reconciliation. This means that resources are needed for understanding what repentance looks like in relation to our oppression of the land and of others. It also means being able to explore what forgiveness might look like in relation to these oppressions. And it means engaging in the deep, imaginative, and difficult work of dreaming what our future can look like together for the good of creation.

DARING TO HOPE

In addition to resources and practices for grappling with climate grief and acknowledging the interconnected nature of our climate crisis with

7. I explore these passages in more depth in my forthcoming book, *Ecological Grief and Creational Hope* (tentative title).

8. See, for instance, Penniman, *Farming While Black*; Heinrichs, *Buffalo Shout*; and Whyte, "Settler Colonialism."

colonialism, our faith communities also need resources and practices for nurturing hope in our midst.

One way to do this is for our communities to reclaim their creational home. We need to recognize again that the biblical story begins in a food forest, in a place that looked something like Turtle Island before contact. We need to remember that the Creator's original plan was to hang out by a river in a food forest with a whole bunch of birds and animals, and a couple of naked vegetarians.

Our biblical imagination needs to be shaped by all those stories where the Creator appears in the wilderness: Hagar, a sexually abused slave, to whom the Creator appears in the wilderness—twice (Gen 16; 21:1–21); Jacob, on the run from familial violence, who is visited by angels in the wilderness (Gen 28:10–22); Moses, who not only encounters the Creator in the wilderness (on sacred ground), but learns the skills needed to lead a people there safely (Exod 3:1–6); Israel, discovering that the Creator is a God of abundance in the wilderness; David, discovering who he himself is in the wilderness (especially 1 Sam 24 and 26); Elijah, fleeing for his life, fed by angels in the wilderness (1 Kgs 19); Jesus, seeking out the Creator in the wilderness (e.g., Matt 14:13; Luke 4:42); John, seeing a vision of the Creator's home on earth, the new Jerusalem, a food forest that creates wilderness in the city (Rev 21; 22:1–5).[9]

Throughout the story, the Creator wants to meet us in the wild spaces, because those are the places where we are most whole. Don't forget that this is how the story ends: God coming again to dwell with all of creation on earth in a food forest city with a river running through it.

What if our liturgies, our preaching, our worship, our missional work, and our pastoral efforts all happened in a way that more deeply rooted us in that vision of the new creation, a vision that in turn nurtures the love of our place and our watershed? And what would a deep grounding in our watershed reveal to us about the love and abundance of the Creator?

This renewal of the biblical vision of hope for a restored earth would mean that we would finally repent of the "heaven after we die" heresy bequeathed to us by a Neoplatonic reading of the biblical text. We need to remember that *Adam* literally means "earth creature" and the earth is where we were created to be. The fact is that the Bible embodies a crazy "against-all-the-evidence" faith that our God specializes in resurrection, especially when things seem hopeless. That also means resurrection for us, the earth-creatures, on the renewed earth.

---

9. Israel: the wilderness wandering make up the bulk of the books of Exod, Lev, and Num.

If we are going to start talking about resurrection, we will need to strengthen our imagination around what climate justice and creational hope look like in our midst. We will need to realize that God's promise of resurrection is deep and wide, which means that climate justice is impossible without racial justice and Indigenous justice. And once we recognize the breadth of the biblical vision, we will understand why our communities are tired of small actions such as changing your light bulbs or recycling, which fail to change the trajectory of carbon capitalism, and the stranglehold of colonialism on creation.

The whole point about the resurrection is that it is so transformative that everything becomes so much more than we can imagine. Jesus was so new they couldn't see who he was. We don't know how to imagine what climate justice will look like: so we need to foster a robust and expansive imagination, and feed that imagination in our neighborhoods. Does this look like a food forest replacing the church parking lot? Challenging developments on wetlands? Giving church lands back to Indigenous peoples? Does it mean settler and Indigenous communities working on a cultural center together? What do reparations and Land Back look like in our context, and does the biblical vision of jubilee have anything to teach us?[10]

There are many resources out there for imagining a flourishing future. We need to be making them available. As others have indicated, we need to be getting on with things and invite all people of good will to join us.

The most ambitious project that the Bishop's Committee on Creation Care has engaged in to date is our "Lent Curriculum for All Ages" entitled "Ecological Grief and Creational Hope."[11] It contains biblical reflection, opportunities for sharing grief, and liturgies that root us in our place. It also provides links to resources that explore ecological degradation alongside racial and Indigenous injustice; the opportunity for repentance and forgiveness, along with actions for children and youth; and resources for further engagement and imaginative hope. Each week begins with a short contemplation on what we love about creation as a way to ground our reflections together. Each week includes activities and reflections that happen outside, rooting ourselves in our watershed. The resource draws together much of what I have been outlining thus far in this paper.

10. "Land Back" is increasingly being used to describe possible paths for reparations for Indigenous peoples. It also includes movements focused on Black and POC liberation as well. See "What Is Land Back?" and https://landback.org/.

11. Keesmaat, "Ecological Grief." This curriculum can be found in two places: on the Anglican Church of Canada, Diocese of Toronto website; and on my website, "Bible Remixed."

Our next project will be a resource for encouraging parishes to engage in a pilgrimage in their watersheds. It is precisely the sort of thing that we think can begin to meet the needs of our communities by creating a biblically grounded, safe, pastoral context for lament, repentance, and hope.

DIGGING DEEPER IN THEOLOGICAL EDUCATION

All of this begs the question, of course: How do our theological colleges engage in the formation of clergy who are best poised to meet the needs of our communities? I will be quite frank here: at the moment the Anglican Diocese is not looking to our theological colleges for any resources or leadership on this issue. This is because there is a sense that *there is nothing in the current curriculum of our Anglican theological colleges that addresses the issue of climate change in any depth.*

Given that this is the defining issue of our time, or, one could say, the last societal issue we might ever grapple with, I am glad that this consultation is exploring how theological education can provide leadership in this area. Let me say, however, that from a curricular standpoint, this could be a large task. Just as addressing anti-Black racism or colonization cannot be accomplished by adding a little section onto each course, so also the climate crisis will not be easily addressed by tweaking the curriculum.

We should not deceive ourselves into thinking that our teaching has been somehow neutral in relation to the current crisis. The roots of our current crisis are deeply embedded in the ways we teach and the content of our courses in theology. My students at seminary, as well as my colleagues at other institutions, share the experience of a disconnect between creation-affirming theology courses, or courses in environmental ethics, and other parts of the curriculum. What changes will be necessary to address this disconnect?

Might our teaching of church history and theology have to abandon the privileging of Platonic and rationalistic trajectories that have resulted in colonial Christianity and theologies that emphasize God's transcendence, omnipotence, and wrath?

What would it look like if our teaching of church history privileged the voices of the vulnerable, the slaves, the colonized? What if our church history centred the voices of those throughout history—many of them women—who celebrated the goodness of God's creation, rather than escape from it?

What might liturgy look like that is shaped by the lament of creation, the lament of the poor, the pain of Indigenous communities, and the passion of Black communities? What might liturgy look like that is deeply rooted in our places, in our watershed, in the land where we find ourselves?

What would sacramental theology look like that takes the indwelling of the Spirit in our places seriously?

How would our pastoral formation change if we were providing pastoral resources for dealing with climate grief and lament, resources for engaging young adults who do not want to have children due to the destruction of creation, and supports for grappling with the despair and hopelessness that climate collapse creates in our communities? How are we equipping our clergy for counseling in the midst of the climate crises—wildfires, floods, avalanches, unbearable heat—that are increasingly challenging our communities?

What does mission look like if we are proclaiming good news to all of creation? How is the gospel proclaimed to our farm animals? What would it look like if our communities were sharing *good news* in the face of climate collapse? What word of hope does the gospel have for climate refugees, for those in Lytton, British Columbia, whose homes burned to the ground, who then were cut off in avalanches, and who then faced fire once again? What does mission look like when it is untethered from its colonial moorings, which have linked the gospel with the commodification of peoples and the land?

What does our preaching look like if creation is a *character* in the biblical story, not just the stage for what human beings are up to? What if our preaching grounded us more firmly in creation, called us into our vocation as servants of creation, opened our imagination to the deep sorrow of creation abused, and the deep hope of creation loved, and prioritized our relationship with creation as much as our relationship with other human beings or with God?

What if our biblical studies abandoned readings of the text as literature, or as sociology, and read the text as a living word, a story that draws us into the passion and joy of a Creator who fiercely loves creation and wants us and all creatures to flourish?

I know of no place that has a curriculum quite like this.

However, I will say this. Any seminary hoping to become a leader in these critical times will need to appoint at least one faculty member who can provide curricular leadership that is biblically deep, theologically vulnerable, missionally imaginative, and pastorally sensitive on creation and the climate crisis. This faculty member should be able not only to teach courses that focus on the climate crisis biblically and theologically, but also to assist colleagues in the exciting work of communally rethinking how each part of the curriculum coheres, intersects, and supports the others as different facets of each discipline engage the story of creation and its abuse and healing.

This is not a task for the faint of heart. It is, however, one that is necessary if theological education is to meaningfully grapple with the overwhelming crisis that the church and our world now face.

BIBLIOGRAPHY

Brueggemann, Walter. "The Costly Loss of Lament." *Journal for the Study of the Old Testament* 36 (1986) 57–71.

Cohen, Leonard. "The Future." In *Stranger Music*, 370–72. Toronto: McClelland and Stewart, 1993.

Davis, Ellen F. *Scripture, Culture, Agriculture: An Agrarian Reading of the Bible.* Cambridge: Cambridge University Press, 2009.

Fretheim, Terence E. *The Suffering of God.* Philadelphia: Fortress, 1984.

Heinrichs, Steve, ed. *Buffalo Shout, Salmon Cry: Conversation on Creation, Land Justice, and Life Together.* Harrisonburg, VA: Herald, 2013

Keesmaat, Sylvia C. "Ecological Grief and Creational Hope: A Lent Curriculum for All Ages." The Diocese of Toronto, 2022. https://www.toronto.anglican.ca/wp-content/uploads/2022/02/LentCurriculum2022.pdf.

———. *Ecological Grief and Creational Hope.* Eugene, OR: Cascade, forthcoming.

Keesmaat, Sylvia C., and Brian J. Walsh. *Romans Disarmed: Resisting Empire, Demanding Justice.* Grand Rapids: Brazos, 2019.

Penniman, Leah. *Farming While Black: Soul Fire Farm's Practical Guide to Liberation on the Land.* White River Junction, VT: Chelsea Green, 2018.

"What Is Land Back?" David Suzuki Foundation. https://davidsuzuki.org/what-you-can-do/what-is-land-back/.

Whyte, Kyle. "Settler Colonialism, Ecology, and Environmental Injustice." *Environment and Society: Advances in Research* 9 (2018) 125–44.

15

A Field Sketch on the Future of Anglicanism in Quebec

What the Woodland Caribou Might Teach Us about Going Extinct

JEFFREY METCALFE

"The highest form of morality is not to feel at home in one's own home."

—THEODORE ADORNO[1]

THOUGH I DID NOT know Ellie Johnson personally, I welcome the opportunity to reflect on how her vision of justice, mission, and partnership might contribute to a vision for the future of our church, indeed, if it has one at all.[2] I have argued elsewhere that statistically, among survival stories, the story of the Anglican Church of Canada is neither the most interesting, nor the

---

1. Nafisi, *Reading Lolita in Tehran,* 88.

2. I would like to thank editors Ken Gray and Maylanne Maybee for this invitation, as well as their generous and extensive feedback on an earlier version of this article. I would also like to thank Bishop Bruce Myers and the Executive Council of the Diocese of Quebec for creating space within our church structures to ask risky questions with uncomfortable answers.

most important.[3] The population of Anglicans in the Diocese of Quebec has collapsed, but so too has the population of our woodland caribou neighbors.[4] Most of our parishes will be closed within ten years, but the woodland caribou might be extinct by the time the book you are reading is published.

Living in the midst of an ecological apocalypse as an ethicist and a church leader working for the Diocese of Quebec, I find myself in the awkward position of identifying with an institution whose colonial presence has contributed to the destruction not only of the woodland caribou, but of the biosphere itself.[5] What does it even mean to identify as a soon to be extirpated regional variant of Anglican in the context of the imminent extinction of the woodland caribou?

In this essay, I will argue that amid the collapse of both our colonial-ecclesial and our natural ecosystems, there lies a potential pathway for reorienting our identity and practice in the Diocese of Quebec, namely by reimagining our sense of belonging in Quebec through the lens of our creatureliness. I will begin with a short description of my experience of walking to work. It is an odd place to begin, to be sure, but interpreted through the lens of Charles Taylor's doctrine of "strong evaluation," that walk will help to expose the crisis of identity I believe the Anglican Church faces in contemporary Quebec and, I suspect, in many other dioceses. After offering a glimpse into this crisis, I will explore Willie James Jennings's hermeneutic of creatureliness as an alternative approach to understanding our sense of belonging, which could potentially guide us towards better navigation through these challenges.

This reflection is not intended to be a definitive documentation of the Diocese of Quebec's contribution to its own demise, nor is it meant to show how Jennings's hermeneutic of creatureliness might help us heal from the wounds of our colonial past. What I present here is more like a field sketch than a scientific diagram—a preliminary impression of how we might reimagine justice, partnership, and mission for Anglicans living in Quebec today.

---

3. Metcalfe, "Living as Footnotes."

4. *Presse canadienne*, "Nouveaux inventaires des caribous."

5. As Willie James Jennings has persuasively argued, colonial missionaries worked perichoretically with soldiers and merchants to create a new world order, an order, I would add, that continues to destabilize our ecologies. As a diocese, we have yet to reckon with our own contributions to that destabilization. See Jennings, "Disfigurations of Christian Identity."

WALKING TO WORK

After a fifteen-minute ride from my home, I get off the 800 metrobus and begin the two-hundred-meter walk up the hill that will lead me into the Old City of Quebec. I turn left, moving past the local concert hall toward the Kent Gate. There are only a few ways into the Old City, four of which pass under the ramparts through large and impressive stone gates. I always take the Kent Gate to avoid the tourists, who tend to impede the flow of traffic. The Kent Gate feels like my own secret entrance: more likely to be frequented by those who call Quebec City their home.

I know I am just about at our cathedral church when I reach the foot of the Price Building. A strong looking man in oxidized bronze always meets me there, riding a skiff of stone logs that seem to be spilling from a gap in the building onto the sidewalk: L'Homme-Rivière. It is a monument to the logging industry and to the Price family whose lumber company helped to build that industry. The Price family and their company are well known within the history of the Anglican diocese as employers of many of its members and generous patrons of several of our churches including our cathedral only a few meters away—it too bears a plaque and an endowment in their honor.

The building the statue juts out from still bears the family's name, although it now serves as the official residence of the premier of Quebec. Occasionally, I have to stop my walk as the premier exits the building and climbs into a black SUV, flanked by plain-clothes police officers, but today I have a clear path, so I keep walking. I turn right. Crossing the shadow of the Price building, I pass through the cathedral gates and from there into the Synod Office.

As I walk down the corridor toward my office, I pass several photos decorating the walls, including a beautiful landscape painting by a Quebec artist, and two plaques created by the national church: the first a timeline of Anglican relations with Indigenous peoples that describes and denounces the doctrine of discovery, the second a timeline of the Indian residential school system. Above the latter is hung a photo of Kawachickamatch, the small town that serves as the current home of the Naskapi Nation—an Indigenous community who nomadically hunted caribou before their forced settlement; a community with whom our diocese has a historic relationship. Each time I walk by this constellation of plaques and posters, it always strikes me that there is nothing on the timeline past 2014, and no indication that any of that work might be ongoing locally.

Entering my office, I sit at my desk, pushing a brochure about the Anglican Communion Forest Initiative off my keyboard. It has been there since the Lambeth Conference of 2022. Each workday I push it aside, and end up putting it back.[6]

TARRYING WITH TAYLOR

I will return to explore this walk shortly, but first, I need to take a further stroll with the Quebec philosopher Charles Taylor, whose doctrine of strong evaluation will help to provide an interpretive framework for my walk. According to Taylor, "in order to make minimal sense of our lives, in order to have an identity, we need an orientation to the good, which means some sense of qualitative discrimination, of the incomparably higher."[7] By nature, we make qualitative distinctions, we are "inevitably evaluative creatures," in the words of the anthropologist Webb Keane.[8] We cannot help placing our perceptions of human and other-than-human activity within a framework of judgement. Taylor uses the term "constitutive goods"[9] to describe those values and ends that help us to strongly evaluate the multiple lesser goods and values that make up our lives, values and goods which we "cannot help having . . . for the purposes of life: deliberating, judging situations, deciding how you feel about people, and the like. . . . You need these terms to make sense of what you are doing."[10] What Taylor means by "strong evaluation" is our capacity and tendency to discriminate our desires and actions and the actions of others in relation to our imagination of "the good" or "goods," our background understanding of what makes for a flourishing life.

For Taylor, our moral orientation constitutes our sense of identity, an idea he presents as the simple maxim: "To know who I am is a species of knowing where I stand."[11] That is, to know where I stand in relation to what I take to be the good, even if implicitly. Self-knowledge is in this sense a kind of moral knowledge—our imagination of who we are is inextricably linked to our moral imaginations. As Taylor describes it, "My identity is defined by the commitments and identifications which provide the frame or horizon

6. Note that this is a composite phenomenology.

7. Taylor, *Sources of the Self*, 47.

8. Keane, *Ethical Life*, 4.

9. Taylor, *Sources of the Self*, 92.

10. Taylor, *Sources of the Self*, 59.

11. Taylor, *Sources of the Self*, 27.

within which I can try to determine from case to case what is good, or valuable, or what ought to be done, or what I endorse or oppose. In other words, it is the horizon within which I am capable of taking a stand."[12]

To describe ourselves as holding a particular identity, such as being a Quebec Anglican, is to name, if only partially, a framework or moral imagination that characterizes the qualitative distinctions we routinely make. "What [we] are saying is not just that [we] are strongly attached to this spiritual view or background; rather it is that this provides the frame within which [we] can determine where [we] stand on questions of what is good, or worthwhile, or admirable, or of value."[13]

Taylor draws on spatial metaphors to describe this dynamic, depicting the questions that arise about our qualitative distinctions in our encounters with others as a moral space of encounter and dialogue we must navigate.[14] Our identity is how we orient ourselves within that space; it is our sense of the moral landscape we use to determine "where we stand," and "where they stand," in relation to what we perceive as the good or goods. "To understand our predicament in terms of finding or losing orientation in moral space is to take the space which our frameworks seek to define as ontologically basic."[15] By virtue of encountering and engaging in dialogue with others— always and already making qualitative distinctions—we are all engaged in navigating moral space. "The issue is, through which framework-definition can I find my bearings in it?"[16] An identity *is* this framework definition—it "plays the role of orienting us, of providing the frame within which things have meaning for us, by virtue of the qualitative distinctions it holds."[17] To identify as a Quebec Anglican is to claim a particular orientation within moral space—to describe the set of qualitative distinctions we make in relation to our sense of "the good" or "goods."

However, as Taylor notes, human beings are not static creatures; we "are always also changing and *becoming*."[18] In order to describe our orientation or identity within moral space, it is necessary to take account not only of our sense of our nearness or farness from the good, but also "as a question of yes or no," to a particular constitutive good or goods.[19] "The yes/no

---

12. Taylor, *Sources of the Self*, 27.
13. Taylor, *Sources of the Self*, 27.
14. Taylor, *Sources of the Self*, 28.
15. Taylor, *Sources of the Self*, 29.
16. Taylor, *Sources of the Self*, 29.
17. Taylor, *Sources of the Self*, 30.
18. Taylor, *Sources of the Self*, 47.
19. Taylor, *Sources of the Self*, 45.

question concerns . . . the direction of our lives, towards or away from it, or the source of our motivations in regard to it."[20] Just like orienteering in a physical landscape, a moral orientation requires two points and a direction: where we have been, and where we are going. This directional "sense of the good has to be woven into my understanding of my life as an unfolding story."[21]

Human identity, Taylor argues, is intuitively understood as an unfolding quest.[22] To comprehend who we are is to understand not only where we currently stand in relation to our perception of the good, but also of how we got there, and where we might project ourselves into the future.[23] This imagination is constructed through personal narratives, which are in turn formed by and nested within wider social narratives and the institutions that bear them. It also includes our moral ontologies, or the stories that help to frame our moral reasoning, which while always implicitly present, when described "offer themselves as correct articulations of our 'gut' reactions of respect."[24] As the American sociologist Christian Smith succinctly summarizes, "Our stories fully encompass and define our lives. They situate us in reality itself, by elaborating the contours of fundamental moral order, comprising sacred and profane, in narrative form, and placing us too as actors within the larger drama."[25]

THE CRACKS IN OUR STORIES

Having tarried with Taylor, we can return to reflect upon and provide an interpretation of my walk to work. The reason for describing the experience of my daily walk to work is to help highlight the social and personal narratives and the qualitative discriminations that give shape to my identity as a Quebec Anglican and to reveal some of the cracks therein. In light of Taylor's work, we can ask ourselves this: What stories can we unearth in the lived experience of my walk? What qualitative distinctions in relation to the good or goods are present? And what might these reveal about the trouble of identifying as "Anglican" in Quebec today?

The first thing we can note in my walk is how the built environment itself tells the city's story as rooted within contested settler colonial projects.

20. Taylor, *Sources of the Self*, 45.
21. Taylor, *Sources of the Self*, 47.
22. Taylor, *Sources of the Self*, 51–52.
23. Taylor, *Sources of the Self*, 47.
24. Taylor, *Sources of the Self*, 6.
25. Smith, *Moral, Believing Animals*, 78.

It reveals the social narrative of the French European theft and resettlement of Indigenous lands, and subsequently, the English European theft and attempted resettlement of French lands. Indeed, the Kent Gate serves as a visualization of this mixture of colonial projects: it bears the name of a British sovereign's father,[26] and was a part of Lord Dufferin's project to preserve the architectural and military history of these initially French fortifications.[27] To pass through that gate is to pass through the fundamental social narrative of the combined legacies of French and English settler-colonialism, regimes of power memorialized in the architecture, urban design, and place names.

This is particularly striking when it comes to the statue of L'Homme-Rivière at the base of the Price Building. The city's historical citation of that statue makes it clear that it is meant to both commemorate and celebrate the "courage and tenacity of the builders of Quebec,"[28] especially regarding the forestry industry, which remains one of the pillars of the Quebec economy. According to the provincial government's statistics, the forestry sector now accounts for "10% of total jobs in 150 municipalities and generates economic benefits in more than 900 municipalities (about 83% of municipalities),"[29] and 5.9 billion dollars of GDP annually. While the Price family name no longer represents the corporation, which has undergone several mergers, acquisitions, and consolidations, those initial foundations remain in its successor company Resolute Forest Products, the largest forestry company in Canada, now owned by Paper Excellence.[30] It seems symbolically fitting that the premier's official residence lies at the top of the Price Building: a spatial arrangement that locates Quebec's colonial foundations within the political economies of resource extraction. Indeed, it is this same forestry industry and the government agencies whose policies support it that has created the conditions for the decline of the woodland caribou.[31]

Each time I pass L'Homme-Rivière, I am reminded of this legacy and of its entanglement within our Anglican history and identity—that is why it jumps out at me as I walk to work. By drawing on the romantic figure of the strong, courageous, and tenacious logger who helped to build Quebec, the statue is, in Taylor's terms, a kind of storyteller, whose narrative helps to

26. That is, Queen Victoria's father, Prince Edward, Duke of Kent and Strathearn.

27. "Héritage."

28. "Répertoire des œuvres d'art public." My translation.

29. "Invest in Québec's Forest Products."

30. Dubinsky and Thompson, "Canada's New Pulp-and-Paper."

31. We need only to recall the words of Pierre Dufour, the former minister of Forests, Wildlife, and Parks, to confirm this: "La forêt, c'est une manière d'exploiter économiquement quelque chose qui repousse" (The forest is a way of economically exploiting something that grows back). See Rémillard, "Caribous forestiers," para. 14.

orient us in moral space in relation to a particular vision of flourishing, one that imagines our belonging in terms of our participation in building Quebec through the process of extraction—a colonial imagination of becoming. The Anglican Church in Quebec has contributed to the cultivation of this imagination, due to its members' engagement in founding and managing the logging industry and their acceptance and celebration of patronage from this industry for the construction and upkeep of its churches.

Yet while I hear the story told by L'Homme-Rivière, I do not find it a compelling one. Rather, my gut reaction is moral revulsion because I have begun to see that narrative through the lens of the caribou's story, a story in which the theft and exploitation of Indigenous land is bringing about the caribou's extinction. That revulsion reveals a qualitative distinction I cannot help but make. Prior to my reflecting upon it, I respond to the constitutive good as told by the story of L'Homme-Rivière with a resounding "no." While my identity as a Quebec Anglican might be nested within the wider social narrative of the colonial building project, I do not desire it to be so.

What Is the Alternative?

But what alternative and compelling vision of Quebec Anglican identity do I have to offer in its place? What constitutive good or imagination of flourishing might orient an alternative framework-definition? At first glance, we might view the space within the diocesan offices as one possible answer to this. Just as L'Homme-Rivière is telling a story of our belonging in this place, so too are our office walls: a narrative that retells the story of the colonial project through the lens of the theft and exploitation of Indigenous peoples and lands. Certainly, this is a story I find more truthful and compelling. Yet here is where the cracks within the foundations of contemporary Quebec Anglican identity become more apparent.

The pictures that frame our office walls are just that—pictures. Whereas the story told by L'Homme-Rivière has shaped the material reality of our churches, city, and province, the pictures that hang on our office walls reflect, at best, a preliminary performance of who we hope to become, and at worst, a decorative obfuscation in becoming it. Each day at the beginning of my work, I push the Anglican Communion Forest Initiative pamphlet off my keyboard. I do so because I am not sure how to take up the call to create an Anglican Communion Forest without first reckoning with the role Quebec Anglicanism has played in the disappearance of the woodland caribou. Yet each day I put the pamphlet back, recognizing that simply pushing it off because it is difficult and complex is not the answer. Like the pictures on the wall of our diocesan office, participating in the Anglican Communion Forest Initiative might be a pathway for telling a new story about how we belong in this place. But unless we find a way of telling a compelling story of our participation that can truthfully describe our transition from one sense of flourishing to another, it is far more likely to merely plaster over the cracks in our foundation.

For those who no longer find the framework-definition provided by our participation in the colonial narrative compelling, the cracks in Anglican identity lie, in Taylor's terms, between where we have been and where we are going. If we look at our material and spiritual foundations truthfully, we know as Quebec Anglicans where we stand in relation to the colonial story (as least to some degree), and how we got there (at least in part). But it is unclear who we might yet become in this place, and it is even more unclear how we might tell the story of transitioning from one point to the other. What we need is an alternative vision of flourishing that can help us to reinterpret our past and present while reorienting our identities in the land. We now turn to an impression of this alternative vision in Willie James Jennings hermeneutic of creatureliness.

RECLAIMING OUR SENSE OF CREATURELINESS

Willie James Jennings is perhaps best known for his theological race theory, which ties the origins of White supremacy to a constellation of historical and theological developments that come to fruition in the colonial moment.[32] Yet it is the hermeneutic of creatureliness[33] underlying his work that I would like to highlight as particularly helpful for reorienting our sense of belonging in the land we now call Quebec.[34] Simply defined, Jennings' "hermeneutic of creatureliness" is an interpretive approach that emphasizes the interconnectedness of human identity with our creaturely nature. As a hermeneutic, it serves as a method for critically rereading our theology, ethics, and daily experiences with the intent to see how our social structures

---

32. See Jennings, *Christian Imagination*.

33. Due to the limitations of space, I cannot delve into the innovative way Jennings develops this hermeneutic in his dissertation on the work of Athanasius of Alexandria and Karl Barth. See Jennings, "Reclaiming the Creature."

34. I do not want to mislead the reader: the story of colonialism in Quebec and the role of the Anglican Church within that project cannot be adequately told outside of a critique of White identity in Quebec and within the Anglican Church. While, due to the limitations of space, I have not engaged in such a critique directly, it nevertheless undergirds my thinking, and remains a necessary area of development for future work.

and histories have concealed our creatureliness from us, in the hopes of regrounding our identities and therefore the way we ought to live. Whereas Taylor offers us an analytical framework to understand how the formation of human identity works in relation to our moral frameworks, Jennings offers us a particular moral story for how that identity ought to be formed and how it has been deformed.

According to this hermeneutic of creatureliness, "the significance of humanity, its authenticity and truth, cannot be assumed, rather it must come as a revelation of our creatureliness rooted in the revelation of the triune God."[35] For Jennings, even though our creaturely status is sometimes cited as a theological fact about the human condition, it too often fails to be taken up as a primary source and method within our theological reflection. It is not enough simply to cite our creation by the triune God as the starting or ending point of our theological reflection, especially regarding human identity. The revelation of our creaturely status is not just *something* we know; it is also *how* we know it. "Believing in the web of life requires that we have theologies of creation that preform that web in their writings."[36] This is why our creatureliness is a hermeneutic for Jennings, rather than only a doctrine—it is meant to actively engage and orient the work of our theological reflection, rather than merely begin or end it.

Drawing on works of anthropology,[37] environmental and cultural history,[38] and Indigenous writing,[39] this hermeneutic of creatureliness leads Jennings to advocate for a place-based identity: "Identity that is constituted in and constitutive of life defined by and coordinated around specific lands, animals, plants, bodies of water, and objects created and situated in specific spaces."[40] In Taylor's terms, our orientation in moral space ought to bear a relation to our orientation in geographic space. In a very real way, to borrow Taylor's phrase, we are where we stand—or at least we ought to be.

One of the great tragedies of the colonial encounter, according to Jennings, was the way Christian settlers failed to listen to, learn from, and join with the place-based identities of the peoples and lands they encountered. "Indeed, it is as though Christianity, wherever it went in the modern colonies, inverted its sense of hospitality. It claimed to be the host, the owner

---

35. Jennings, "Reclaiming the Creature," 2.

36. Jennings, "Reframing the World," 407.

37. Basso, *Wisdom Sits in Places*.

38. Melville, *Plague of Sheep*. Jennings draws on Melville as a negative example: how colonial ungulate pastoralism destabilized both the ecology and identity of Indigenous peoples.

39. Deloria, *God Is Red*.

40. Jennings, "Binding Landscapes," 217.

of the spaces it entered, and demanded 'native' peoples enter its cultural logics, its ways of being in the world, and its conceptualities."[41] Animated by a supercessionist habit of mind in which European peoples imagined themselves as called by God to replace the idolatrous Indigenous peoples and their relations with the land, European peoples practiced a theology of abstraction and extraction: the land was exorcised of its animacy and communicability, abstracting both lands and peoples from the community of relations in which all creatures are formed and sustained in their being. This made way for both the land and peoples to be transformed into and sold as commodities. Said differently, forest homes came to be seen as lumber yards and forest peoples came to be seen as either laborers or, like many other forest creatures, obstacles to development marked for extirpation.

Jennings's hermeneutic of creatureliness is helpful because it allows us to see both how our creatureliness has been concealed from us as place-based identities were uprooted and reoriented in the New World to better align with the colonial building project, and, through the revelation of that concealment, points the way toward the cultivation of an alternative sense of belonging. What is needed, Jennings's work suggests, is for us to reclaim our sense of creatureliness by realigning our orientations in moral space with our orientations in geographic space. We need to recultivate place-based identities.

Here, I suggest, our Anglican tradition might contain within its history and theology some redemptive resources, such as its recognition and practice of geographic expressions of Christian identity through the ecclesial structures of diocese, deanery, and parish. What might those structures look like if they were realigned through a bioregionalist lens? How might the relations of creation where we find ourselves reshape our ecclesiology and our ethics? Yet as Jennings rightly notes, there can be no romantic return to a past prior to the colonial fragmentation of place-based identities. Repairing the cracks in our foundation cannot be brought about by simply hanging pictures of the woodland caribou on our walls: real repairs will require real reparations.

Moreover, we must be clear that while our Anglican tradition might have within it some helpful resources to contribute to this task, our internal resources are not sufficient. Here is where partnership comes to the fore: we must join with our neighbors in the land in order to learn how to retell our story as Quebec Anglicans. In Jennings words: "This joining involves first a radical remembering of the place, a discerning of the histories and stories of those for whom that land was the facilitator of their identity. This

---

41. Jennings, *Christian Imagination*, 8.

must be done to gather the fragments of identity that remain to learn from them (or at least from their memory) who we might become in that place."[42] We must cease to feel at home where we find ourselves, and consciously move from the position of being hosts and teachers in the land to that of being students and guests of the peoples who still bear a historic witness to a place-based identity. For those whose paths cross under the shadow of the Price Building, this includes becoming "second readers of creation"[43] under the tutelage of the Huron-Wendat, whose place-based histories, stories, practices, and contemporary political struggles will be required reading in reshaping our own.[44]

CONCLUSION

In this brief field sketch, I have argued that amid the collapse of our colonial ecclesial and natural ecosystems, reimagining our sense of belonging in terms of our creatureliness offers us a potential pathway for reorienting our church identity and practice in the Diocese of Quebec. A description of my experience walking to work, interpreted through the lens of Charles Taylor's doctrine of strong evaluation, helped us to glimpse the cracks and the crisis at the foundations of Quebec Anglican identity. I then turned to Willie James Jennings's hermeneutic of creatureliness as providing a particular story that might help us to better navigate this crisis. Finally, I suggested, in the spirit of Ellie Johnson's work, that the reorientation of our identity and mission in the Diocese of Quebec will require a particular kind of partnership with the Indigenous peoples of the lands in which we find ourselves.

Yet it must be said that even if as church members and leaders we have the desire and will to move forward with this reorientation, it is unclear whether, under the burden of our histories as well as our material and organizational structures, we will find the capacity to do so. This is not unlike the story of the woodland caribou. Like many creatures facing extinction, the woodland caribou are dying because they *cannot adapt quickly enough* to the changing material conditions within their habitats: logging roads have increased predation on dwindling herds, and the clear-cutting of old growth boreal forest has reduced and fragmented the habitat they need to successfully raise new generations of young. Unless their habitat is protected, or

---

42. Jennings, *Christian Imagination*, 286.

43. For a fuller account of what being a "second reader" entails, see Jennings, "Reframing the World."

44. Here, I suggest, the works of the Wendat scholar George Sioui will be of particular importance. See in particular Sioui, *Eatenonha*, and Sioui, *Les Hurons-Wendat*.

they suddenly learn to overcome centuries of practice encoded into their DNA, they will not survive.

So too, I suggest with the Quebec subspecies of Canadian Anglicanism: our evolution has been bound up within the political economies of extraction—the colonial project is our natural habitat. While these political economies still define Quebec and Canada, our church's prominent role in those projects has definitively ended. The question remains, however, as to *whether we can adapt ourselves quickly enough* to develop new ecclesial niches in our changed environment. And perhaps more provocatively, if we can, will we still be identifiable as Quebec Anglicans, or will we have evolved into something else?

BIBLIOGRAPHY

Basso, Keith H. *Wisdom Sits in Places: Landscape and Language among the Western Apache.* Albuquerque: University of New Mexico Press, 1996.

Deloria, Vine, Jr. *God Is Red: A Native View of Religion.* 30th anniversary edition. Golden, CO: Fulcrum, 2003.

Dubinsky, Zach, and Elizabeth Thompson. "Who's behind Canada's New Pulp-and-Paper Powerhouse, and Where's the Money Coming from?" *CBC News,* Mar 9, 2023, https://www.cbc.ca/news/business/paper-excellence-pulp-china-1.6772654.

"Héritage." Ville De Québec. https://www.ville.quebec.qc.ca/en/citoyens/patrimoine/quartiers/vieux_quebec/interet/fortifications_de_quebec.aspx.

"Invest in Québec's Forest Products Industry." Québec, last updated Apr 26, 2023. https://www.quebec.ca/en/agriculture-environnement-et-ressources-naturelles/forets/entreprises-industrie/invest-forest-products.

Jennings, Willie James. "Binding Landscapes: Secularism, Race, and the Spatial Modern." In *Race and Secularism in America*, edited by Jonathon Samuel Kahn and Vincent W. Lloyd, 207–238. New York: Columbia University Press, 2016.

———. *The Christian Imagination: Theology and the Origins of Race.* New Haven, CT: Yale University Press, 2010.

———. "Disfigurations of Christian Identity: Preforming Identity as Theological Method." In *Lived Theology: New Perspectives on Method, Style, and Pedagogy,* edited by Charles Marsh et al., 67–88. New York: Oxford University Press, 2017.

———. "Reclaiming the Creature: Anthropological Vision in the Thought of Athanasius of Alexandria and Karl Barth." PhD diss., Duke University, 1993. ProQuest. https://www.proquest.com/openview/85f14cf81560e390f54f691e7264 0c8c/1?pq-origsite=gscholar&cbl=18750&diss=y.

———. "Reframing the World: Toward an Actual Christian Doctrine of Creation." *International Journal of Systematic Theology* 21 (2019) 388–407.

Melville, Elinor G. K. *A Plague of Sheep: Environmental Consequences of the Conquest of Mexico.* Cambridge: Cambridge University Press, 1994.

Metcalfe, Jeffrey. "Living as Footnotes to the Story." *Anglican Journal,* Jan 22, 2020. https://anglicanjournal.com/living-as-footnotes-to-the-story/.

Nafisi, Azar. *Reading Lolita in Tehran: A Memoir in Books*. New York: Random House, 2003.

La Presse canadienne. "Nouveaux inventaires des caribous: le déclin continue." *ICI Côte-Nord*, Jan 14, 2023. https://ici.radio-canada.ca/nouvelle/1948413/inventaire-caribou-gaspesie-cote-nord-declin.

Rémillard, David. "Caribous forestiers: le ministre Dufour s'en prend à un expert national." *ICI Quebec*, Dec 11, 2019. https://ici.radio-canada.ca/nouvelle/1428968/caribous-charlevoix-ministre-dufour-tour-ivoire-rimouski-court-solutions.

"Répertoire des œuvres d'art public." Ville de Québec, 2023. https://www.ville.quebec.qc.ca/citoyens/art-culture/art-public/repertoire/index.aspx.

Sioui, Georges E. *Eatenonha: Native Roots of Modern Democracy*. Montreal: Mcgill-Queens University Press, 2019.

———. *Les Hurons-Wendat: l'héritage du cercle*. Laval, QC: Presses de l'Université Laval, 2019.

Smith, Christian. *Moral, Believing Animals: Human Personhood and Culture*. Oxford: Oxford University Press, 2003.

Taylor, Charles. *Sources of the Self: The Making of the Modern Identity*. Cambridge: Cambridge University Press, 1989.

Webb, Keane. *Ethical Life: Its Natural and Social Histories*. Princeton: Princeton University Press, 2016.

16

From Homelessness to Homefulness
Faith and Housing

MICHAEL SHAPCOTT

"Shout out, do not hold back! Lift up your voice like a trumpet! . . .
Look, you serve your own interest on your fast day
and oppress all your workers.
You fast only to quarrel and to fight and to strike with a wicked fist. . . .
Is not this the fast that I choose: to loose the bonds of injustice,
to undo the straps of the yoke, to let the oppressed go free,
and to break every yoke?
Is it not to share your bread with the hungry and bring the homeless
poor into your house;
when you see the naked, to cover them and not to hide yourself
from your own kin? . . .
If you remove the yoke from among you, the pointing of the finger,
the speaking of evil,
if you offer your food to the hungry and satisfy
the needs of the afflicted,
then your light shall rise in the darkness and your gloom
be like the noonday. . . .

Your ancient ruins shall be rebuilt; you shall raise up the foundations
of many generations;
you shall be called the repairer of the breach,
the restorer of streets to live in."

—EXCERPTS FROM ISA 58.

"Home. Homelessness. Longing for home. Ours is a culture of displacement, exile and homelessness. Socioeconomic homelessness is growing with many people seeking adequate housing. Ecological homelessness is increasing, with its sense of alienation from a degraded and defiled earth. And a profound spiritual homelessness pervades postmodern culture."

—STEPHEN BOUMA-PREDIGER AND BRIAN WALSH,
BEYOND HOMELESSNESS[1]

IN THE BEGINNING: THE SOCIAL RIGHT TO HOUSING

The beginning of Canada's golden era of social housing came in 1973 when Canada's national housing minister, Ron Basford, rose in the House of Commons to introduce amendments to the National Housing Act. He included these words: "Good housing at reasonable cost is a social right of every citizen of this country.... [This] must be our objective, our obligation, and our goal. The legislation which I am proposing to the House today is an expression of the government's policy, part of a broad plan, to try to make this right and this objective a reality."[2]

Imagine that! Housing as a right for everyone, and an obligation and goal of government is to ensure that everyone has a good place to call home.

Minister Basford's amendment to the National Housing Act in 1973 was a step toward realizing substantial rights for "every citizen of this country." Yet our market-based and segmented societies now create divisions and inequities. Private markets are the only place for most people to find

---

1. Bouma-Prediger and Walsh, *Beyond Homelessness*, 40.
2. Basford, "House of Commons," 2557.

housing, shutting many others out of a place to call home. Private markets commodify and financialize basic needs, such as housing. Housing and land are financial assets to be bought and sold to the highest bidder. The danger of consigning something as fundamental and important as housing to private markets is that housing gets detached from its human and social dimensions. Housing becomes a commodity, detached from its moral and social qualities as home, a place of belonging, a place of comfort.

People of faith understand that housing has a physical expression—the roof, the walls, the plumbing, and the electricity are very important. Yet there is so much more, as Stephen Bouma-Prediger and Brian Walsh note: "Home is a place of belonging, of recognition and acceptance, rather than disdain and rejection. At home we feel included, we belong, and we have friends."[3] "Home" is elevated from an individual entitlement and a market commodity to a social and moral duty that we owe to one another. Homemaking, as it is practiced by faith communities, is more than building structures. It is about mending and building relationships with people and communities.

Canada's nationwide housing crisis and homelessness disaster is as relentless as it is all-pervasive. To make this terrible and immoral situation even worse, those who are forced to the economic and social margins with all the consequent suffering are blamed as authors of their own misfortune.

And yet, we keep hearing, there is no alternative—except there is—and we had a brief glimpse of that in 1973, and at a few other moments before then and in subsequent years.

In those different times, the minister's words appealed to a higher moral good and a moral duty on the part of government. His words ushered in legislative changes, new programs and plenty of funding, creating almost six hundred thousand community-based homes across the country over the next two decades.[4] People were housed and communities were engaged; government, corporate, and community sectors, including faith groups, had practical structures that allowed them to collaborate for the common good.

Taking up the prophetic challenge from Isaiah to house the houseless and repair the streets of our communities, churches and other faith communities seized on Minister Basford's words and converted parking lots and other pieces of land into new housing. They established housing

---

3. Bouma-Prediger and Walsh, *Beyond Homelessness*, 65.

4. There is no reliable federal database of housing. Policy experts estimate between four hundred thousand and six hundred thousand new homes were created from 1973 to 1993, directly under federal programs and through allied provincial or municipal initiatives sparked by the federal action.

development groups in many parts of the country and created coalitions to tackle housing, hunger, income, and inequity as justice and human rights issues.

It was an era when community groups, cooperatives, and municipalities focused on building houses and creating homes as never before, starting with local churches offering the basics of shelter and food for those who were homeless and hungry—meagre comfort, assuredly, but necessary until new homes could be built.

CANADA'S LONG HISTORY OF FAITH-BASED INITIATIVES

More than a hundred years ago, during the economic recession of the late nineteenth century, volunteers in Toronto and Montreal started modest food programs. Over the years, with vision and energy, Fred Victor Centre in Toronto and the Old Brewery Mission in Montreal moved from food charity and temporary shelter to housing and homes. For almost 140 years, First United Church in Vancouver's Downtown Eastside has worked on justice and advocacy, while delivering practical support. They seek to put reconciliation into action in their work alongside Indigenous people.

In 1981, seven faith-based groups came together to create Ecuhome in Toronto. They manage a large portfolio of houses and apartment buildings. More recently, in 2001, the Multifaith Alliance in Ottawa was formed and has grown into a coalition of more than seventy faith communities. They manage almost two hundred homes. Opened in 2022, one of the newest housing initiatives in Canada was developed by Halifax's Ummah Masjid and Nisa Homes to serve Muslim and other newcomer women.

Housing instability is closely linked to hunger and food insecurity. Canada's first food bank was created in Edmonton in 1981 and has grown to be a truly multisectoral effort, linking more than 250 churches and other faith groups with community agencies and others. In the relatively small town of Salmon Arm in the central interior of British Columbia, a group of visionaries associated with the Salvation Army joined with Shuswap Food Action to create a community food forest.

And the list goes on, in big cities, small towns, and remote and rural regions, there are plenty of inspiring examples of faith communities in action on housing and ending homelessness.

Given that long and brilliant history, and the brave words of Minister Basford in 1973, how did Canada descend to the depths of the third decade of the 2000s and a nationwide "culture of displacement, exile and homelessness," to quote theologians Stephen Bouma-Prediger and Brian Walsh?

That is a cautionary moral tale, and in the telling of it are signs of a more hope-filled future.

THE VIEW FROM 2023: CANADA'S HOMELESSNESS DISASTER

Before the 1980s, few Canadians were unhoused and almost none were born homeless. The word "homelessness" was hardly used in the news media. Some people, mostly men, struggled to find secure housing, some were itinerant workers who moved from city to city and would gather in "skid row." The cost of housing was beyond the reach of some, many of whom lived in rooming or boarding houses. Numbers fluctuated as people moved in and out of housing—those who grew up during the Great Depression of the 1930s and after the Second World War when troops were demobilized, falling with the rise of social housing in the 1960s.

Churches and other Christian agencies provided support in the form of hostels and missions to those who were precariously housed or unhoused. Governments funded various initiatives over the decades. Though it is always terrible if even one person goes without shelter, nevertheless, the numbers were relatively low, victims of housing insecurity were largely hidden from view, and the issues of homelessness and affordable housing fell below public and political attention.

Then, in the 1980s, circumstances began to change radically, leading to the mass homelessness in the second decade of the twenty-first century. From the relatively small numbers of people who were homeless before the 1980s, the more recent national estimates from the Canadian Observatory on Homelessness report that 235,000 Canadians experience homelessness annually (some for brief periods of time, others longer-term). There are an estimated 35,000 "unsheltered" homeless people on a given night, sleeping in shelters, or rough on the streets. There are another 50,000 "hidden" homeless, sleeping on couches or otherwise without a place to call home.[5]

Absolute homelessness represents the tip of the iceberg when it comes to widespread housing insecurity across Canada. According to the 2021 census, one-in-ten Canadian households are in core housing need—defined as housing that is inadequate, uninhabitable, or unaffordable. While they may have some form of shelter, but they are, for all practical purposes, homeless.

---

5. See "How Many People."

By the 1990s, the profile of homeless people was no longer mostly middle-aged men. It was a shock when pregnant women became part of the growing ranks of the homeless, joined by newborns, children, youth, adults, and seniors crowding into homeless shelters and spilling onto the streets. Tent cities emerged in large urban areas and in small rural communities in the 1990s and remain a fixture in many parts of the country three decades later.

Dr. David Hulchanski, one of Canada's leading housing policy experts, calls homelessness a "human-made problem" and refers to the processes and people behind it as "homeless making" and "homeless makers."

> Since the 1980s there have been a number of homeless-making processes set in motion. . . . People in public and private institutions and organizations large and small, from households to corporations and governments, have set in motion and have left unchecked these homeless-making processes. People able to stop or redress the harm fail to do so. . . . They are Canada's homeless makers. Canada's homeless makers prefer to believe, and take every opportunity to promote the belief, that the men, women and children who are homeless did this to themselves. It is their fault they are homeless. . . . This self-serving ideology deflects the blame and protects those who benefit from the homeless-making processes.[6]

The strange thing is that Canada's homeless makers, the forces and processes that generate mass homelessness, did not set out to force millions of people to become precariously housed, nor did they intend that hundreds of thousands of people would live without shelter. There was no organized lobby advocating for more homelessness, yet that is precisely the reality of today. Dr Hulchanski notes:

> Homelessness is the "natural" outcome of the way we have organized our housing system, and the way we allocate or fail to allocate income and support services when they are desperately needed. Though no one favours homelessness, many contribute to it by doing what societal norms and government laws and regulations allow.[7]

When referring to the economic, social, and political forces that brought about the scourge of modern-day homelessness, people of faith might reach for the old fashioned language of demons, powers, and principalities (Eph

---

6. Hulchanski, "Did the Weather," 1.

7. Hulchanski, "Homelessness in Canada," 9.

6). Yet these forces are not horned devils; they are respected parts of society, going about their daily business.

Until the 1960s, most low-, moderate-, and even middle-income people who were excluded from the ownership market were finally able to find a home through the private rental housing market, in an era when major businesses invested in the development and leasing of rental housing. Then, in the early 1970s, large investors began to shift funding away from private rental housing toward shopping malls and commercial properties. They did not intend to generate homelessness; they simply wanted a better return on their investments. Commercial real estate was more lucrative than private rental housing. And yet, the erosion of private rental markets, and the conversion ("gentrification") of previously affordable housing, pushed more people into housing insecurity.

The economic and social systems that efficiently and relentlessly created housing insecurity and homelessness have worked effectively over the years. Despite the words of Minister Basford in 1973, the key actors did not accept that they had a moral duty toward those pushed aside by their social and economic policies and practices.

Homelessness is not just a social, economic, and political concern for those seeking a place to live; it is a profoundly *moral question for everyone.* It is part of the pervasive culture we live in, one of "displacement, exile and homelessness," as so aptly put by Stephen Bouma-Prediger and Brian Walsh, with its swirl of forces that create social, economic, ecological, and spiritual homelessness.

And so, on that day when Minister Basford rose in the House of Commons to proclaim housing as a human right for every citizen of this country and declare that his government would take on the obligation to realize that right, he set a powerful moral tone that challenged the dominant practice of private and government sectors when it comes to housing policy.

ANOTHER PERSPECTIVE: THE HUMAN RIGHT TO HOUSING

While the forces seeking to commodify housing, with all the attendant costs, have been powerful, there is another narrative that recognized home and homemaking as basic moral duties. In Minister Basford's 1973 statement he stressed that it is the "objective, obligation, and goal" of government is to ensure everyone has a good place to call home.

His commitment to a rights-based approach to housing policy in 1973 did not come to him in a vision one night. Nor did it spring from the benevolence of the government of the day, led by Prime Minister Pierre Trudeau. The New Democratic opposition, led by David Lewis, was applying pressure to the minority Liberal government to tackle housing issues. For the sake of their political survival as a government, the Liberals needed to collaborate with the opposition.

Politicians on both sides of the house reached back to the words of the Universal Declaration of Human Rights, proclaimed by the United Nations in 1948, for practical inspiration.

And so, the golden age of social housing in Canada, from 1973 to 1993, was built on the foundation of internationally recognized human rights.

The Universal Declaration of Human Rights is the most important articulation of the universal rights of all humans in the modern world. Hundreds of other covenants, treaties, declarations, statements, and legally binding agreements have followed at the international level, and some countries have recognized the right to housing in national legislation.

Canada was one of the first to sign on to the Universal Declaration of Human Rights. This is not entirely surprising, as it was a Canadian, John Peters Humphrey, who drafted the original words for the declaration. The international discourse on human rights gathered strength in Canada and helped to power the 1973 national housing initiative.

The discourse of international human rights is steeped in statements of neighborly love that form the foundation of many faiths. Jesus, when summarizing the religious law, reached back to ancient Jewish Scripture: "You shall love your neighbor as yourself" (Lev 19:18). Reciprocity—the moral duty human beings have toward each other and to the world around—is a common theme in all the great faiths.

In the early decades of the twentieth century, the social gospel movement emerged in the US and Canada from a world wracked by war, economic crises, and divisions. It was a new theology that applied the Christian gospel to the issues of the day, with the goal of realizing the common good, or, in Christian terms, to realize God's reign on earth. Theologian Walter Rauschenbusch described the social gospel movement in these words:

> The social gospel is the old message of salvation but enlarged and intensified. The individualistic gospel has taught us to see the sinfulness of every human heart and has inspired us with faith in the willingness and power of God to save every soul. . . . But it has not given us an adequate understanding of the sinfulness of the social order and its share in the sins of all individuals

within in. It has not invoked faith in the will and power of God to redeem the permanent institutions of human society from their inherited guilt of oppression and extortion.[8]

The sinfulness of the social order includes private housing markets that exclude great numbers of women, men, and children, rising homelessness and housing-based discrimination based on religious, cultural, gender, or other grounds. Rauschenbusch's words echo those of the prophet Isaiah, bringing them into the twentieth century.

In Canada, the social gospel was an inspiration to a generation of Christian leaders, including Tommy Douglas, widely recognized as the father of public health care in this country. Many local church leaders across Canada took up the moral challenge to create a caring and just society. Rev. John Frank preached the social gospel from the pulpit of Toronto's Church of the Holy Trinity, Trinity Square in the 1930s—from which the message was carried into the streets and alleyways in practical actions.

Similarly, in postwar Britain, the theologian and archbishop of Canterbury, William Temple (1881–1944) sought to realize God's reign on earth working with many others towards a new kind of government in Britain to address the practical needs of people. He was a mid-twentieth century Isaiah:

> The existing system is [to be] challenged on moral grounds. It is not merely that some who "have not" are jealous of some who "have." The charge against our social system is one of injustice. The banner so familiar in earlier unemployed or socialist processions—"damn your charity, we want justice"—vividly exposes the system as seen by its critics. If the present order is taken for granted or assumed to be sacrosanct, charity from the more or less fortunate would seem virtuous and commendable; to those for whom the order itself is suspect or worse, such charity is blood-money. Why should some be in the position to dispense and others to need that kind of charity?[9]

Temple's vision of the common good centered on a society in which every person has equitable access to education, housing, health care, and income. In 1945 (just after Temple passed away), the Labour government of Clement Atlee was elected to create what would be called the "welfare state"—that is, a state in which the common good and general welfare of all

8. Rauschenbusch, *Theology for the Social Gospel*, 5.

9. Temple, *Christianity and Social Order*, 36.

the people is the foundation for public policy. Atlee's agenda was propelled forward by Anglicans and others of good faith.

THE RIGHT TO HOUSING IN CANADA

The Universal Declaration grew out of the horrors of the Second World War—a violation of our moral duty to one another. This acknowledgement was central in the development of declaration. The question remains, how do these words apply to housing in Canada in the twenty-first century?

In 2007, the United Nations Special Rapporteur on the Right to Adequate Housing, Miloon Kothari, made an official fact-finding mission to Canada at the invitation of the government. While he was impressed with a history of successful housing practices, including the 1973 program, he noted that funding and program cuts starting in the 1990s led to growing housing insecurity and homelessness.

Canada was failing in its human rights obligations to many people, he warned, especially the housing rights of Indigenous peoples and others. Canada must enshrine the human right to housing directly in its national law, and not just leave it to the political whims of the government of the day and to opposition parties, he added. He called for Canada to reinstate the successful programs of the 1970s to create more homes.

International human rights, as articulated in Kothari's report and Basford's amendment to the National Housing Act, were based on a simple structure. First, they recognize that human rights are inherent in the dignity and worth of all people; they are neither bestowed by benevolent governments nor plucked out of the air, but are the moral foundation of our world. And second, they recognize that it is those with power—governments, businesses, and others—who have the moral obligation to realize human rights, in this case, the right to housing.

The moral underpinning of modern human rights, including the internationally recognized right to adequate housing, is drawn from an ancient religious understanding that all humans have inherent dignity and value. The Abrahamic faiths trace it back to Gen 1:27: "So God created humankind in his image, in the image of God he created them." Humans as image-bearers of God mean that all people are very special indeed. To then assert that every human has inherent worth and dignity raises the discussion around housing to a new level.

More than a feel-good emotion, the right to housing is a fundamental recognition that human beings belong together, living in homes in communities, in dignity and with respect.

THE EROSION OF THE MORAL FOUNDATION OF HOUSING POLICY

Regrettably, the successful policies and practices that grew out of the 1973 commitment, built on a moral proclamation of the human right to housing, did not survive Canadian politics. Just a decade after Canada's rights-based national housing policy was launched, a new federal government led by Conservative Prime Minister Brian Mulroney was elected. Their moral vision included small government, with deep cuts to national housing and other government spending.

This notion of the atomized individual seeking their own interests in private markets was embraced with increasing fervor across the political spectrum and among the most powerful in economic and social circles. Called "Thatcherism" in the UK, and "Reaganism" in the US, Canada's own brand sought to reduce or eliminate any notion that we have a collective moral duty to each other, or that governments have an obligation to help realize the right to housing. Private markets, which place their highest value in maximum private profit, became the center of economic, social, and political policy.

By 1993, more than $1.8 billion had been cut from federal housing spending, with no new funding for affordable housing. Many provinces followed with their own cuts. Political leaders claimed that government withdrawal from housing programs and funding would "free" private housing markets to make new investments. Private housing markets did boom (until the global recession of 2008 triggered a meltdown in housing markets). Many profited handsomely.

As the private markets in housing boomed, the governmental responsibility for homemaking faded. Inequality and inequity boomed, as did mass homelessness and housing insecurity.

The 1993 federal election saw the return of a Liberal government—the same party that twenty years earlier launched Canada's successful national housing strategy. Liberal Paul Martin had toured the country before the election, calling for a renewed federal role in housing programs and funding. Yet after the election, Paul Martin, as finance minister, embraced the market-based economic orthodoxy of the day, and his government continued to erode federal housing funding and programs through the 1990s.

The federal government's departure from housing programs and funding, with its decision to neglect its obligation to realize the housing rights of all people, had a profound impact on people and communities. By 1998, the mayors of Canada's largest cities, acting at the urging of homeless advocates, declared homelessness a national disaster and called for federal relief. Local municipalities were facing an escalation in local homeless encampments as they struggled to deal with the fallout from the growing devotion to the ideology of private markets.

While governments in Canada and in many parts of the world were cutting initiatives aimed at ensuring equitable access to good homes, the facts on the ground demonstrated that private housing markets could not, and would not, meet the housing needs of a growing number of Canadians.

And so, there were downs, and then some ups, in housing policies and funding in the early years of the twenty-first century. Advocates, including churches, began a relentless campaign for a rights-based approach to housing. In 2017, after concerted pressure from these advocates, the federal government announced a multiyear, multibillion dollar National Housing Strategy. There are some important achievements in this latest National Housing Strategy, but on the basic metric of number of new homes created, it falls well short of the 1973 program.

While Canada's housing crisis and homelessness disaster is nationwide, the funding was targeted to a handful of large urban areas. The financial commitment seems impressive: the latest numbers from the federal government promise $82 billion over multiple years. But the flurry of political pronouncements have not generated a significant number of new homes, nor have the press releases stopped the growth of homeless encampments in large cities and small towns and even in rural areas.

All, however, is not bleak. Two years after the strategy was announced, and after a decade-long campaign by secular and faith-based housing advocates, Canada's Parliament formally adopted the internationally recognized right to housing into national law in 2019. New Democrat MP Libby Davies had worked with many outside Parliament over the previous ten years to enshrine this international right in Canadian law.

This is an important achievement. Even though a Canadian helped to draft the Universal Declaration of Human Rights in 1948, the right to housing never made it into Canadian law until June 21, 2019, when the National Housing Strategy Act was proclaimed.

Governments come and go, and politics sweep and sway. Economic, social, and cultural forces rise up and dominate our lives and the lives of our communities. The human right to housing is a moral calling to rise above politics, to rise above business as usual, and to fully embrace our duty to respect each other in profound and practical ways.

THE PROPHETIC AND MORAL VOICE IN 2023 AND BEYOND

The duty of Christians to raise their prophetic and moral voices has not been superseded by the 2019 parliamentary decision to bring the internationally recognized right to housing into Canadian law. Proclaiming the right to a home is a major step forward. Now, more urgently than ever, *churches and people of faith need to enter the public square with confidence, to seek to ensure that the newly recognized right is fully realized.*

The first task is to speak truth to power, to challenge the "culture of displacement, exile and homelessness," the powers and principalities that grimly and effectively generate more housing insecurity and homelessness.

"Shout out, do not hold back! Lift up your voice like a trumpet!" says the prophet Isaiah (Isa 58:1).

Afflicting the comfortable, forcing them to regard the needs and human rights of others, is an ancient and important calling. In the parable of Lazarus and the rich man (Luke 16:19–31), we read of a poor man who sits hungry and in poor health at the very doorstep of a rich man. Lazarus dies and ascends with angels to be with Abraham. The rich man dies and falls into a fiery pit. The rich man was not being punished for being a bad rich man. He was a busy rich man, fully occupied with the business of his household. Even in the afterlife, his concern is for his immediate family, that his brothers might be forewarned and avoid a similar fate. The sin of the rich man was neglect. He didn't even notice poor Lazarus at his doorstep.

That is the sin of many contemporary economic, political, social, and cultural structures. They are consumed with themselves and do not regard the lives and needs of others outside their circle.

The second task of the faithful is to put loving-kindness into practical action—feeding the hungry, housing the homeless, comforting the afflicted. The church often does a very good job in this, but too often falls into the charity trap, letting governments and others shrug off their responsibilities. So, practical actions fused with a commitment to justice: that is the way forward.

The focus needs to be enlarged from house-building to homemaking, the rebuilding of communities with a wide web of belonging. House-building is about physical structures; homemaking is about people and their value, dignity, and diversity of needs: physical, security, cultural, economic, and spiritual.

The ancient message from the sacred Scripture of many traditions is that we belong together. As we realize that sense of reciprocity in tangible ways, then we can also realize the words of Isaiah: "Your ancient ruins shall be rebuilt; you shall raise up the foundations of many generations; you shall be called the repairer of the breach, the restorer of streets to live in" (Isa 58:12).

BIBLIOGRAPHY

Basford, Ron. "House of Commons Debates, 29th Parliament, 1st Session : Vol. 2." Library of Parliament, orig. pub. March 15, 1973. https://parl.canadiana.ca/view/oop.debates_HOC2901_02/1105.

Bouma-Prediger, Steven, and Brian J. Walsh. *Beyond Homelessness: Christian Faith in a Culture of Displacement.* Grand Rapids: Eerdmans, 2008.

"How Many People Are Homeless in Canada?" Homeless Hub. https://www.homelesshub.ca/about-homelessness/homelessness-101/how-many-people-are-homeless-canada.

Hulchanski, David. "Did the Weather Cause Canada's Mass Homelessness? Homeless-Making Processes And Canada's Homeless-Makers." TSpace, Mar 2000. https://tspace.library.utoronto.ca/handle/1807/126268.

———. "Homelessness in Canada: Past, Present, Future." Toronto Disaster Relief Committee, Feb 18, 2009. http://www.tdrc.net/uploads/file/2009_hulchanski.pdf.

Rauschenbusch, Walter. *A Theology for the Social Gospel.* Louisville: Westminster John Knox, 1997.

Temple, William. *Christianity and Social Order.* London: Shepheard-Walwyn, 1987.

17

Ecojustice and Mission

Thoughts on a Relevant Missional Terminology

KENNETH GRAY

LANGUAGE IS IMPORTANT. The language humans use to communicate is broad, ranging from small talk, to academic arguments able to communicate complex ideas supported by research and analysis. Analytical language requires the skill of lawyers, politicians, and policy makers, of scholars, and of content creators of all sorts, some holding influential positions while others speak from more humble spaces. This is true in the church and in other faith communities. In the Anglican literary and spiritual trove, names such as C. S. Lewis and Annie Dillard are now accompanied by the likes of Rowan Williams, Barbara Brown-Taylor, and Malcolm Guite. All these authors use words to bring worlds to life for readers and listeners as they draw from the Western European literary tradition. The increasing attention paid to global authors continues to enrich the content of theological, philosophical, and missional dialogue.[1]

Words, even individual words, can function as rallying points and icons for generations and movements. Think, for instance, of words or couplets like *hippie, neoliberal, space-age, populist, religious, woke,* or *capitalist.* Used inappropriately, they can insult, stigmatize, and injure. Used well, they can serve as fulcrums for movements and causes. Closer to the theme of this collection are words like *justice, partnership,* and *mission.* In today's

---

1. See Beros et al., *International Handbook on Creation Care.*

hyper-connected world, there is no shortage of opportunity to probe and explore each of these terms in order to discover and compare our experience of faith and (in)justice. Through partnership, as part of both a global communion and a national church, Canadian Anglicans can transcend and celebrate the gift of cultural differences as we share God's witness-in-Christ all over the world.

Such conversation, however, is not always easy. Yet even when serious disagreements erupt, tension can lead to a fruitful outcome when the conversation occurs in a context of trust and inclusivity. I think of the varying, though growing, support of LGBTQ2S+ persons and communities worldwide. I recall the energy of the Jubilee 2000 Initiative which advocated for new economic realities for heavily-indebted countries and for reform within the World Bank system. I celebrate the growing influence of healing and reconciliation initiatives between Indigenous peoples and settlers in Canada. The church must work hard to foster such a welcoming and safe conversational space for peace and justice to appear.

CHURCH AND SOCIETY

The Anglican Church of Canada remains a forum for social and ecological justice debate, but there is considerable rivalry between the two, a competition highlighted when the funding of programs occurs. Such decisions regarding the distribution of fiscal and human resources were a large part of Ellie Johnson's responsibility as director of Partnerships, and later during her time as interim general secretary. The availability of resources has often been stretched in our church, affecting dioceses and parishes as well as General Synod, and no less so in the present moment. Fiscal challenges, however, are not all bad. Colloquially, I hear from clergy colleagues that our church is at its best when we fret not on how much we possess, but on how we steward what we have been given.

If finances sometime stretch our ability to witness, our sphere of influence has also subsided in recent years. The church operates more on the sidelines of secular life than it once did. Even in the UK, where the Church of England is an established political entity, its influence and ability to garner respect is increasingly diminished. In Canada our reputation and influence shrinks day by day. Take the press, for instance, who in Canada typically pay attention to church-related matters when personnel are under sanction or discipline. In the Global South, by comparison, especially in regions of South Africa that I have visited, the church is still held in high regard and considered authoritative. Today, the Canadian church faces a particular challenge: How might we extend our witness to all Canadians and our global partners, especially regarding creation care and the climate crisis? With what language and images should we speak? Put another way, in places where it is possible to speak of faith in the public square,[2] how might thinkers, teachers and influencers powerfully and accurately describe the need for social and environmental justice?

I will argue in what follows that the church needs new missional language to strengthen our witness and assist our own reflection and understanding. The time is surely ripe to develop and reshape our language in a way that connects with current realities and with the passions of those who can contemplate the common good. We need to find fresh post-colonial speech and breath, a language which does not require social and economic power to drive change, which inspires and convinces, is inclusive of all creation, and connects to the "heart's desire" (Pss 37:4, 20:4; Matt 6:21) of humanity and of all creation. I suggest that the single term *ecojustice* is a timely, effective, and persuasive term that can explain, inspire, and move us towards the destination to which we all must travel.

THE TERM: ECOJUSTICE

When the General Synod Ecojustice Committee was formed in 1995, its name was changed on the floor of General Synod from the "Social Justice" to the "Ecojustice" Committee, to reflect a wholistic or ecological framework from which to pursue justice issues. The change owes much to the efforts of then General Synod staffers Peter Hamel and Joy Kennedy.[3] It was a name that leapt ahead of its time, but sadly is no longer in use. Instead, General Synod now uses the language of *public witness*, a term that describes an advocacy process, but lacks a focus for that witness. There are obvious limits to the effectiveness of a single term in attempting to unite social and ecological concerns. It was the late Dr. Christopher Lind who opined, "Adopting the language of ecojustice does not end all debates. It signals a profound shift in thinking, and makes new solutions possible."[4] A colleague, mentor, teacher, and friend, Lind first challenged me to consider the value—and the spelling—of ecojustice. Today, the word is variously found as "eco-justice," "EcoJustice," "Ecojustice," or "ecojustice." For Lind, the issue was the letter J. If J is capitalized, *eco* is simply a prefix indicating a particular form or

2. For views of Canadians on faith in the public square see "Faith in the Public Square?" Also see Williams, *Faith in the Public Square*.

3. In conversation with Peter Hamel.

4. See Lind, "Ecojustice," 1–3.

subspecies of justice. To retain the word in lowercase form–"ecojustice"– suggests some sort of organic union between the experience of earth as our home (*eco* from the Greek word *oikos*, meaning family, house, or household) with the necessary appeal for justice, meaning right relationships.

Lind shaped his findings in a curriculum for a November 2007 synod of the Anglican Diocese of Niagara. Having explained the growing theological focus on Creation from the 1960s onwards, during a time when American Protestants increasingly raised concerns about the health of the planet and pointed to destructive human effects on sensitive ecosystems, Lind cites the German Protestant theologian Jurgen Moltmann: "What we call the environmental crisis is not merely a crisis in the natural environment of human beings. It is nothing less than a crisis in human beings themselves. It is a crisis of life on this planet. . . . As far as we can judge, it is the beginning of a life and death struggle for creation on this earth."[5]

Regarding his own stance, Lind writes, "I have become convinced that the developing concept of ecojustice can be a way forward, beyond the false dichotomy of social justice vs. ecological justice, as long as it is understood as a term that can include both human suffering and the groaning of the Earth." He continues: "Speaking as someone who comes to this debate after decades of involvement in issues of social justice, I can say that the movement to an Earth-centred consciousness is as profound a challenge as I have encountered."[6] Given his previous work on the *Moral Economy*,[7] he extends his purview to include Creation. "All life has moral value and therefore a claim on humans as moral agents. Again, from a Christian point of view, all Creation comes from God and all Creation bears the marks of God. Creation gives witness to the Creator (Acts 14:17) and makes plain God's power and nature (Rom 1:19–20)."[8]

Lind goes on to explain the Earth Bible Project, conceived by Dr. Norman Habel, a biblical scholar from Flinders University in Adelaide, who developed a set of six ecojustice principles for interpreting sacred texts—for example, *the principle of voice* (earth is a subject capable of raising its voice in celebration and against injustice) and *the principle of resistance* (earth and its components not only suffer from injustices at the hands of humans, but actively resist them in the struggle for justice).[9]

5. Lind, "Ecojustice," 2.

6. Lind, "Ecojustice," 2.

7. Lind, *Rumours of a Moral Economy*; Habel, *Inconvenient Text*, 60–63.

8. Lind, "Ecojustice," 3.

9. Nieuwerth et al., *Every Part of Creation Matters*.

MOVING TO AN EARTH-CENTERED CONSCIOUSNESS

Other scholars have followed similar paths. A discussion paper *Every Part of Creation Matters*, published by the Conference of European Churches, argues, "We suggest an eco-centric spirituality in which humanity is part of creation and in which we rethink our place within it." The authors seek "common ground with others concerned by injustice and [urge] deep social, political, and economic change as we know that the burden of ecological crises will fall disproportionately on the poorest and on those whose lives are yet to come." They argue for a "Christocentric understanding of the relationship between God and the world [that] leads to a new ethos, where everything that exists constitutes an element of loving communion, necessary for the divine plan to become true."[10]

In his 2010 Sarum Lectures, Richard Bauckham joins together recent earth science understanding with the Biblical text. "The biblical writers did not, of course, know what recent science has taught us about the ways in which these complex interrelationships work. (We ourselves are doubtless only near the beginning of this contemporary journey of scientific understanding, which is steadily revealing more and more aspects of the delicate web of creation within which we belong.) But the Bible does evince a strong sense of the interconnectedness of all creatures and relates this to their common dependence on God their Creator."[11]

The Rev. Stan McKay, former moderator of the United Church of Canada, breathes the spirit of Ezek 37:9: "Prophesy to the breath, prophesy, mortal, and say to the breath: Thus says the Lord God: Come from the four winds, O breath, and breathe upon these slain, that they may live." McKay writes, "It is said that when the four winds blow the people will be healed and the Earth will be healed. . . . The elders teach that you must include Creation in the conversations about reconciliation and healing."[12] Such an understanding opens up a new conversation and appreciation of the relationships found within what many call the *web of creation*.

During a trip to South Africa in 2002 I was introduced to the concept of *Ubuntu*, "I am, because we are." This single word describes an experience of community, where the ultimate hope for justice is expressed in a context of trust and social reciprocity, in a forum of shared values and assumptions. It is now possible—actually it is necessary—to extend such a practice and

10. Nieuwerth et al., *Every Part of Creation Matters*, 12, 27.

11. Bauckham, *Bible and Ecology*, ix.

12. McKay, "All My Relations," 159.

understanding beyond human relations to the relationship between humans and Creation.

Turning to the arts, and especially photography, as a novice photographer I typically placed human subjects in the center of the camera viewfinder when composing an image. Such a strategy made the human figure the most important element in the resulting portrait. I have since learned that interesting portrait photography is environmental, where the human figure still appears in the frame though in a manner that allows other elements of the setting to be clearly seen and observed.

I now experiment with placement of the human in relation to other elements—the natural environment, furniture and decor, the task at hand such as carpentry or fiber-art creation. The result is visually rewarding and more interesting and informative. I see this same dynamic in conversations around ecojustice generally. To keep the human central in conversations around resource management, for instance, often at the expense of nonhuman creatures, continues to protect and privilege human needs and wants over and above all other claims for care and attention. The word *ecojustice* creates a "new frame" for viewing the community of the planet, where humanity finds its proper place within creation and is no longer considered the sole focus and primary subject of creation.

THE WORLD COUNCIL OF CHURCHES

For decades the World Council of Churches has sought to advocate for right relationships between people and the earth. "The Christian perspective that has valued humanity over the rest of creation has served to justify the exploitation of parts of the earth community."[13] Their work exposes a sinister competition between the gifts and needs of creation itself, especially as human ingenuity continues to develop more "efficient" extractive processes, against the ability of the earth to rejuvenate itself. Creation can respond and adapt to some human practices, but we now see more clearly the limits of such resilience in light of human overconsumption and ecological exploitation. "Human existence is utterly dependent on a healthy functioning earth system. Humanity cannot manage creation. Humanity can only manage their own behaviour to keep it within the bounds of earth's sustenance."[14]

The positive contribution of the World Council of Churches, especially around the theme of justice, peace, and the integrity of creation, cannot be overstated. During the WCC Vancouver Assembly of 1983, and

13. World Council Of Churches, "Statement On Eco-Justice," para. 3.
14. World Council Of Churches, "Statement On Eco-Justice," para. 3.

continuing with the establishment of the Climate Change Programme in 1998, the WCC gave ecojustice work high priority, "as part of a common effort to promote Justice, Peace, and the Integrity of Creation . . . and to promote the transformation of socioeconomic structures and personal life-style choices that contribute to global warming." A more recent declaration, entitled "Listening to the Cries of Mother Earth: Towards a New Spirituality of Respectful Co-Existence," was presented on Earth Day, April 22, 2010, by a coalition of ecumenical organizations including the WCC. It declares, in part, "the desire to increase wealth, the comfort of a luxurious lifestyle, con-sumerism, indiscriminate exploitation of natural resources and pollution of air, water and soil have brought our planet Earth to the edge of climate breakdown. . . . We call, together with indigenous peoples and their wisdom, for a deep conversion of the ruling paradigm and of oppressive structures, as well as our mentality, attitudes and way of life, so as to bring our lives into harmony with Nature, the cosmos and the great mystery of life."[15]

This beautiful and prescriptive language helps us to appreciate and ar-ticulate a mutual, organic, and reciprocal relationship between human and nonhuman species within Creation. If the unifying term *ecojustice* can claim any effect on the speech and actions of policymakers in the church and elsewhere, it behooves me to suggest some instances where such language has already had good effect. It is helpful to see how organizations are using ecojustice language in programming decisions and in advocacy positions.

ECOJUSTICE IN ACTION

Since its formation in 2003, the Catherine Donnelly Foundation, a Ca-nadian lay-religious alliance, has been supporting programs "designed to promote social and ecological justice and to engage those that have been overlooked and excluded."[16] They now promote an ecojustice approach that represents "an inseparable bond between nature, justice for the marginal-ized, a commitment to society and reconciliation with Inuit, First Nations and Métis people."[17]

I first encountered the Christian Reformed Church's Committee for Justice and Liberty while a student during 1979. Now reconfigured as Citi-zens for Public Justice (CPJ) based in Ottawa, they continue to advocate for public justice throughout Canada, including environmental justice. CPJ describes its approach as follows:

15. "World People's Conference," paras. 1, 4.
16. "Story of CDF."
17. "Our Work."

The biblical foundations for creation care unite spirituality with scientific, ecological, and political insights. Through a sense of wonder with creation, we are invited to seek God's will for a flourishing ecological community. In the face of climate change, this need has never been more urgent. . . .

We must take a holistic approach that respects the rights of Indigenous peoples, considers the health of the economy, the well-being of plants and animals in our natural environment, as well as sustainable livelihoods, health of individuals, families, communities and future generations.[18]

One final example of effective integration of social and ecological advocacy is the Anglican Franciscans, a worldwide community in three orders, all drawing strength and focus from the story of St. Francis (1181–1226), recently brought to prominence through the writings of Pope Francis, SSF. Of creation, justice, and peace, the community proclaims, "[Francis] had an intuitive grasp of the relationship between all the parts of creation, and their creator. Everything in creation is part of an intricate web created by God. Each part speaks of God's presence and purpose. This presence and purpose is best expressed when all parts of creation are in right relationship with each other and witness to the peace and righteousness which is God's will for creation."[19]

Religious communities and individual authors from both Catholic and Protestant traditions continue to integrate ecojustice demands and advocacy as part of their spiritual life. In his 2023 BBC Reith lecture, former Archbishop of Canterbury Rowan Williams sets the scene: "A private oil company has seized some farmland to build a natural gas pipeline. The landowners are not happy and have gone to Court. So far, so familiar, but here's what's unusual, the farmland belongs to a Catholic women's religious order, and the nuns have argued that the pipeline violates their rights to liberty, specifically religious liberty. 'Every day since October 2018,' said one of the sisters, 'as fossil fuel and gas flows through our farmland, so also flows Transco's blatant disregard and trampling of our religious beliefs.'"[20]

18. "Climate Justice," paras. 1, 5.
19. "Creation, Justice and Peace," para. 1.
20. For lecture transcript, see Rowan, "Lecture 2."

BEYOND ECOJUSTICE? HEALING JUSTICE!

In those situations where ecojustice can effectively unite ecological and social justice in a binding whole, it remains possible that any outcome might simply be a mechanical or political solution, something like a negotiated settlement. There is an important difference between an agreement such as an armistice, and a new and strengthened relationship of former enemies possibly including postwar Vietnam. In historical terms, how might the First World War have ended more justly? More recently how might the civil rights movement in the US have brought persons of mixed race into a deeper and stronger relationship instead of simply allowing for social integration. Might some of the current racially motivated violence have never occurred? From the perspective of 2023 how might the invasion of Ukraine be ended, with justice for all and the real prospect of peace? Present tensions on the Korean Peninsula since 1953 continue to threaten an increasingly fragile and tenuous peace.

Justice requires the mending of relationships, the practice of truth-telling, and a persistent desire to live, move, and breathe better, now, and at all times. Peacemaking, ecojustice, healing, and reconciliation form a powerful transformative unit. The Canadian Anglican Church has learned so much in facing the legacy of the residential schools. Certainly response varies from place to place. Yes, racism often catches me off guard, but in my experience I increasingly find that people are curious about Indigenous peoples and are keen to learn from and move beyond the mistakes of history. In my lifetime I have seen significant healing in the Anglican Church among Indigenous peoples and settlers. The emerging Indigenous Anglican Church is but one example of ongoing reconciliation.

As a former resident of Kamloops, British Columbia, I remember the announcement of the 215 burial sites at the Kamloops Indian Residential School in 2021. For a few days, life in that city of one hundred thousand people slowed down and took a deep breath. How might ecojustice encourage such a reflective breath as it names the struggle for justice and encourages the work of relationship building? Jaren Sawatsky, a onetime university professor, author, and researcher in peace and conflict studies who now lives with Huntington's Disease through which he views life and healing, argues that healing justice will offer opportunities and a way forward in the pursuit of justice and peace. Specifically, he brings together spirit with land: "Healing justice does not begin with states and institutions. Healing justice . . . begins and ends with the Spirit and the land. . . . This kind of justice is not primarily about social control but more about cultivating a life that acknowledges and responds to the gift, beauty, and fragility of life."[21]

Sawatsky includes a poem by Rebeka Tabobondung, a beautiful reflection on healing, reconciliation, suffering, lament, and tears.[22] I quote the poem in full as I will use the text in my final section in this essay, an inquiry into how ecojustice and healing figure in the rebuilding of the town of Lytton, British Columbia, following its destruction in 2021.

Reconciliation

We are waking up to our history
from a forced slumber
We are breathing it into our lungs
so it will be part of us again
It will make us angry at first
because we will see how much you stole from us
and for how long you watched us suffer
we will see how you see us
and how when we copied your ways
we killed our own.

We will cry and cry and cry
because we can never be the same again
But we will go home to cry
and we will see ourselves in this huge mess
and we will gently whisper the circle back
and it will be old and it will be new.

Then we will breathe our history back to you
you will feel how strong and alive it is
and you will feel yourself become a part of it
And it will shock you at first
because it is too big to see all at once
and you won't want to believe it
you will see how you see us
and all the disaster in your ways
how much we lost.

---

21. Sawatsky, *Healing Justice*, 123.

22. Sawatsky, *Healing Justice*, 120. The poem opens the book *Nation to Nation: Aboriginal Sovereignty and the Future of Canada*.

And you will cry and cry and cry
because we can never be the same again
But we will cry with you
and we will see ourselves in this huge mess
and we will gently whisper the circle back
and it will be old and it will be new.
(Rebeka Tabobondung, 2002)

ECOJUSTICE AND HEALING AT LYTTON, BRITISH COLUMBIA, CANADA

On June 30, 2021, wildfire destroyed the village of Lytton, British Columbia, a historic settlement especially for Indigenous people nestled in the Fraser Canyon in the British Columbia Interior. The fire erupted as part of a "heat dome" causing temperatures to rise as high as 49.6 degrees Celsius (an all-time Canadian record). Ninety percent of the village was destroyed. Two years later, progress towards rebuilding remains slow and frustrating for residents and community leaders alike.

The cultural tapestry of Lytton is complex and beautiful. Living alongside the descendants of settlers, Lytton First Nation (LFN) is located on 14,161 acres of land divided into fifty-six reserves. The reserves are located at the site of the Indian village of Kumsheen, meaning "where the Rivers Cross." According to the LFN website, "the Lytton First Nation is a culturally orientated, secure community with a strong community identity and sense of place. The vision of Lytton First Nation is to have a viable residential community with the foresight, and resources to meet new challenges and opportunities in accomplishing its mission." The vision of the community is inclusive and dynamic: "Lytton First Nation will continue to practice mutually beneficial relationships with local, provincial and federal governing bodies. These in combination, will achieve the desired quality of life. To serve the best interest of our Tl'kemtsin Nation by preserving, promoting our cultural heritage, and building a healthy and a sustainable economy through transparent and good governance."[23]

Given the destruction of the village and the effects on those presently living elsewhere who hope to return, the question remains—how can settler and Indigenous communities function best as plans for rebuilding emerge. Also, how have environmental, social, economic, and bureaucratic factors blended together? A quick examination of the town of Lytton and Lytton

23. "About Us."

First Nation websites suggests two different worldviews, each with little reference to the other. At least online, the two are not yet one.

Speaking with the local Anglican priest, the Rev. Angus Muir,[24] I learned that the recovery and rebuilding progress has been very slow to respond to the immediate and future needs of all residents and those living nearby. After the customary photo ops with provincial and federal government officials, tangible results are hard to find. Necessary archaeological work has hampered access to sites—in several instances property owners are required to submit site development plans without the ability to physically examine the site itself. Multiple layers of bureaucracy have intersected poorly creating mistrust, frustration, and occasionally anger. Relationships have been strained everywhere. One could well say that such tension is typical of post-catastrophic experience, though that does not mean that such behavior is acceptable or that such frustration is inevitable. For Angus, "Lytton has been a failure for government, and the people suffer."

I cannot imagine a community more aware of the healing and reconciliation journey than Lytton and area First Nations. Truth and reconciliation are familiar words in church, coffee shops, and online.

> The New England Company, a missionary organization associated with the Church of England, opened the St. George's [Indian Residential School] in Lytton, British Columbia in 1901. The school had ongoing sanitation, fire safety, and overcrowding problems. An influenza epidemic at the school over the 1926–1927 school year led to the deaths of thirteen children. During the 1930s, runaways were forced to march back to the school ahead of the principal who drove behind in his car. . . . In 1993, a former St. George's employee pled guilty to charges of sexually abusing students at the school when he worked there.[25]

The legacy of physical, sexual, cultural, and emotional abuse at the school is legendary and dark, and it continues to affect survivors and their descendants to this day.

Lytton residents have known despair before. How then might some of the words of the Tabobondung poem help Lytton come back to life? I am not qualified to suggest solutions. This role falls to others, such as pastoral elders Ernie and Pauline Michell (Sn'k'yep and Quey'stala) who initiated a prayer walk through town, done with a unified healing voice, as "one people" working together . . . some have now understood that particular plea.

---

24. Angus Muir, email to the author.

25. "St. George's."

But we will go home to cry
and we will see ourselves in this huge mess
and we will gently whisper the circle back
and it will be old and it will be new.

While disaster sometimes brings people and communities together, the opposite can also become real. Lytton Creek fire survivor Michele Feist worries divisions will form among people affected differently by the catastrophe.

> I worry that there's becoming various categories of people that could divide us. There's the people who lost their houses, the people who didn't lose their houses, people on the west side of the river who still have their places but they've lost the community. And people all around because Lytton was a hub for 3,000 people. So they've all lost, even if they've got a home. I know people that want to rebuild, that are trying to rebuild. I also know people that just want to put it all behind them. I'm somewhere in the middle.[26]

LAND AND SPIRIT

And then . . . there is the land—how might it recover? Has the relationship between the land, humanity, and creation changed following the fires? Can Indigenous and settler communities unite not just with each other, but in a unique way with the land upon which they depend, the land which they love? If the earth is resilient, how might such God-given energy affect all who gather in this sacred place? Where and how is healing justice to be found? Again, Sawatsky:

> Healing justice does not begin with states and institutions. Healing justice . . . begins and ends with the Spirit and the land . . . If one wants to create and sustain a healing kind of justice, one needs to be in a particular relationship with Spirit and land. Both Spirit and land push a sense of justice beyond the individual orientation and beyond the state orientation. In fact, this kind of justice is not primarily about social control but more about cultivating a life that acknowledges and responds to the gift, beauty, and fragility of life.[27]

---

26. Feist, "Back of My Head," para. 22.
27. Sawatsky, *Healing Justice*, 123.

Beyond Lytton and the experiences of all affected, in a more general way how might we "all return home?" Do we know where "home" is? In the midst of a global and local mess, how might we see ourselves in a new way? And how shall we speak as we gently whisper the circle back? Old and new unite in the present. Ecojustice will become more present, more real, more inclusive, and more effective, if and when we make healing in every sense a priority. As we all pay attention to what is there before us, drawing others into this same orbit, justice can and will be done. All my relations.

BIBLIOGRAPHY

"About Us." Lytton First Nation. https://lfn.band/about-us.

Bauckham, Richard. *Bible And Ecology: Rediscovering the Community of Creation.* London: Darton, Longman and Todd, 2016.

Beros, Daniel, et al. *International Handbook on Creation Care and Eco-Diakonia: Concepts and Theological Perspectives of Churches from the Global South.* Oxford: Regnum Books International, 2022. https://www.ocms.ac.uk/wp-content/uploads/2022/07/Handbook-of-Creation-Care-and-Eco-Diakonia-PDF-for-distribution-A.pdf.

Bird, John, et al., eds. *Nation to Nation: Aboriginal Sovereignty and the Future of Canada.* Toronto, ON: Anansi, 1998.

"Climate Justice." CPJ. https://cpj.ca/climate-justice/.

"Creation, Justice and Peace." Society of Saint Francis. https://anglicanfranciscans.org/index.php/creation-justice-and-peace.

"Faith in the Public Square? A Comprehensive Study of the Segments of Canadian Society." Angus Reid Institute, Nov 23, 2018. https://angusreid.org/public-faith-debate/.

Feist, Michele. "I Knew in the Back of My Head That Lytton Was Gone." The Tyee, May 22, 2023. https://thetyee.ca/News/2023/05/22/Michele-Feist-Wildfire-Escape/.

Habel, Norman. *An Inconvenient Text: Is a Green Reading of the Bible Possible?* Hindmarsh, SA: Australian Theological Forum, 2009.

Lind, Christopher. "Ecojustice: A Presentation." Synod of the Diocese of Niagara, Nov 2007. https://niagaraanglican.ca/climatejustice/docs/animating/LIND_NiagaraEcoJustice_v3web.pdf.

——. *Rumours of a Moral Economy.* Winnipeg, MN: Fernwood, 2010.

McKay, Stan. "All My Relations: Living Respectfully on the Earth with All Creation." In *For the Sake of the Common Good: Essays in Honour of Lois Wilson,* edited by Kate Merriman and Bertha Yetman, 159–68. Montreal: McGill-Queens University Press, 2022.

Nieuwerth, Kees, et al., eds. *Every Part of Creation Matters: A Discussion Paper.* Geneva: Conference of European Churches, 2022. https://www.globethics.net/documents/10131/26882184/GE_CEC_8_isbn9782889314904.pdf.

"Our Work: Environment." Catherine Donnelly Foundation. https://catherinedonnellyfoundation.org/our-work/environment/#why-we-support-change.

Sawatsky, Jarem. *Healing Justice: Stories of Wisdom and Love.* Toronto: Red Canoe, 2018.

"St. George's (Lytton)." National Centre for Truth and Reconciliation. https://nctr.ca/residential-schools/british-columbia/st-georges-lytton/.

"The Story of CDF." Catherine Donnelly Foundation. https://catherinedonnellyfoundation.org/who-we-are/our-story/.

Williams, Rowan. *Faith in the Public Square*. London: Bloomsbury Continuum, 2015.

———. "Lecture 2: Freedom of Worship." By Anita Anand. *The Reith Lectures 2022: The Four Freedoms*, BBC, 2022. https://downloads.bbc.co.uk/radio4/reith2022/Reith_2022_Lecture2.pdf.

World Council of Churches. "Statement on Eco-Justice and Ecological Debt." Geneva, Sep 2, 2009. https://www.ecocongregationireland.com/2009/09/04/world-council-of-churches-issues-statement-on-eco-justice/.

"World People's Conference on Climate Change and the Rights of Mother Earth: Listen to the Cry of Mother Earth—Towards a New Spirituality of Respectful Co-Existence." *Earthcaremission's Blog* (blog), Dec 8, 2010. https://earthcaremission.wordpress.com/2010/12/08/ecumenical-declaration-presented-at-the-world-people%E2%80%99s-conference-on-climate-change-and-the-rights-of-mother-earth-listen-to-the-cry-of-mother-earth-%E2%80%93-towards-a-new-spirituality-of-res/.

18

The Mission and Hope of Ecojustice
A Franciscan Perspective[1]

JEFF GOLLIHER

WHEN TAKING UP A new challenge, or taking up the same challenge again, hoping to be more effective, it is wise to proceed on solid spiritual ground. Otherwise, frustration will quickly build, and we will give up, or give in to discouragement. For that reason, we need to discern what "solid ground" means in practice—and why it seems so difficult to find in these disruptive times of climate and ecological emergency.

I am writing from a personal, Franciscan perspective. The word "personal" here does not mean "subjective" as opposed to "objective." Rather, it involves the whole of our experience and the *conversion of life*, which is the penitential heart of the order's *charism*. Exemplified by St. Francis and St. Clare, a life lived in this way is a journey with Christ. It helps us to recover our diminished humanity and to rediscover (or remember) our shared existence within the whole fabric of life. Both are interwoven dimensions of our challenge to create effective ministries in ecojustice.

I remember hearing about Navajo elders who perceived us, the colonizers, as having a weak, rather than a healthy, sense of self. We're so wrapped up in ourselves that we're disconnected from the sacred reality

1. For their editorial assistance and support, I would like to thank Janet Fedders, Asha Golliher, Ken Gray, Rachel Mash, Masud Syedullah, chapter members of TSSF in the Province of the Americas, and the minister general and minister provincials of the global Provinces of the Third Order.

we all share. I also think of Dietrich Bonhoeffer, the Lutheran martyr and resister of Nazism. His simple words—"life together"—point us in the right direction. St. Francis and St. Clare in the 1200s wanted to live holy and respectful lives, so they struggled to unwrap themselves from the crusading forms of domination that emerged in their time. They struggled to find solid spiritual ground, and they succeeded.

We are mistaken to believe that crusading and colonizing are relics of the past. "Settler colonialism" has been replaced by "extractive" or "resource colonialism," in which the political and economic exploitation of people and the land continues in pursuit of profit. The "invisible hand" of Wall Street has become the world's moral compass. The guiding principle offered in this chapter is that effective ecojustice depends on how willing we are to find solid spiritual ground, which depends, in turn, on our willingness to decolonize ourselves.

HOPE AND MISSION IN THESE UNTHINKABLE TIMES

According to Paulo Freire, genuine hope must be grounded in the truth about the reality we face.[2] If we avoid that, fearing that "too much reality" will throw us off course, then our efforts are based on an illusion of hope. Our words become just "talk," whether in everyday conversations or on policy levels. We treat the symptoms, rather than the causes. Freire's perspective resonates with the lives of St. Francis and St. Clare, suggesting that true hope requires us to discern not only the difference between morally right and wrong, but also our illusions and delusions.

Let's consider our global crisis in the context of Freire's understanding of hope. We are already living in a climate emergency, which is the outcome of greenhouse gas emissions combined with economic exploitation and habitat destruction. The work of the United Nations demonstrates that the whole fabric of life is affected: food and agriculture, water, energy, economics, human rights, poverty, gender, race, migration and refugees, land use, and population growth. According to the UN, carbon emissions must be halved by 2030 and reduced to zero no later than 2045 or 2050 to prevent a total catastrophe. Some scientists suggest that this time frame could be understated and that "tipping points" may be reached sooner than predicted. We live in a period of earth history called the "sixth great extinction." A recent UNESCO analysis reports that over one million species currently

2. Freire, *Pedagogy of the Oppressed* and *Pedagogy of Hope*.

face extinction. The number of climate refugees will continue to rise dramatically reaching into the millions each year.

In light of Freire's teaching, the recent work of Wallace-Wells[3] takes on unexpected significance, together with the helpful controversy, summarized well by Paoletta,[4] that arose in response to it. Wallace-Wells originally said that unless we take substantial action now, then the earth could become uninhabitable by the end of this century. Scientists generally believe that this time frame for "uninhabitable" is much too soon. Nevertheless, the most recent IPCC report—described as their "final warning"—emphasizes that disastrous changes will likely occur to ecosystems and human life if greenhouse emissions are not halved by 2030 and brought to "net zero" (an ambiguous term) by 2050.[5] The point is that the emergency we face is very real. Are we telling ourselves, in effect, that it's okay to continue basically on our present course—making "some" changes, losing "some" ecosystems, species, and people—while we postpone truly substantial action? "Hope," in that context, means making "some" adjustments in how we live, while keeping everything essentially the same. That amounts to a form of gambling. Our sacred, biblical directive to "care for" God's creation cannot truthfully translate into "gamble with."

We must always discern what scientific reports really mean, but the issue goes deeper than optimism or pessimism about the future. Wallace-Wells actually pointed to the critical challenge before us by his choice of the word "unthinkable" to characterize the consequences of failure. Our climate and ecological emergency represents something that humankind has never faced until now. It might be "thinkable" for members of the scientific community, yet "unthinkable," in a manner of speaking, for the large majority of people. One huge psychological challenge is that those of us who begin to perceive the "unthinkable" possibility often experience denial, grief, and fear that can be disorienting emotionally and intellectually. Our consciousness and conscience are affected, while we are subjected to the profit motives of the media and manipulation by authoritarian powers. This reality must be confronted in order to strengthen our capacity for discernment and faithful, effective action. So, should we debate and discern the nature of the emergency that we face so we can act together? Of course—that's the whole point. Wallace-Wells made an essential contribution by moving the discussion, as Hayhoe (2019) aptly put it, into the mode of "story": a deeply personal, honest testimony that guides our search for solid spiritual

---

3. Wallace-Wells, *Uninhabitable Earth*.

4. Paoletta, "Incredible Disappearing Doomsday."

5. The Core Writing Team, "AR6 Synthesis Report."

ground.[6] That is the story that we should all strive to tell, because we are all living it, for better or worse, each and every day.

As Jamail and Rushworth and others demonstrate, Indigenous peoples are good at discerning the "unthinkable."[7] This is because they're more respectful and aware than we are of the world as a sacred body of life; and they have suffered the disastrous impacts of colonialism for a long time. Until the recent presidency of Lula da Silva in Brazil, who has begun to change the nation's course, the exploitation of Indigenous peoples and their land continued as a result of greed, renewed deforestation, cattle ranching, and gold mining, and they speak out. Julian Brave NoiseCat echoes their cries as the "genocide of colonization and the ecocide of climate change," which go hand in hand.[8] Another Indigenous writer, Natalie Diaz, put it this way: "The Earth [is] telling us it's exhausted. It's ready to start cleaning itself."[9]

In the wake of the 1992 Earth Summit, some economists and cultural analysts clearly perceived the implications of the challenge. The hope was and is that sustainable development guided by human rights and the elimination of poverty could be accomplished in an ecologically sound way. David Korten courageously wrote *When Corporations Rule the World*[10] and *The Great Turning: From Empire to Earth Community*.[11] He hoped for a "Great Turning" away from the "global suicide economy" as he put it. Nevertheless, an intensive process of transnational economic globalization proceeded with little restraint as new forms of extractive colonialism intensified. Governments and corporations often encouraged (and still do) the misleading assumption that the crisis is "manageable" and that we can find technological fixes. More recently, authoritarian governments have flatly rejected the vision of global cooperation on which resolving our shared crisis depends. While some corporations have rejected or ignored the science (often using "corporate greenwashing" as a misleading screen), others have acknowledged the truth and made wise changes in their policies and behavior.

Nearly sixty years ago, Thomas Merton, the renowned Trappist monk, pointed to the last issue we need to consider concerning discernment. His *Conjectures of a Guilty Bystander*[12] was written before the reality of the climate and ecological crisis was widely known. Since that time, it has

6. Hayhoe, "David Wallace-Wells."

7. Jamail and Rushworth, *Middle of Forever*, 290.

8. NoiseCat, "How Indigenous Peoples Are Fighting," para. 1.

9. Diaz in Jamail and Rushworth, *Middle of Forever*, 290.

10. Korten, *When Corporations Rule the World*.

11. Korten, *Great Turning*.

12. Merton, *Conjectures*.

magnified greatly. Our instinctive response when reading the words "guilty bystander" might be something like, "well, that's not me!" There can be some truth in it, despite the fact that the developed world shares the responsibility in different degrees. As much as many people organize and protest, most are still "watching" the crisis unfold. This is how Merton perceived that dilemma in his time:

> The greatest need of our time is to clean out this enormous mass of mental and emotional rubbish that clutters our minds and makes of all political and social life a mass illness. Without this housecleaning we cannot begin to see. Unless we see we cannot think.[13]

He was reflecting on the mass media and its impact on our minds long before the Internet. One might argue that our greatest need is not to clear our own mental rubbish, but to heal Mother Earth. In practice, they go hand in hand. The corporatization of the media since Merton's time and its impact on politics has a profound impact on our life together. Merton was pointing prophetically to one reason why Wallace-Wells described our emergency as "unthinkable." Let's keep in mind that some aspects of Francis's life and experience could have been "unthinkable" for him too. We will see below that his "conversion of life" encourages us to clean out the "rubbish" in our minds and lives so we can discern more clearly. He also laid the groundwork for the "Great Turning" that the whole fabric of life desperately needs.

THE FRANCISCAN "CONVERSION OF LIFE"

Stories about St. Francis offer signposts on a spiritual journey that we, as followers of Christ, are all meant to make.[14] Perhaps the pivotal story took place in the very heart of Assisi. He had been a rowdy youth, a troubadour, a would-be crusader and an imprisoned soldier. After a difficult period of soul searching, St. Francis entered the town square for a public hearing involving money owed to his father. He removed his bourgeois clothing in the presence of the bishop, his father, and many onlookers. That in itself was a proclamation—that he was leaving behind one way of life in search of another. There was no outward appearance of official religious meaning. Yet, the implications would have been self-evident for those who knew and observed him through the eyes of the Spirit.

13. Merton, *Conjectures*, 77.

14. Cowan, *Saint's Way*; Sweeney, *Francis of Assisi*; Sister Joyce, "Walking in the Footsteps."

The Spirit helped St. Francis break through the hard shell that the worldly powers of domination had wrapped around him. Then, after he retreated to a nearby mountain, his deepening soul began to flower. Having once heard the divine voice say, "Rebuild My Church," he began rebuilding the dilapidated church in San Damiano with meaning that must be discerned from the evidence of his life. St. Clare would join him, along with many others. Together, their lives left a distinctive mark on the church and history.

The soul of Francis flowered in many ways: befriending lepers, strangers, and the Wolf of Gubbio, visiting Muslim leaders, and writing the "Canticle of the Creatures." These expressions of his "conversion of life" exemplify the unfolding of a deeply relational "life together," to borrow Bonhoeffer's words. His story contradicts the exploitation of God's creation that has magnified in our day, sometimes applauded as the will of God. St. Francis discovered that to be humanely human is to enter into relationships of kinship with the whole fabric of life.[15] His "conversion" exemplifies what we call "decolonization," revealing the solid spiritual ground on which our lives depend.

In recent times, the UN's work in cultural and biological diversity has been grounded in a similar vision, drawing upon the life of St. Francis, as well as eco-philosophers and Indigenous peoples. In a vision statement arising from the UN's Biodiversity Convention, both biological and cultural diversity are understood as having "intrinsic value," rather than the commodified for-profit value customarily assigned by the marketplace.[16] That same vision is central to the traditions of Indigenous peoples who the Euro-American colonizers once called "savages." In ways that resonate with St. Francis, Chief Oren Lyons (Faithkeeper of the Turtle-Clan, Onondaga Council of Chiefs), who contributed to the UN's work, describes the Indigenous perspective in this way:

> The Lakota end all their prayers with "all my relations." This means more than their families or extended families. It includes all life upon this earth. It is the recognition, respect, and love for the interconnected "web of life" that Chief Seattle spoke of. It is the instruction to the human community of our relationship to the earth.[17]

15. Horan, *Francis of Assisi.*

16. Posey and Darrell, *Cultural and Spiritual Values*; and Golliher, "Church as Renewed Creation."

17. Lyons, Oren. "All My Relations," 450.

St. Francis could have prayed with the Lakota as brothers and sisters. He departed boldly from colonizing assumptions, while remaining true to the Holy Sacraments. His decolonized vision of our life together suggests that the larger "church" is the whole of God's creation in a process of renewal.[18] This includes interfaith relations, issues of racial and gender justice, ecojustice, and "all our relations." Our church buildings and gatherings of the faithful, customarily called "the church," are obviously sacred too. There, we are called "to remember deeply" (in the Greek sense of *anamnesis*) the inward and outward dimensions of our lives in Christ. Jesus instructed us to do precisely that in the Holy Eucharist: "*Do this in remembrance of me.*" The remembering that St. Francis and St. Clare experienced was gradually revealed as their transformed, decolonized lives flowered. This became the essence of the Franciscan charism of *penitence*, which means the *conversion of life*.

FINDING SOLID SPIRITUAL GROUND FOR ECOJUSTICE

We now move more deeply into the essential qualities of a solid spiritual ground on which ecojustice depends—and we must do this at a time when solid ground seems difficult to find. Solid spiritual ground is not disappearing. Rather, the climate and ecological emergency combined with an intensely recolonizing period in history make it seem "unthinkable." For many, this can make the essential teachings of spiritual traditions seem simpleminded or irrelevant, as if they won't help us now. Yet, the life of St. Francis contradicts all kinds of "mental rubbish," as Merton put it. His life reminds us to put our desire to good and holy uses, to overcome fear, and to live respectfully by turning our attention to experience as it is lived each day.[19] The practical implications of this will become apparent as we take it several steps farther. The World Council of Churches, for example, has posted on their website a very helpful *Roadmap for Congregations, Communities and Churches for an Economy of Life and Ecological Justice*.[20] This is how the WCC summarizes the roadmap's essential features:

1. Living in accordance with the covenant with God and creation [small scale agriculture, community gardens, clean water]

---

18. Golliher, "Church as Renewed Creation."
19. Sweeney, *Feed the Wolf.*
20. Tendis, *Roadmap for Congregations,* 5.

2. Renewable Energy and Climate Protection [energy consumption, renewables, climate friendly mobility, conscious
   energy]

3. Just and Sustainable Consumption [buy ecological, fair and
   regional, reduce waste, re-use and recycle]

4. Economies of Life [create places for moneyless interaction,
   practice alternative economic models, practice just nature]

5. Networking [name contact persons for economic and ecological justice, raise voices in communities and beyond,
   network with other communities and beyond]

Notice the wide-ranging content that the WCC briefly recommends. *Notice also that to follow through in any of these areas of work requires us to gain knowledge of our local ecosystems, cultures, and economies, including the political dynamics that shape them.* The efficacy of Dubos's famous dictum for sacred ecology immediately comes to mind—"think globally, act locally." A good example involves the emergence of numerous youth groups in many parts of the world that have learned to organize passionately for political action. We urgently need to join efforts of that kind. I also think of Karen Armstrong's exploration of our need for ecological healing in *Sacred Nature: Restoring our Ancient Bond with the Natural World.*[21] All these efforts ask us to use our discernment with prayerfully conscious intent. How can we do that? What do we actually need to do in order to make ecojustice ministries effective?

The Principles of the Franciscan Third Order (Anglican)[22] offer sub-stantial assistance. I'm thinking specifically of *Humility, Simplicity,* and the three Forms of Service: *Prayer, Study, and Work.*[23] Below, you'll find the tra-ditional meaning of those principles, followed by an in-depth discussion of how they can be lived in perilous times. As Merton understood in relation to the media, the temptation today is to overlook the deeper meaning—and the solid spiritual ground—by looking only on the surface.

Humility: "We always keep before us the example of Christ, who
emptied himself taking the form of a servant, and who, on the
last night of his life, humbly washed his disciples' feet."

Simplicity: "The first Christians surrendered completely to our
Lord and recklessly gave all they had, offering the world a new

21. Armstrong, *Sacred Nature.*
22. Brother Geoffrey, *Way of St. Francis.*
23. Golliher, "Franciscan Forms of Service."

vision of society in which a fresh attitude was taken towards material possessions."

Prayer: "Tertiaries recognize the power of intercessory prayer for furthering the purposes of God's Kingdom, and therefore seek a deepening communion with God in personal devotion, and constantly intercede for the needs of his church and his world."

Study: "True knowledge is knowledge of God. Tertiaries therefore give priority to devotional study of scripture . . . some of us accept the duty of contributing, through research and writing, to a better understanding of the church's mission in the world: the application of Christian principles to the use and distribution of wealth; questions concerning justice and peace; and of all other questions concerning the life of faith."

Work: "Tertiaries endeavor to serve others in active work. . . . The chief form of service which we have to offer is to reflect the love of Christ, who, in his beauty and power, is the inspiration and joy of our lives."[24]

The meaning and practice of these principles are interwoven signposts for finding solid spiritual ground in our journey with Christ. As basic as they are, it is important to keep in mind that they are not the ground itself. For example, the principle of *humility* speaks to our tendency to overstate what we think we know, a form of ego-inflation. Making the point in a different way, Korzybski, the philosopher, reminds us of perennial wisdom: "The map is not the territory."[25] The territory we seek—solid spiritual ground—reveals itself when we put our faith into practice. Another example: intellectual insight alone into what carrying the cross might mean is not the same as actually carrying it. The point is that we need to be careful not to overly-intellectualize any of this, which often makes our colonized wrapping tighter, as we "wave flags" of self-righteous religious identity. Let me share what Sweeney said about St. Francis and his views on *study* in this regard:

> Francis was not a man of many words. . . . In fact, it is impossible to imagine Francis sitting in a library or with a pen in his hand. . . . Some have even accused Francis of being anti-intellectual, and for good reasons: he often warned his brothers against owning books and excessive reading. He counseled his brothers

24. Society of St. Francis, *Living with the Principles.*

25. Korzybski, *Science and Sanity.*

again and again to study only if they could do so without it ruining their spiritual lives. And yet he wrote.[26]

St. Francis was encouraging us to reflect deeply on our life together. Today, we might ask this about our lives everyday: how much do we stereotype others by projecting our own predispositions and opinions onto them based on what we've heard or read? Do we even bother to ask what they really think or believe? I had my own experience with this years ago, ironically, during my doctoral training. I asked my mentor, a highly skilled cognitive analyst of meaning, how I should proceed with my study. Her answer was direct: "Don't read." She was serious, but she didn't mean it literally. She was drawing upon the practical wisdom of some founders of her field of study who were resisters of the Nazis and propaganda decoders. She wanted me to take responsibility for how much more our minds have been colonized than we realize. It's likely that St. Francis would have given the same advice for much the same reasons.

The same perspective applies to the Franciscan principle of *prayer*. To unwrap ourselves from our colonized baggage, it is important to free ourselves of our incessant inner dialogue, which keeps our heart and minds wrapped up tightly. Ross, the Anglican solitary, explains how silent prayer and meditation are a great help in that regard, as is the traditional Jesus Prayer.[27] The principle of *work* involves weaving together—and weaving back together—our communities, bioregions, and political systems that have suffered the destructive consequences of exploitative profit at the expense of our life together. Similarly, the principle of *simplicity* asks us to examine and act upon our relation to the material world, which includes our use of greenhouse gases, plastics, and consumerism generally.

Based on this understanding of Franciscan principles, the solid ground that we seek involves three simple but unexpectedly revealing questions:

1. Do we really know where we live?

2. What do we see?

3. Who are our neighbors?

Our discernment of genuine answers to those questions depends on our willingness to practice *humility*, which can carry us into the heart of effective ecojustice ministry.

---

26. Sweeney, *Francis of Assisi*, 4.
27. Ross, *Silence*, vols. 1 and 2.

OUR FIRST RESPONSIBILITY: DO WE REALLY KNOW WHERE WE LIVE?

Our best starting point is the creation story in the opening chapters of Genesis. This story is part of our shared cultural and religious heritage, including the patriarchal portion, discussed so well by Fox, that blames Eve for the "fall."[28] Translated and interpreted in different ways, the meaning at the heart of the story is that creation is God's, not ours, and God bestowed on us the responsibility to care for creation. The pivotal symbol is the primordial tree of life at the "center" of the cosmos, which has parallels in the sacred traditions of many Indigenous peoples. In some Franciscan traditions, the cross of Christ transforms into the tree of life as we carry it to the heart of our life together.

In most public discourse, the sacred ecological significance of this story has been largely ignored or lost. Often, the story we think we know is understood as "so basic that everyone knows it," or "we learned it in Sunday school." The underlying assumption is that it's a "kid's story." However we rationalize it, our first responsibility in life has essentially been overlooked. This has parallels in the widely shared linguistic usage of the word "environment" among English speakers. I'm not criticizing the work of environmental organizations, but reflecting on the culturally defined meaning of the word. It overlooks the essential part/whole relationship of our life together, of our complete dependence on the living earth—God's creation—that we live within. Instead, "environment" usually suggests something that is object or thing-like, existing exterior to and separate from us. This represents a historical disruption in the collective wisdom of humankind.

From a Franciscan perspective, this ordinary usage of the word "environment" opens the surface of a deep wound, which raises a serious question for discernment: *Do we really know where we live?* In the English-speaking West, our immediate answers often reflect official meanings. We might answer with a street or mailing address, which is what we would say to a traffic cop. The fact that we do this so routinely suggests that the immediate spiritual reality of the creation story is far from our thoughts. By extension, we probably overlook or ignore our God-given responsibility. It's not that we don't "know" in the abstract. We just don't think about what it means very often with regard to our life together.

If we were to ask Chief Oren Lyons that question, his answer would involve actual relationships. In addition to his earlier quote, this is what he says:

---

28. Fox, *Original Blessing*.

All relationships are forms for kinship—a family of God in which no one is left out and everyone and all creatures are welcome. The spiritual traditions of Indigenous peoples express this plainly.[29]

St. Francis would agree with Chief Lyons, as he would with the late Archbishop Emeritus Desmond Tutu. Reflecting on the ecological implications of the African word *Ubuntu* and its current context, Tutu writes,

> Ubuntu acknowledges what we are, biologically. We are not individual beings; we have evolved as a social organism. This is the literal meaning of Ubuntu. . . . Shouldn't we extend Ubuntu beyond people to all other living beings? . . . If Ubuntu encourages us to cultivate and care for ourselves, for our families and our brethren, so too should we care for our larger, extended body—the veld, bush soil, air, water, and the wetlands.[30]

Scientists began to "discover" the foundation of Indigenous wisdom—the fact of the interwoven fabric of life—about two centuries ago. Humboldt's description of the "web of life"[31] comes to mind first, and then Dubos and his vision of "sacred ecology,"[32] which helped to shape the policies of the UN's response to the climate and ecological crisis. More widely known is the vision of the biosphere proposed by Lovelock as an interwoven and self-regulating body of life known as "Gaia."[33] It suggests that when disruptions in the biosphere threaten the balance of life, the biosphere employs its own agency, making adjustments within the living system to maintain its balance.

The looming question now falls squarely on our own agency: on our willingness and capacity to pursue ecojustice in sound and effective ways. The first step is to know where we live in a more ecologically realistic sense; the second step follows from the prophet Amos.

THE QUESTION GOD ASKED OF AMOS: "WHAT DO YOU SEE?"

The historical context of Amos, the great eighth century BCE prophet of social justice, was very different from ours; but in other ways, it's much the

29. Lyons, "All My Relations," 450.
30. Tutu, "Eco-Ubuntu," 2.
31. Humboldt, *Views of Nature*.
32. Dubos, *Celebrations of Life*.
33. Lovelock, *Ages of Gaia*.

same. The divide between the wealthy and the poor was large then and now, and the poor along with foreigners were treated with disrespect. Because Amos left a written record of his vision of God, we can consider its implications for our time:

> This is what he showed me: the Lord was standing beside a wall
> built with a plumb line, with a plumb line in his hand. And the
> Lord said to me, "Amos, what do you see?" (Amos 7:7)

The larger symbolism of Amos's vision includes the throne of God with justice and righteousness at its foundation. With the plumb line measuring justice and injustice, he saw a world out of balance. Taking this living image to heart in our time, the same question that God asked of Amos is asked of us—"what do we see?" The answer: a world hugely out of balance, much more so than in the time of Amos. Have we been fulfilling our responsibility to care for creation with justice and respect? The answer is clearly "no" to an unthinkable extent. In our out-of-balance world, the hidden hand of Wall Street plays a large role. Consumerism, including its impact on the media, subsumes citizenship and community. Exploitation in the name of democracy gains power over genuine relationships with God's creatures. In many countries, intensifying resource extraction and habitat destruction have become "legal," but that doesn't make them just. In some countries it is illegal to nonviolently protest unjust laws regarding fossil fuel pipelines and water rights. According to Amos (5:24), when the plumb line is out of balance, the judgment of God can be harsh: "Let justice roll down like water, and righteousness with an ever-flowing stream."

We have the capacity to act and bring the plumb line back into balance, but doing so depends on our agency—which depends on our willingness to form genuinely respectful relationships with each other and Mother Earth. Writing recently in *The Christian Century*, Preston, an associate of the Iona Community, got to the heart of it in two ways. In the first, she writes about our agency in relation to the interwoven fabric of life. "The most miraculous part of Earth's agency is not how she makes mountains rise and streams curve. It's how she offers humans an invitation to intimacy. In the second: Reciprocity is a far more powerful expression of kinship than right. . . . Love is more powerful than laws."[34]

Honest, uncorrupted legal systems are desperately needed to protect ecosystems and the people that live within them, as is nonviolent protest and resistance to loosen the hold that corruption has on us. However, changes in legal systems alone will not be enough in a world where corporate power

---

34. Preston, "Earth's Self-Care," 44.

seeks control over politics and the courts in the name of freedom. One immediate response for ecojustice ministry should be steps towards bioregional awareness and justice, as the World Council of Churches suggests: organizing friends and neighbors, working and networking with local farmers, youth, civic organizations, and protecting the rights of nature. We need to organize globally and locally, while walking together on the solid spiritual ground that brings about a genuine "conversion of life."

THE TWO GREAT COMMANDMENTS: WHO ARE OUR NEIGHBORS?

Let's remember again the Indigenous voice of Diaz: "The Earth [is] telling us it's exhausted. It's ready to start cleaning itself."[35] The response that the Earth needs can only come from us. To do this, we must reach a tipping point in how we put our faith into practice. It centers on the questions of whether we—together—can really know where we live, know what we see, and then act on the knowledge that our responsibility is for the whole living earth.

For that reason, these reflections come to a conclusion with the two great commandments of Jesus: *to love God and to love our neighbors as ourselves* (Matt 22:36–40; Mark 12:29–31; Luke 10:25–28). Remember that in the context of Amos's prophetic vision, the life and teachings of Christ are traditionally elevated to the right hand of God, with justice and righteousness at the foundation. This vision for the practice of loving-kindness should guide us in all dimensions of our lives, including the pursuit of ecojustice through right action.

Jesus's teaching is also based on a warning clothed in discernment: *you cannot serve God and wealth* (Matt 6:24). It should be obvious that we're living at a time when the "principalities and powers" have created a profit-driven world based on an "us versus them" calculus. In practice, this means that our neighbors and their land can be exploited, even sacrificed, in the name of God and profit. This flatly contradicts the relationships of kinship that are the essence of solid spiritual ground.

The two great commandments and Jesus's teaching about wealth should also be a warning about the distinct possibility of authoritarian movements becoming "eco-fascist." "Mental rubbish" of that kind appeared in the 1930s and it can happen again. For that reason, we must remember that our sacred Mother Earth cannot be politicized into the equivalent of "motherland" or "fatherland" ideologies. Dangers of that kind arise when we restrict and diminish the meaning of "neighbor" for our own self-righteous purposes. In

---

35. Diaz in Jamail and Rushworth, *Middle of Forever*, 290.

effect, people pose the deceptively rhetorical question: "Well, who actually are my neighbors anyway?" (Luke 10:29). We've all heard many versions of it, which amount to asking whether Jesus really meant that our neighbors include people we don't know, or those with a different skin color or nationality, or of different religious faiths, or creatures of a different species. And especially now, when so many climate refugees are seeking sanctuary: Are they all our neighbors too? Of course they are!

That our lives can be rooted in a vision encompassing the whole fabric of life is much more than an ideal to be brokered or decided in a court of law. We need good, effective laws, but we cannot depend on them to be solid spiritual ground. *The practice of loving-kindness is the foundation of the solid ground on which our life together depends.* In my lifetime, the leaders of the world's religions have sometimes taken steps towards this vision of a life together. Today, in the midst of an "unthinkable" emergency, we must all join together in that shared vision for the sake of our survival. St. Francis and St. Clare, Indigenous peoples, and countless others have understood what is at stake. It's time for us all to join them, speak out, resist evil, and organize.

BIBLIOGRAPHY

Armstrong, Karen. *Sacred Nature: Restoring Our Ancient Bond with the Natural World.* New York: Knopf, 2022.

Bonhoeffer, Dietrich. *Life Together.* New York: HarperCollins, 2008.

Brother Geoffrey. *The Way of St. Francis.* Norwich: Edmund Norvic, ca. 1986.

Cowan, James. *A Saint's Way.* Liguori, MO: Liguori/Triumph, 2001.

Dubos, Rene. *Celebrations of Life.* New York: McGraw Hill, 1981.

Fox, Matthew. *Original Blessing: A Primer in Creation Spirituality.* Santa Fe, NM: Bear and Company, 1983.

Freire, Paulo. *The Pedagogy of Hope.* New York: Continuum, 1992.

———. *Pedagogy of the Oppressed.* New York: Continuum, 1979.

Golliher, Jeff. "Ethical, Moral, And Religious Concerns." In *Cultural and Spiritual Values of Biodiversity,* edited by Darrell Posey, 437–50. Nairobi, Kenya: United Nations Environmental Program, 1999.

———. "The Church as Renewed Creation." In *Crisis and the Renewal of Creation: Church and World in the Age of Ecology,* edited by Jeff Golliher and William Bryant Logan, 96–100. New York: Continuum, 1996.

———. "The Franciscan Forms of Service: Hopeful Reflections in a Perilous Time." Third Order, Society of Saint Francis, 2022. https://tssf.org/wp-content/uploads/2022/03/Franciscan-Times-Winter-Lent-2022-final.pdf.

Hayhoe, Katherine. "David Wallace-Wells: The Uninhabitable Earth." Jun 28, 2019. Climate One, podcast, 51:26. https://www.climateone.org/audio/david-wallace-wells-uninhabitable-earth.

Horan, Daniel P. *Francis of Assisi and the Future of Faith: Exploring Franciscan Spirituality and Theology in the Modern World.* Phoenix: Tau, 2012.

Humboldt, Alexander von. *Views of Nature: Or Contemplations on the Sublime Phenomena of Creation; With Scientific Illustrations*. London: Bell and Sons, 1884. https://www.ncbi.nlm.nih.gov/pmc/articles/PMC5185371/.

IPCC: The Core Writing Team. "AR6 Synthesis Report: Climate Change 2023." https://www.ipcc.ch/report/sixth-assessment-report-cycle/.

Jamail, Dahr, and Stan Rushworth, eds. *We Are the Middle of Forever: Indigenous Views from Turtle Island on the Changing Earth*. New York: The New Press, 2022.

Korten, David. *The Great Turning: From Empire to Earth Community*. Oakland, CA: Berrett-Koehler, 2006.

———. *When Corporations Rule the World*. Oakland, CA: Berrett-Koehler, 1995.

Korzybski, Alfred. *Science and Sanity: An Introduction to Non-Aristotelian Systems and General Semantics*. New York: Institute of General Semantics, 1994.

Lovelock, James. *The Ages of Gaia: A Biography of Our Living Earth*. London: W W Norton, 1995.

Lyons, Oren. "All My Relations: Perspectives from Indigenous Peoples." In *Cultural and Spiritual Values of Biodiversity*, edited by Darrell Posey, 450–52. Nairobi, Kenya: United Nations Environmental Program, 1999.

Merton, Thomas. *Conjectures of A Guilty Bystander*. Garden City, NY: Doubleday, 1968.

NoiseCat, Julian Brave. "How Indigenous Peoples Are Fighting the Apocalypse." *Emergence Magazine*, Nov 23, 2021. https://emergencemagazine.org/op_ed/how-indigenous-peoples-are-fighting-the-apocalypse/.

Paoletta, Kyle. "The Incredible Disappearing Doomsday: How the Climate Catastrophists Learned to Stop Worrying and Love the Calm." *Harper's Magazine*, Apr 2023, 25–31.

Posey, Darrell, ed. *Cultural and Spiritual Values of Biodiversity*. Nairobi, Kenya: United Nations Environmental Program, 1999.

Preston, Katharine M. "Earth's Self-Care." *The Christian Century*, Sep 2022, 40–45.

Ross, Maggie. *Silence: A User's Guide; Volume 1; Process*. Eugene, OR: Cascade, 2014.

———. *Silence: A User's Guide; Volume 2; Application*. Eugene, OR: Cascade, 2018.

Sister Joyce. "Walking in the Footsteps of Christ: The Historical Documents of the Society of Saint Francis." Dorchester, UK: The Society of Saint Francis, Hilfield Friary, 2003.

Society of St. Francis. *Living with the Principles of the Order*. N.p.: Society of St. Francis, 2005.

Sweeney, John M. *Feed the Wolf: Befriending Our Fears on the Way of Saint Francis*. Minneapolis: Broadleaf, 2021.

———. *Francis of Assisi: The Essential Writings; In His Own Words*. 2nd ed. Brewster, MA: Paraclete, 2018.

Tendis, Norman, ed. *Roadmap for Congregations, Communities, and Churches for an Economy of Life and Ecological Justice*. Geneva: WCC, 2019.

Tutu, Desmond. "Eco-Ubuntu." Ubuntu Society. https://www.ubuntusociety.nl/public/files/Eco-%20Ubuntu%20Desmond%20Tutu.pdf.

Wallace-Wells, David. *The Uninhabitable Earth: Life after Warming*. New York: Penguin Random House, 2019.

Three honorary doctorate recipients, photographed at a COGS meeting
Ellie Johnson, Esther Wesley, and Alyson Barnett-Cowan

The Partnerships team:
Top row: Andrea Mann, Maylanne Maybee
Middle row: Esther Wesley, Theresa Mandricks, Ellie Johnson
Front row: Meagan Blais, Lydia Kiden Laku, Clem Thomas, Jill Cruse

Anti-Racism Working Group meeting in Winnipeg
BACK ROW: Murray Still, Isaac Kawuki-Mukasa, Klaus Gruber
FRONT ROW: Ellie Johnson, Maylanne Maybee, Esther Wesley, Susan Barclay, Yves-Eugene Joseph

V. ELLIE, IN HER OWN WORDS

19

A Presentation on Mission

ELLIE JOHNSON

In this undated workshop format on mission found in the papers of Maylanne Maybee we see how Ellie unpacked "mission" for her listeners. Imagine her audience as being the House of Bishops, or a group of theological students, or members of her home parish of St. Simon's, Oakville. The notes below are edited for length and detail.

WHAT DO WE MEAN BY MISSION?

There are more definitions of mission than you could shake a stick at, and I'm going to avoid adding to the list. What I want us to do today is to think about mission as first and foremost what God is doing in the world. God is at work in the world, bringing healing, hope, transformation in many different place and many different ways. God is calling each and every one of us to be active participants in the work of God's mission. So first and foremost we name mission as God's transformative action in the world. And in addition, we acknowledge that God is calling all of us to active participation in that transformative action.

ASSUMPTIONS UNDERLYING THIS UNDERSTANDING OF THE MISSION OF GOD

First, we assume that God is in charge of God's mission, that God has a vision and a plan, and that God is working towards the fulfillment of that plan. Secondly, we assume that we are able, at least partly, to understand God's plan because we are created in God's image as rational beings. This is very different from starting with the concept of the church's mission.

We have got ourselves in a lot of trouble by focusing on the "church's mission," which seems to be based on the assumption that whatever the church decides to do is blessed by God. The sad history of the Indian residential schools is an example. And I know that it's easy to look back and criticize what our predecessors did. On the other hand, I also think that in the present we can lose our perspective, and get sidetracked into concerns about our declining membership and budgets, rather than trying to figure out what the Risen Christ is doing today in our communities right now, and figuring out how to become involved in what God is already doing. We need to listen to and reflect on the *word of God*.

Second, we need to listen to and observe how God seems to be intervening in the struggles people face, especially during significant moments in their lives. In other words, we need to *pay attention to peoples' life-stories* and examine God's interventions in those stories.

Third, we need to *pray for, and look for signs of the Holy Spirit*.

Fourth, we need to *learn to like change*, because this ecosystem that we live in, including human culture, is ever changing. That's how God made it; God embraces change and also expects us to embrace change and work with it.

THE WORD OF GOD—SCRIPTURE

We listen to God's word every Sunday and remind ourselves that we are doing so by saying, "This is the word of the Lord," or "Hear what the Spirit is saying to the church," or some such phrase. We also read or listen to other peoples' reflections on God's word, as well as offering our own reflections in sermons, study groups, or conversations. There are many passages in Scripture that give us clues about God's mission in the world. Here are three that I particularly like.

The first is from Luke 4, where Jesus quotes a passage from Isa 61, which is his own mission statement:

> The Spirit of the Lord is upon me,

Because he has chosen me
to bring good news to the poor,
He has sent me to proclaim release to the captives
And recovery of sight to the blind; To set the oppressed free,
And announce the year of the Lord's favour.[1]

In this passage Jesus defines his mission in terms of bringing healing and liberation to the sick, the poor, and the oppressed. He identifies himself as chosen by God to be an agent of God's mission in the world, and by doing so, he becomes a role model for us.

The second passage is also from Luke 10, the parable of the good Samaritan. In this well-known passage, Jesus teaches the meaning of loving one's neighbor by telling the compelling story of how the Samaritan, a social outcast, saved the life of a total stranger, after the priest and the Levite both turned a blind eye and walked away. Jesus then instructs us to "go and do likewise" (Luke 10:37).

The third passage is the short summary statement from Mic 6: "What does the Lord require of you, but to do justice, and to love kindness, and to walk humbly with your God" (Mic 6:8).

PAY ATTENTION TO PEOPLE'S LIFE-STORIES

A second way we can discern what in the world God is doing is by paying close attention to people's life stories. I really believe that God is especially close to people in their times of struggle, and at significant moments in their lives, so if we watch and listen attentively to their stories, we may catch a glimpse of what God is doing and perhaps discern what our own role in that story might be. Personal stories are sacred gifts and need to be handled with care. The people I'm going to speak about have given me permission to share their stories.

The first story is about a woman from Sri Lanka, Rani Srikantha, whom I met in Honduras many years ago. At that time I was teaching high school in San Pedro Sula, and Rani's son attended the school. One day another teacher told me that Rani had suffered some kind of emotional breakdown and was in the hospital. I went to visit her. She told me that she had discovered that her husband was in a relationship with a Honduran woman that had been going on for four years and he had fathered two children with that woman. Rani was deeply shocked and depressed. After she came out of hospital we continued to meet and talk. She told me that in the past she had

---

1. Ellie's own translation of Luke 4:18.

been unable to get pregnant, and so she and her husband had gone back to Sri Lanka and adopted a boy. But it was important for her husband to father children, so he had done so without telling her.

I suggested to her that she go home to her family in Sri Lanka, but she refused, saying that in her culture, she would be blamed for the breakdown of the marriage, and her parents would also experience great shame. She was in great distress, and I really didn't know how to help her, so I asked her if I might pray with her. She was not a Christian but was very open to having me pray with her. So we began to meet regularly to talk and pray for God's guidance.

One day she announced she wanted to tell her whole story to God so she prostrated herself flat on the floor, as was the custom in her culture, and speaking in her own language, she poured out her heart to God. Although I did not understand a single word, I was very moved to witness this event. Sometime after this, she told me that she wanted to be baptized and become a Christian. She asked me to be her sponsor, and I was honored to accept.

So Rani became a Christian. With the support of our small house church, she eventually was able to ask her husband to move out. He continued to give her financial support, but she also got a job as a teaching assistant in the school where I worked. It was truly awesome to watch this woman recover her dignity and self-esteem as God worked within her to bring healing.

What did I learn from this experience? Well, God truly works in mysterious ways, and when I am drawn into events, then my role will be shown to me even when I don't fully understand what is going on.

ANOTHER STORY

The second story is about one of my sons-in-law. It is not so dramatic as Rani's story, but is very important to me. My youngest daughter, Emily, married a very nice young man Daniel just over three years ago. Both Emily and Dan are high school teachers and they met at the school in Brampton where they both work. Emily was raised in the Anglican Church, including attending the youth group at the Parish Church in Fredericton many years back when I worked in that parish. Daniel was raised by a single mother who was not a regular churchgoer, but occasionally took him along to the local United Church.

Through their work, Emily and Dan became good friends with another teacher couple in Georgetown where they live, and were invited to the baptism of this couple's baby, held at St. George's Anglican Church. Dan was intrigued to see that the young father was baptized along with the baby. Emily and Dan began to attend St. George's Church along with these same friends. About eighteen months ago, they had a beautiful baby girl of their own, Devon Susan Earle. And I have to say that this child is absolutely gorgeous, incredibly smart, and happy as the day is long—not that I'm in any way biased, of course. They decided to have Devon baptized at St. George's, and in the course of the baptismal preparation, Daniel decided that he too wanted to be baptized. He invited me to be his sponsor, again a great honor to me. This is a story not of a time of great struggle, but rather, of a significant moment in the life of this young father. God was active in Dan's heart. Their teacher friends were the agents of God's actions. My role was again to act as sponsor, but also to watch and wait quietly—not easy for me!

WAITING ON THE SPIRIT

A third way we can discern what in the world God is doing is to wait expectantly for a sign of the Holy Spirit. It's difficult to figure out what God is doing in your local context, and it's equally difficult to figure out what you yourself and/or the church is being called to do as participants in God's work where you are. I believe that while the Holy Spirit is invisible, there are visible and "knowable" signs of its work. If we pay attention and expect signs, we will occasionally catch a glimpse. This is similar to listening to people's stories, except that it's perhaps more immediate, "happening right now," so to speak.

Here is a story about me and how I came to work for the Anglican Church. In 1982, my (then) husband and I were living and working in Kenya. At this time, our first two girls were in boarding school in England, and the third, Emily, was at the age when she also needed to go away to school. So we decided to try to come back to England or Canada. After much letter writing that produced nothing, my husband was finally offered a post-doctoral fellowship at the University of New Brunswick in Fredericton. It wasn't going to pay enough, but I hoped to find some sort of a job once we got there.

During the time when we were preparing to leave Kenya, I had a dream. In my dream, I was reminded that in Canada, some churches hire laypeople to do Christian education and other program work. When I arrived in Fredericton (ahead of my husband and kids who were not Canadians and had to wait for their immigration papers), I decided to see if I could get a job in a church. I walked into Wilmot United Church, and told the minister that I had just arrived from Africa and was looking for a job.

He said that he had just hired a Christian education director, but thought that the Anglican Church down the street might have such a job vacant. So I walked down the street into Christ Church Parish Church, and got the job.

And I kid you not! It happened almost exactly like that! Every time I tell that story, I am amazed at how I dreamed the idea, and then how it worked out so easily! Whenever I tell this story to Aboriginal people, they just nod calmly and smile, because they are very familiar with how God uses dreams to give us guidance.

This next story happened recently, in 2008, and it is about reconciliation that occurred before my very eyes. The last big project I worked on before I retired was an Aboriginal and Church Leaders' Tour to prepare the way for the Truth and Reconciliation Commission on Indian residential schools that is now underway. The four churches that were involved in running residential schools decided that we needed to do some kind of educational project to prepare our church members for the TRC. So we began meeting as an ecumenical planning group to figure out what we could do.

Eventually we decided to organize public events in four different cities, and have the leaders of our churches speak about the specific role of their own organization in the running of the schools, offer appropriate words of apology, and speak about the current work of healing that the churches are involved in. Our ecumenical planning group was joined by staff members from the Assembly of First Nations, and the National Residential School Survivors' Society. Our planning group got off to a pretty slow and rocky start, but suddenly things began to fall into place. This big project came together in ways that left all of us breathless, so there are many stories I could tell you about the Remembering the Children Leaders' Tour.

A VERY SPECIAL STORY

But the one story I want to focus on is the relationship between our primate, Archbishop Fred Hiltz, and the executive director of the National Residential School Survivors' Society, Ted Quewezance, and the work of the Spirit in that relationship. These two men had never met each other until they found themselves on the same stage in the Museum of Civilization in Ottawa at the event to kick off the tour. The primate was nervous, having not had much time to learn all the history of the Anglican involvement in residential schools. Ted Quewezance was angry and skeptical, having been sexually and physically abused in an Anglican-run school in Saskatchewan. He did not intend to say much of anything at this event. But he listened quietly to Fred Hiltz who offered a heartfelt apology on behalf of the Anglican Church. Ted was moved by Fred's sincerity, and so he got up and told a portion of his story of abuse. There were about five hundred people in the audience.

The second stop of the tour was in Vancouver, with a smaller crowd, but still well over two hundred people present. Again the primate spoke with deep sincerity. Ted spoke boldly and revealed more of his story. At the end of the evening, all the leaders embraced one another.

The third stop was in Saskatoon and the fourth in Winnipeg. Big crowds turned out in both places. All the leaders got better as they went along. What I witnessed was a deep respect growing between Fred Hiltz and Ted Quewezance. At the end of the whole thing, both men embraced and shed tears of deep emotion.

I believe the Holy Spirit was actively guiding the interaction between these two men, and it was truly amazing to watch the transformation happening to the leaders right before my eyes. Now, I want you to sit quietly for a moment with your eyes closed, and remember a moment when you think you felt the nudging of the Spirit in your own life, or observed the Spirit at work in someone else's life.

LEARN TO EMBRACE CHANGE

A fourth way we can figure out how to participate in God's mission in the world is to learn to embrace change. Living systems are constantly changing. When they stop changing they die. That is true of organisms like our bodies, and also of sociocultural systems like our human communities. Like it or not, God created an ever-changing world. Change is part of the plan. Transformation is another word for change. So, if we want to participate in God's mission of transforming the world, we have to expect change, strangeness, and strangers. In fact, we will need to become agents of change and motivate others to embrace change and to become involved in the world beyond their own homes and their own church families. I have a hard time understanding why some people are so resistant to change. I like change and find it very energizing, but I realize most people don't feel this way.

WHAT CAN I DO? USEFUL MISSION ACTIONS

If you do a good job of motivating people to become engaged in mission, then someone is sure to ask you, "What can I do?" Everyone can do at least one of these useful acts, and some people can do all of them.

Prayer—pray intentionally and intelligently. There are resources to help, such as the Anglican Cycle of Prayer, the various diocesan cycles of prayer, and Praying with Our Partners. People can also pray about world affairs at all levels. We all can pray, and as you know, prayer does have a variety of results and leads to a variety of other actions.

Hands-on service—this is a broad category involving everything from volunteer work in one's own community to full-time missionary work somewhere else. Many Christian people perform many acts of service. I sometimes think we in the church don't give enough recognition to our members for their volunteer work outside of the church. Positive reinforcement and public recognition is a good way to encourage more service.

Financial support—give to enable the mission work of others, whether in your home community or in other places. Most, though not all, of our members already do this. Some are not able to.

Advocacy—raising one's voice to bring about policy and structural changes in our social systems. This is hard work, and is often thankless as well. But it is very important, and in our nation, Christian social justice advocates have made and continue to make significant contributions to social transformation.

I have a hunch that many of you, along with other Anglicans across Canada, faced with declining membership in your parishes, may feel that you have no energy for the work of mission. However, it is important to remember that without mission, the church will decline further. I think it's also important to remember that God's mission is to the whole of creation. God so loved the world that he sent his Son out into the world. As agents of God's mission in our own times, we too need to be focused outward and be active in the world, addressing injustices, and bringing hope to those in despair.

20

An Address to the Convocation of Montreal Diocesan Theological College, Montreal, May 8, 2006

ELLIE JOHNSON

IT IS A GREAT honor to be speaking to you this evening. I bring you greetings from our primate, Archbishop Andrew Hutchison, and from my staff colleagues at Church House in Toronto. My thanks to your principal John Simons, to Bishop Barry Clarke, to my friend Sue Winn for her kind words, and to my family and friends who made time to be here.

When Bishop Clark phoned to invite me to give this address I said, "But I'm not a theologian, I'm a social anthropologist," to which he replied, "We are all theologians." So I accepted the invitation because I do subscribe to the view that we are all theologians, in that we are all capable of seeking to know God, and reflecting on what we think we know. Then when I asked the bishop what topic or theme he wanted me to address, he replied, "Missiology, [so] reflect on mission from your own experience, and don't forget the residential schools!" So that is what I will try to do.

But right at the outset, I want to direct a few comments to those who are graduating today. Congratulations on successfully completing the goals you have set for yourselves. I know only too well that there is a lot of work behind these achievements! This day marks the end of one chapter for each of you, and at the same time, the page is turning and the next chapter is

beginning. That too will have both challenges and rewards, some anticipated, but many quite beyond your expectation or imagination.

In my years of working for the Anglican Church, I have experienced a
constant tension between the needs of the institutional church and the needs
of the world. Although the church is my employer, I have always felt that my
calling was to serve the world. I do believe that our purpose, as the people
of God, is to serve the world. The institutional church exists to facilitate
that service. The tension exists because social institutions become increasingly institutionalized, or "fixed in stone," to the point that they eventually
become self-serving, rather than other-serving. So as you graduate from
this academic institution, which too is somewhat fixed in stone, I encourage
you to embrace change, to take risks, to walk lightly on the earth, and to
learn to "turn on a dime" when a new direction is called for. The Anglican
Church needs to change, and you have an opportunity to give leadership to
that movement for change. But now, something about mission.

The conceptual framework of mission with which I am most comfortable is the current popular thinking about the *missio Dei*, the mission of
God in the world, and God's call to us to participate in that mission. This
concept of *missio Dei* assumes that God is in charge (and thank goodness
for that!), that God has a plan or mission, and that the plan is good. It also
assumes that we humans can, at least partly, understand God's mission
plan, because we are created in God's image and therefore, we think, at least
partly, the way God does.

We need to stop talking about the mission of the church, and start
talking about the mission of God. We have got ourselves in a lot of trouble
talking about the mission of the church, especially where the church was
part of colonial expansion, which the Anglican Church most certainly was.
The legacy of empire building continues to haunt us. Our church needs to
change! We need to stop talking about the church's mission and start talking
about God's mission—and following from that, it seems to me that the first
challenge facing anyone who feels called to mission (and I hope all of you
feel that call), is to figure out what in the world God is doing in that particular, local context. This has to come first before you or I can start thinking
about what we ought to be doing.

So how do we figure out what in the world God is doing? It seems to
me that there are two ways of learning this, and both are necessary. The first
is to listen to, and reflect on what God is saying, and the second is to listen
to, and observe or participate in the experiences people are having. And
we need to be lifelong learners because the world is ever-changing, cultural
contexts are ever-changing.

We listen to God whenever we read Scripture. When we do that collectively in our parish congregations, we remind ourselves what we are doing by saying, "This is the word of the Lord," or "Hear what the Spirit is saying to the church." There are many, many passages in Scripture that give us clues about God's mission in the world. One of the best known is the passage from Isaiah that Jesus used to define his own mission:

> The spirit of the Lord is upon me,
> Because he has chosen me to bring good news to the poor,
> He has sent me to proclaim release to the captives
> And recovery of sight to the blind;
> To set the oppressed free,
> And announce the year of the Lord's favour. (Isa 61:1–2a)[1]

In this passage, Jesus defines his mission in terms of bringing healing and liberation to the sick, the poor, and the oppressed. He identifies himself as chosen by God to be an agent of God's mission in the world, the *missio Dei*. Another one that I like is the parable of the good Samaritan in Luke's Gospel (Luke 10:25–37), in which Jesus teaches the meaning of loving one's neighbor by telling the compelling story of how the not-so-socially-acceptable Samaritan saved the life of a total stranger. Jesus then instructs us to, "go and do likewise." So, that's the first way we figure out what in the world God is doing. We listen to the *word of the Lord*, listen to the *word of God Incarnate*.

The second way we learn what God is doing in the world is to listen to and observe what people are experiencing in their lives, in their daily struggles. God is always present with people in the struggles because, as you know, God has a preferential option for the broken and marginalized. Listening and observing are not always as easy as they sound. People don't share their experiences unless they feel safe in doing so, unless they trust the listener or the observer. Building trust can be a long, slow process, and trust is a fragile commodity, easily broken, difficult to repair.

During the past few years, I have had the good fortune to be part of an international sharing circle where trust was built and stories were shared. This is a group of people from many different parts of the worldwide Anglican Communion, each of whom, like me, has some responsibility for the mission work of their churches. For some, it is a local responsibility, for others it is diocesan responsibility, for still others, it is a national responsibility. We have spent a lot of time listening to each other talk about the mission challenges we are facing. The questions we asked ourselves were these:

1. What is the mission of God in your place?

---

1. Ellie's own translation.

2. How is the church participating in God's mission where you come from?

3. What is Good News in that situation?

We met roughly every eighteen months, each time in a different country. This gave us opportunities to experience a variety of local cultural contexts. Over the years we managed to build a circle of trust where we could share our stories, and where we observed how the church is engaged locally with the struggles of the people. I want to share with you some of the things I learned from this circle of people.

The first thing I learned is that there is no such thing as "global mission." There is only "local mission." When people answer those three questions, they talk about their reflections, observations, and experiences, obviously coming from their own frame of reference, which is first cultural, and secondly Christian. We are human before we are Christian, and to be human is to have a cultural frame of reference. That is most obvious when we think about how language shapes the way we understand the world beyond self. The Cree speaker does not inhabit the same universe as the Hindustani speaker. Christianity is another type of language. It overlays and modifies, but does not replace the language of culture. Of course the whole thing is more complicated than that, but it's good to remember that God understands and works in all cultures and in all languages. What we understand of God through our own local, cultural lens is only a small part of the whole picture. One of the exciting things about cross-cultural experiences is that if we listen and watch carefully, we will learn something new about God and about what God is doing in another culture.

That is why I found the international mission group so interesting—and I learned a lot. For example, our South African member talked about the HIV/AIDS pandemic in her country, and how the church has responded by recruiting and training teams of women to provide home care to HIV/AIDS patients. She also talked about how the church is advocating for cheap and accessible antiretroviral drugs. When we asked her what is good news in that situation, she replied that because of stigmatization, and fear of catching the disease, family members often abandon HIV/AIDS patients, who are left to die alone, with no one to care for them. The good news is that through this home-based care program, patients are nursed, their physical needs are met, they do not feel as lonely, they understand that they are loved and valued. It is a much better way to die. And every success in the campaign to provide cheap, accessible drugs is also good news.

At another meeting I listened to a priest from Gulu in the northern part of Uganda. That is the part of Uganda where a rebel group called the

Lord's Resistance Army is terrorizing local communities and seizing children whom they force to join their army. The young boys are given guns and taught to shoot. The young girls become sex slaves. The priest I met is trying to protect children by gathering them up in the evenings and taking them to his house to sleep. For some reason that wasn't clear to me, the priest's house is considered out-of-bounds by the Lord's Resistance Army. I asked him what, if any, good news he had for these children. He looked at me in surprise and said "but of course I tell them that God loves them and does not want them to be seized. That is why I am working to protect them." But the sad news is that the Ugandan government in Kampala is not doing enough to stop this horror.

Another member of our group, from the Solomon Islands, talked about how God is using the Melanesian Brothers, an Anglican religious order, to bring an end to violent conflict between ethnic groups in several of the islands, particularly Guadalcanal and Malaita. His reflection was that this had become possible because the brothers are highly respected and trusted in that society. Building trust is a long, slow process, but essential in order to participate successfully in the *missio Dei*. When I talked about what God is doing in Canada, I explained the mission history of the Anglican Church of Canada, our participation in the Indian residential schools system, and our current struggle to repent, to make amends, and to work towards reconciliation. It is a story I have told many times and in many places. I have been engaged in work with the Aboriginal members of our church for about twelve years, and it is certainly the most challenging work I have ever done.

The full story of the long history of relations between the Aboriginal[2] peoples of Canada and the Anglican Church of Canada is not all bad. But within that fuller story, there is a sad substory of mission gone wrong, a story of the disastrous consequences of blending the goals of colonialism and evangelism. And yet even within that sad substory, we have experienced the remarkable power of the Holy Spirit, which has prodded and pushed, supported and encouraged people to keep their eyes on the goal of reconciliation and to persevere in the face of setbacks, mistakes, resistance, and discouragement. I am not going to review this history, because I think most of you are quite familiar with it. Instead I want to say a few things about what I have learned from my own involvement.

I have learned quite a bit about power and the abuse of power. Colonialism in this country (as well as in other countries) was an abuse of power, and because the descendants of the colonizers are still here and still

2. Indigenous Nations prefer to be called either First Nations, Metis, or Inuit. In this instance, "Aboriginal" is left as found in the text, recognizing, however, it is no longer appropriate.

run the country and the Anglican Church, this abuse of power continues. Bishop Steven Charleston, [former] dean of the Episcopal Divinity School in Cambridge, Massachusetts, and himself an Aboriginal person, wrote in an article a few years ago: "Colonialism is historically radioactive. It has a long half-life that continues to poison the relationships between human beings even generations after the fact." In my observation, there continues to be poison affecting relations between Aboriginal and non-Aboriginal people in this country and in our church. Building trust is long, hard, and humbling work, especially when trust has been so badly betrayed, but that is what God is calling us to do. There will be no reconciliation without it. I have also learned quite a bit about the consequences of childhood trauma. Those of you who are social workers know more than I do.

I want to mention three reasons why the residential schools system has had such devastating consequences.

Firstly, many children were forcibly removed from family and community and placed in an alien cultural environment where they were not allowed to speak their own languages, and from which they did not return home for a very long time. Some even died at the schools, and the families are still searching for their graves. Think of what I said about language a few moments ago, and how it shapes our view of the universe. How confusing and frightening it must have been for those children to have been unwillingly thrust into an alien universe!

Secondly, quite a few of those vulnerable children were also abused physically and sexually.

Thirdly, for the most part they did not get a decent education, nor learn a decent trade. So by the time they had finished school, they were alienated from their families and communities, and on top of that, they were unemployable. They literally didn't fit in anywhere. In Matthew's Gospel we read that Jesus drew a little child into the circle and said, "If any of you puts a stumbling block before any of these little ones, you will be held accountable for that failing. The little ones are especially precious to my loving Father who does not want to see any one of them lost in fear, anger, loneliness or self-hatred."[3]

I've also learned that healing can be a very long process. Those of us in our "quick fix" culture don't want to hear that. But Aboriginal people have been saying for quite some time that the healing will take seven generations. My observation is that within our church there continues to be a strong commitment to support healing work, and I pray that will continue because that is good news for the broken ones.

3. Ellie's own translation of Matt 18.

I've also learned that we all need healing, and until we acknowledge that, there will be no reconciliation. White people in particular, and I'm one of them, need to learn about white privilege and entitlement. For the past five years I've been part of a group doing anti-racism training in our church, and my experience has been that working with stubborn white people in denial about their privilege is, to be truthful, more exhausting than working with angry and broken Aboriginal people. I have days when I tell God that "enough is enough" and I don't want to do this anymore! But I guess we all have days like that. Maybe God has days like that too!

There is a lot of racism in Canada, and there is a lot of racism in the Anglican Church of Canada. Most white people deny this and find all sorts of reasons to explain the whiteness of our membership. One time not long ago I was in Jamaica and met the local Anglican bishop. He said to me, "You need to do something up there to hold on to Anglicans coming from Jamaica. Thousands of Jamaicans who have been Anglicans for generations are going to other churches because they don't feel welcome in your churches. What are you going to do about it?" I did not have a ready answer for him, but today I'm passing this challenge along to you. What are we going to do about it? And not just about the Jamaicans. Our Church needs to change! God is pushing us to acknowledge our racism and our failure to be inclusive.

Last weekend I went to an anti-racism conference in Winnipeg put on by an Aboriginal NGO called Ka Ni Kanichikh. The conference was called Building Inclusive Schools and was aimed at teachers and high school students. I went because they had some excellent keynote speakers. I also went because from time to time I need to get outside the churchy environment to keep myself grounded in the "real world." In Canada, race works within well-rehearsed narratives and through well-established channels to position whites on top. Whiteness is a system of dominance, and yet many, if not most, white people are not aware of the privileges that are attached to whiteness.

One of the speakers, Dr. George Sefa Dei, said that there is a moral imperative to reflect the diversity of the population in the leadership. (Now, he was talking "school," but you need to think "church.") Bodies matter because we experience life in our bodies. Black bodies have different life experiences in Canada than Aboriginal bodies, or Chinese bodies or white bodies. Think about that. The leadership in our Church is primarily white and male. Among our bishops, there are a few Aboriginal bodies, and now one Chinese body. There are also two women. That does not reflect the diversity of the membership in our church. Leaders can only lead from their own experiences and perspectives. The Anglican Church needs to change!

Racism affects the lives of many, many Canadians on a daily basis. How often do we talk about it in our churches? Dr. Sefa Dei at the Winnipeg conference said—and he was talking about youth in high schools, but I want you to think "church members"—he said, "Many youth have a perception that 'education sucks,' due to the silences and omissions of the issues that youth really need to talk about. This makes education irrelevant to the students." Think about that—are we preaching irrelevancies in our churches? The church is a voluntary organization, and those who find it irrelevant to the issues they are struggling with, they will vote with their feet and go someplace else. The Anglican Church needs to change. God is at work in Canada, transforming our culture and our society. That is happening in thousands of different local contexts. We need to be willing workers in that transformation. Our calling is to serve the world, as part of God's transforming action.

To you who are graduating today, who are moving on to the next stage of your journeys, again I want to say, "Congratulations on the completion of your studies." There are wonderful opportunities for change awaiting you, so welcome those, and trust God to guide you. I pray that you will receive guidance and blessings and firm nudging, more than you can ask or imagine. I want to close with three quick quotes about mission.

The first one is from the Swiss theologian, Emile Brunner, and will be familiar to many of you. He wrote, "A church exists by mission as a fire exists by burning."

Bishop Simon Chiwanga from Tanzania, former chair of the Anglican Consultative Council, added his own comment saying, "When the burning ceases, there is no fire. If mission ceases, there is no church."

The third quote is from Christopher Duraisingh, who ran the Gospel and Culture project at the World Council of Churches in Geneva. Christopher said, "Mission is not a function of the church; the church is a function of mission."

To all of us, the prophet Micah has said, "What does God require of us? To do justice, to love kindness, to walk humbly with God" (Mic 6:8).

Ellie with Maylanne Maybee and Lydia Kidden Laku, program associate

Index

Printed in the USA
CPSIA information can be obtained
at www.ICGtesting.com
JSHW010939090224
56986JS00001B/4